Metropolitan Denver

METROPOLITAN PORTRAITS

Metropolitan Portraits explores the contemporary metropolis in its diverse blend of past and present. Each volume describes a North American urban region in terms of historical experience, spatial configuration, culture, and contemporary issues. Books in the series are intended to promote discussion and understanding of metropolitan North America at the start of the twenty-first century.

Judith A. Martin, Series Editor

Metropolitan Denver

Growth and Change in the Mile High City

Andrew R. Goetz
and
E. Eric Boschmann

PENN

UNIVERSITY OF PENNSYLVANIA PRESS

PHILADELPHIA

Published by
University of Pennsylvania Press
Philadelphia, Pennsylvania 19104-4112
www.upenn.edu/pennpress

Printed in the United States of America on acid-free paper
10 9 8 7 6 5 4 3 2 1

Library of Congress Cataloging-in-Publication Data
Names: Goetz, Andrew R., author. | Boschmann, E. Eric,
    author. Title: Metropolitan Denver : growth and change
    in the Mile High City / Andrew R. Goetz and E. Eric
    Boschmann. Other titles: Metropolitan portraits.
Description: 1st edition. | Philadelphia : University of
    Pennsylvania Press, [2018] | Series: Metropolitan
    portraits | Includes bibliographical references and index.
Identifiers: LCCN 2018002981 | ISBN 978-0-8122-5045-9
    (hardcover : alk. paper)
Subjects: LCSH: Denver (Colo.)—History. | Denver
    (Colo.)—Economic conditions—21st century. | Denver
    (Colo.)—Social conditions—21st century. | Regional
    planning—Colorado—Denver. | Human geography—
    Colorado—Denver.
Classification: LCC F784.D457 G64 2018 |
    DDC 978.8/83—dc23
LC record available at https://lccn.loc.gov/2018002981

Contents

Preface

Perhaps no city symbolizes the American West more than Denver, Colorado. It was founded in 1858 during the Pikes Peak gold rush, and its origins and early growth were tied to mining, railroads, agriculture, and cattle ranching. It has grown in step with the growth of the West from frontier outpost to major metropolis, driven by an economic base in the energy, defense, aerospace, government, telecommunications, information technology, medical, tourism, and recreation industries. Its proximity and orientation to the Rocky Mountains has provided Denver with its essential identity as the Mile High City, where the blending of Old West imagery and New West reality is on full display.

As we contemplated our approach to creating a portrait of metropolitan Denver in this book, the themes of growth and change emerged as the dominant story line. While growth and change are evident for virtually all metropolitan areas, they are especially relevant for Denver, with its history of extreme boom-and-bust cycles, including its current major boom. Grappling with growth and its challenges are an ever-present concern, and the lessons of Denver's experiences have significance for other cities that are faced with extreme growth pressures. The purpose of this book, therefore, is to capture an image of contemporary Denver through its interrelated human, social, economic, and physical landscapes and to provide a geographic perspective on growth and change in the Mile High City.

Among large urban places in the United States, Denver has been one of the top three fastest growing from 2010 to 2016. For cities over 500,000 in population, Denver's rate of growth trails only Austin and Seattle. For metropolitan areas over 2.5 million, only Houston and Dallas had faster growth. And for combined statistical areas over 3 million, Houston, Orlando, and Denver were the fastest growing. Denver has become a destination of choice for millennials, consistently ranking as one of the top metro areas for in-migration among eighteen- to thirty-four-year-olds. Outdoor recreation, especially skiing, snowboarding, camping, hiking, and rafting, are major attractions, in addition to a vibrant arts and music scene, a thriving micro-brewing industry, and the recent legalization and growth of the recreational marijuana business.

The current wave of growth has created significant challenges, especially affordability, equity, mobility, and sustainability. The rapid influx of population has increased demand for housing, but supply has not kept pace, leading to sharply increased prices for houses and apartments. Demand for housing in the city of Denver has resulted in neighborhood gentrification and displacement of lower-income residents who can no longer afford the higher rents or property taxes. Increased population has led to more traffic congestion and demands for improved transportation infrastructure. Expanding urbanization has contributed to urban sprawl and increased pressure on resource consumption and impacts on the natural environment. Denver is trying to address some of these concerns through a smart growth strategy emphasizing the development of higher-density pedestrian- and biking-oriented urban centers served by an expanding rail transit system. While some progress has been achieved, many of the growth challenges still remain.

We hope that this exploration of Denver's past and contemporary identity sheds new light on what the poet Walt Whitman first described as "this curiously attractive region."[1]

From "Queen City of the Plains" to the "Mile High City"

The headline of the *Denver Post* on September 18, 2015, read: "Denver is flourishing." In fact, the beginning of the twenty-first century marks a high point in the history of Denver, Colorado. Population is booming, with a diverse influx of young millennials, older baby boomers, and new immigrants from across the globe. The region has a strong and diversified economy, resulting in rising median household incomes that are 25 percent higher than the national average, and a local poverty rate and unemployment rate well below national averages.[1] The city celebrated its sesquicentennial anniversary in 2008, at a time when Denver was acquiring newfound national and international recognition as a successful city. New transportation infrastructure developments, including new light rail lines, and exciting growth of mixed-use high-density housing developments illuminate the city's attitude toward eco-friendliness and growth consciousness. Like other cities of the New West, Denver offers a variety of lifestyle choices in a place where the Old West mystique is mixed with the urban and high tech, where people can encounter both rugged landscapes alongside ideal urban or suburban lifestyles. And on those days where sunny skies, mild weather, and a clear view of the nearby Rocky Mountains fill the landscape, Denverites might feel the sentiment reflected in publisher Frederick G. Bonfils's oft-repeated phrase from the 1930s: "'Tis a privilege to live in Colorado."[2]

A variety of reasons might help explain why Denver seems to be flourishing. Denver has benefited from strong civic leadership, an early and successful spirit of entrepreneurialism, a legacy of charitable philanthropy, a favorable location with proximity to an abundance of natural resources, an enviable mild and sunny climate, quick access to mountain-based recreation, and successes in regional collaboration, including planning for future urban growth.

But at the same time Denver has also experienced many challenges, some quite common to other growing cities. Economic inequalities and social segregation have persisted, and communities have been marginalized or displaced. Rapid population growth is sprouting ongoing traffic congestion and sprawl, and metropolitan political fragmentation stymies regional progress on pressing issues. Air pollution has spoiled the region's crisp, clean air; surrounding land degradation is resulting from overuse for resource extraction and agriculture production; and urban development is encroaching into nearby open space, which continues with ongoing growth.

These successes and challenges are both Denver's legacy and its future. The purpose of this book, therefore, is to capture an image of contemporary Denver through its interrelated human, social, economic, and physical landscapes. In doing so, we also trace historical elements that centrally play into the identity of what Denver is today. In short, the guiding questions are: What is Denver today in regards to its people and culture, its economy and politics, and its environment and resources? And how did it historically evolve? Such a project could be approached using themes, perspectives, and story lines as diverse as the city itself. And many Denver-focused books have been written from a variety of important angles.[3] This book uses a geographic perspective to illuminate the changes in both space and time of the city's spatial dimensions, place identity, human interactions with the natural environment, and social, economic, and political relations that shape the varied human landscapes in Denver and its surrounding communities.

Multiple visions of Denver exist, and comprehensive coverage is not possible here. The perspective in this book focuses on several key themes that help narrate our interpretation of Denver's history and current identity; this is one articulation of "urban place" expressed in Denver and its surrounding metropolitan area. The next section provides a brief glimpse of these themes threaded throughout the book and is organized around two halves of Denver's history: Denver as the "Queen City of the Plains" up to World War II, and Denver as the "Mile High City" in the years since.

The Queen City of the Plains

The city of Denver was founded on the western frontier of the United States in 1858. As it did with San Francisco, the discovery of gold turned Denver into an "instant city." It emerged suddenly from a rapid influx of disparate groups of individuals who came seeking personal riches. Isolated in the wilderness, with little common history or traditions, early Denverites found social cohesion through their common vision of pursuing individual economic freedom. It was an unlikely city, located at the convergence of the impenetrable Rocky Mountains and the eastern plains, once perceived as uninhabitable and unfit for cultivation. But upon the founding of Denver City in 1858, William H. Larimer Jr. predicted, "Everyone will soon be flocking to Denver for the most picturesque country in the world, with fine air, good water, and everything to make man happy and live to a good old age."[4] Within a single generation Denver overcame its isolation in the frontier and transformed into a bustling city connected to the national market economy, becoming the Queen City of the Plains, an urban oasis in the wilderness of the Wild West.[5] Numerous factors led to the early success and survival of Denver.

While it first existed as a dusty, brawling mining camp and supply center along the South Platte River, Denver quickly established itself as the finance, transportation, and communications hub for the Rocky Mountain region. The vast hinterland of natural resources, including minerals from the mountains and cattle and sugar beet agriculture from the plains, flowed through Denver, where they were processed, refined, and loaded onto trains bound for distant markets. The Denver and Pacific Railroad was the first linkage to the transcontinental Union Pacific Railroad in 1870, ensuring the city's vital role as a transportation center and stimulating many more railroad lines and communications investments. Denver's financial stability and regional importance was further enhanced when the federal U.S. Branch Mint was established in 1863 and the First National Bank of Denver opened in 1864.

Great entrepreneurial leadership from William Larimer, William Byers, John Evans, Horace Tabor, Eben Smith, Jerome Chaffee, David Moffat, Walter Cheesman, and many others modeled the spirit of laissez-faire capitalism, which offered growth and prosperity across the region. As owners of the mining, railroading, banking, newspaper publishing, merchandising, or warehousing industries, they worked to establish a strong local economy that serviced the regional resource extraction activities of the hinterland, where

Denver's role as "gateway to the mountains" was solidified. Their entrepreneurial leadership helped secure outside investments and diversification of the economic base that ultimately enabled the city to withstand a long series of boom-and-bust economic cycles.

Colorado was branded the "Switzerland of America," initiating a robust tourism industry centered on the majestic Rocky Mountains, and all the scenery, splendor, and recreation they offered. For early Denver, the attractive climate generated a significant population influx of so-called health seekers. The tuberculosis epidemic of the nineteenth and early twentieth centuries sent sufferers ("consumptives") and their families from their homes in eastern industrial cities to locations in the West with more favorable climate. It was believed that Denver's dry climate, high elevation, clean air, mild weather, and abundant sunshine provided therapeutic relief to consumptives. Eventually tens of thousands of health seekers would descend on Colorado, stimulating an extensive health industry of hospitals and relief societies.

The rapid economic growth and prosperity from establishing an urban frontier and reaping the hinterland bounties came with tragic exploitation. Mining and smelting wastes polluted nearby land and water supplies, and overuse of dry agricultural lands exacerbated the challenges of drought years. Native Americans were "vanquished" from the plains, as justified by racist ideologies, in order to remove obstacles of progress and develop commercial agricultural activity that diversified Denver's economy.[6] The Sand Creek Massacre of 1864 was the most horrific anti-Indian event in which over 160 Cheyenne and Arapaho, mostly women and children, were killed during a nighttime military ambush led by U.S. Army colonel John Chivington.

In the city itself, many persons who never benefited from capitalist opportunity suffered marginalization or exploitation; others became the unlucky ones, losing everything during periods of crushing economic busts. In the midst of this poverty of the early gold rush era, many individuals started charities to give help to others.[7] Elizabeth Byers founded the Ladies Union Aid Society to help down-and-out gold rush families, and Ella Vincent's Ladies Relief Society helped mining widows and prostitutes. Seeing all the great and varied need in Denver, Frances Wisebart Jacobs, along with a priest, two ministers, and a rabbi, established in 1887 a "community chest" to consolidate all the local charities and better serve the community. This was the very beginning of the United Way.

As in most cities, Denver's philanthropic legacy helped provide for the people in need and build a better society. J. K. Mullen, a Denver-area flour mill industrialist, was a great philanthropist, who among other things established what is known today as the Little Sisters of the Poor Home for the Aged and gave funds to build Saint Cajetan's Catholic Church, which long served the local Hispanic parish. Helen and May Bonfils, daughters of *Denver Post* owner Frederick G. Bonfils, were extremely benevolent women who shared their wealth with Denver, including funding the Church of the Holy Ghost, the Denver Center for the Performing Arts, hospitals, health clinics, and the ongoing legacy of a $100-plus million foundation for arts and creativity.

The Denver of today also exists in part from a long legacy of great civic leadership determined to keep Denver beautiful. Mayor Robert Speer (in office 1904–12 and 1916–18) was one of the most prolific in this regard. Influenced by the 1893 Columbian Exposition held in Chicago, Speer sought to bring the City Beautiful vision to the dusty cow town of Denver and make it a "Paris on the Platte" or "Rome of the Rockies." At the beginning of the twentieth century Denver was a dirty city, with limited street and sanitation planning, and a dearth of green spaces and city parks. Speer sought to bring order and beauty to the center of the city (Figure 1). This he did with the Civic Center, an open park space downtown surrounded by government buildings (including the City County Building and the state capitol), museums, and monumental neoclassical architectural structures. It was designated a national historic landmark in 2012. He built the Auditorium Arena (today the Ellie Caulkins Opera House) to bring culture to the masses with free plays and operas. He also built parks (City Park, Cheesman Park) and parkways radiating out from the city to help make neighborhoods beautiful and establish Denver as a great place to live. Finally, Mayor Speer held a strong vision of preserving the natural beauty of the mountain landscape, and to make it more accessible to Denver's residents and better promote tourism. This culminated in the creation of the Denver Mountain Parks, a collection of twenty-two parks over fourteen thousand acres owned and maintained by the City and County of Denver, but completely in the mountains and outside the municipal boundaries. This vision of keeping Denver beautiful and providing access to nature remained a key theme of civic leadership over the next one hundred years and more.

Figure 1. Welcome Arch. Made of steel, the lighted arch stood outside Union Station from 1906 to 1931. The reverse side said, "Mizpah," a Hebrew expression of kind feelings and good wishes between loved ones while they are apart. (Image source: Denver Public Library, Western History Collection, [X-25212].)

The Mile High City

Another enduring theme of Denver's past, present, and future is rapid population growth and the accompanying challenges. This is particularly true in Denver since the mid-twentieth century as continuous debates center on how to balance the economic benefits of growth with the impacts on the environment and regional quality of life. Also during this period, a new identity of Denver emerged, one that moves beyond its Wild West cow town roots. The Mile High City nickname has branded the city as a place set apart, even as it moves toward becoming more globally connected and an attractive destination city.

For much of urban America the end of World War II was a major turning point. In Denver, "massive federal spending, an influx of newcomers, and a pent-up demand for new cars and new housing led to a boom that would change this drowsy cow town into a sprawling metropolis."[8] Military and federal expansion in Denver led to significant job growth in the area. And suburbanization trends coupled with the in-migration surge expanded the Denver region further from the central city to the surrounding suburbs and exurbs.

This metropolitan-wide residential reshuffling began to reveal racial tension in Denver, a place people had perceived to be free of the segregation and urban crisis issues experienced in other U.S. cities. But underneath, Denver had long been a socially fractured city. Many Native American and Spanish Mexican communities in the area predated the establishment of Colorado and were marginalized after the founding of Denver. By the 1920s more Latinos/Hispanics and African Americans migrated seeking economic opportunities. It was the 1970s school desegregation fights that exposed the depths of Denver's racial divide (see Chapter 3). The 1973 U.S. Supreme Court case *Keyes v. Denver School District No. 1* not only set a precedent for busing desegregation in northern states, but it also articulated that Denver was a triracial city—a reality previously unacknowledged. A strong antibusing movement in the region led to the 1974 Poundstone Amendment to the Colorado Constitution, which effectively ended Denver's ability to annex land from suburban counties.

In the final decades of the twentieth century Denver faced a new population growth surge during the Sun Belt migration trend of the 1970s and early 1980s. This Sun Belt migration saw a dramatic population redistribution shift from northern and eastern cities and states to locations in the South and West, including cities such as Los Angeles, San Diego, Phoenix, Dallas, Houston, Atlanta, and Denver. For new residents these locales had the allure of sunnier and warmer climates with many natural amenities. They also offered new and diverse economic opportunities, as the national economy restructured from heavy industry to light manufacturing and service-based activities. The Sun Belt was particularly attractive to businesses owing to lower energy costs, non–labor union states, probusiness politics, and proximity to international trade partners of the South and the Pacific Rim. Some of the Sun Belt states' economies emphasized military, aerospace, development of domestic fossil fuel resources, or establishing retirement communities.

Denver's specialization in the industries of banking, oil and mineral extraction, federal services, telecommunications, and transportation escalated the city to the ranks of the largest U.S. metropolitan areas through its position as the major regional commercial center for the plains and the Rocky Mountains. The city's booming oil economy even became the setting of the popular 1980s American prime-time soap opera *Dynasty*, which revolved around the oil-wealthy Carrington family. Although Denver grew rapidly as an important economic center, it remained perceived by many as a sleepy cow town out on the western frontier. It also faced many of the challenges similar to other Sun Belt cities, including poverty and segregation, economic recessions due to resource base dependencies, or the negative impacts of population growth and development including suburban sprawl, traffic congestion, pollution, environmental degradation, or the loss of traditional regional characteristics and identity. And, tragically, Denver was also the site of two of the worst mass shootings in the United States: Columbine High School in 1999 and the Aurora Theaters in 2012.

The substantial population growth, expansion of the regional freeway system, and continued outward sprawl has not pleased everyone. Locals lamented the loss of their quiet and slower-paced city that once existed and targeted their frustration at the city's numerous transplants from elsewhere. The undercurrents of antigrowth disdain have played out in local area bumper stickers. Some, with a green-and-white silhouette of the mountains, simply say: "No Vacancy" or "Native" (Figure 2). And others, with anger directed at what seemed an adoption of California-style highway and car culture, read, "Don't Californicate Colorado." An environmental consequence of Denver's growth was a massive air pollution problem worsened by a booming automobile culture resulting in a ubiquitous brown cloud of haze hanging over the city during winter months. In 1987—for all the world to see—a two-page photo appeared in *National Geographic* magazine of Denver's congested highways with the skyline barely visible through the haze.[9] And after the Denver Broncos football team lost the 1989 Super Bowl, a CBS sportscaster quipped that Denver had "never been No. 1 in anything—but carbon monoxide."[10] Much to the dismay of city leaders and boosters, Denver and its dismal air quality became a national joke.

By the 1990s city leaders had several negative images to overcome: Denver's enduring legacy as a sleepy and unsophisticated cow town, its infamy as a dirty-air suburban-and-highway mush trending toward a Little Los Angeles, and Denver as merely the gateway—or worse, the "locker room"—to the Rocky Mountains.[11] Thus began a determined push to make Denver an attractive city to live in and a destination for tourism and business.

Major urban revitalization and megaprojects focused on Denver as easy to get to, easy to get around, competitive, cool, and livable, with numerous choices for entertainment, culture, and recreation. Mayor Federico Peña's (1983–91) "Imagine a Great City" vision resulted in many transformative in-

Figure 2. Two antigrowth bumper stickers observed in the Denver metropolitan area. (Photo reproduction: E. Eric Boschmann.)

frastructure projects, including a new convention center, the Coors Field baseball stadium, new libraries, and the Denver International Airport (DIA)—the first completely new U.S. airport in over twenty years. Mayor Wellington Webb (1991–2003) extended Mayor Speer's City Beautiful movement by adding extensive parkland to the city, established a vision for downtown revitalization and economic prosperity, oversaw the construction of DIA and several downtown professional sports stadiums, expanded the convention center, and supported the 2004 FasTracks plan to construct 122 miles of new rail transit in the region. And as a preservationist and developer, Dana Crawford's tireless work saved much of Lower Downtown Denver from urban renewal demolition, revitalizing old streets and buildings into vibrant and economically prosperous gathering spaces such as Larimer Square and Union Station. In fact, former Denver mayor and Colorado governor John Hickenlooper noted that the impact of Crawford is immeasurable, as she "single-handedly saved lower downtown Denver."[12]

The remaking of Denver into a destination city also created it into a lifestyle city, attracting imaginations of Americans as one of the most enviable places to live. For decades the Rocky Mountains of Colorado held national allure. The popularity of folk musician John Denver, who "embodied Colorado's recreational-environmental ideal," highlighted to mass audiences the majesty of the Rocky Mountains and the human endeavor to escape the city and engage nature. Eventually the tourism activities of camping, hiking, skiing, or white-water rafting stimulated a trend of living where tourists play and shifted Denver-as-urban-gateway to Denver-as-residential-vacationland.[13] This New West city (Figure 3) offered opportunities to live, work, and play in a bustling urban center with quick access to endless amenities of recreation, environment, scenery, and entertainment out in the vast Colorado backyard. It became a place where people visited and never wanted to leave: "How we came to Colorado is the same old story. Boy and girl come to visit Colorado, boy and girl fall in love with Colorado, boy and girl realize, 'Hey! We could live here!' and boy and girl move to Colorado."[14] And to counter the antigrowth sentiment, bumper stickers of newcomers staking their own claim to Colorado appeared, proclaiming: "I'm not a NATIVE, but I got here as fast as I could!"

Future population growth is perhaps the greatest challenge ahead for the Denver region. Colorado added one hundred thousand new residents in a twelve-month period (July 2014–July 2015) representing a 1.89 percent growth rate, twice the national average of 0.79 percent. Much of this is due to in-migration, rather than higher fertility rates. The Colorado population is expected to grow from just over five million residents in 2010 to almost eight million in 2040. And with an average annual growth rate of 1.5 percent, the

Figure 3. A New West city: Denver's past meets Denver today. (Image courtesy of Colorado Public Radio; photo by Nathaniel Minor.)

2010 Denver metropolitan area population of 2.6 million will increase to 3.4 million in 2030, and 4 million by 2040. Looking more broadly, the Front Range megaregion that extends from Albuquerque and Santa Fe, New Mexico, in the south, to Cheyenne, Wyoming, in the north, is expected to grow 87 percent by 2050, from 5.4 million in 2010 to 10.2 million people.[15] The majority of today's new Colorado migrants are eighteen- to thirty-four-year-olds with bachelor's degrees who come from California, Texas, Florida, Arizona, and New York.[16] They settle in the Denver area counties drawn not simply to the nearby skiing, urban hiking, or microbreweries, but also by the many opportunities in a strong regional jobs market.[17]

There are many particular challenges ahead in preparing for explosive population growth in the Denver region. The first is transportation. In recent years the region has increased its alternative and public transportation options. Light rail and commuter rail lines are expanding, as are bus rapid-transit lines. Denver is considered bike friendly; new bicycle corridors are being established throughout the city, and an extensive bike-share program has been in place for a decade. New street designs are placing more emphasis on walkability, and use of car-sharing programs is gaining popularity. And new high-density mixed-use developments have focused on providing access to daily activities without the need of an automobile. But this growing alternative transportation infrastructure does not reach vast swaths of the extended Denver region. For many, Denver remains a very car-dependent place. And this is a source of great concern over future traffic congestion given the projected population growth.

Another issue is rising inequality, particularly as it relates to housing in a booming real estate market. With the influx of new residents, housing and rental costs are already skyrocketing (some years with double-digit growth), and vacancy rates are at a record low. In the suburbs new housing and apartment construction is swift, and the city is expanding through high-density infill residential developments. But construction has not kept up with demand, and in 2015 Denver was listed among the nation's "hottest" housing markets. Older and centrally located neighborhoods are undergoing dynamic transformations. In these newly desirable areas, older homes are refurbished or demolished and replaced with larger modern homes ("scrape and build"). Property value increases are resulting in gentrification-driven displacement. With this growth and changing real estate geographies, there are deep concerns over the availability of affordable housing and proximity to jobs and public transit options. And further, there is concern that the housing affordability equation will even squeeze out middle-class workers in favor of the elite.

Future population growth also places greater pressure on protecting the natural environment and managing scarce resources. Growth management agreements such as the Mile High Compact have potential to direct the location and density of new urban developments (see Chapter 5). But suburban and exurban sprawl will likely continue into a variety of sensitive locales. Further human encroachment into unoccupied territory in the mountain foothills will expand the wildland-urban interface and the disasters that culminate from naturally occurring wildfires. And finally, with the unending scarcity of water in a semiarid region, there is a paradox of living in the West: large populations are supported by massive water infrastructures (including dams, reservoirs, tunnels, or ditches), but those infrastructures disrupt the very ecosystems and landscapes that lure people to live in the West.[18] The water resource challenge will possibly be the most pressing issue in the upcoming decades in Denver and all Colorado.

Regional Overview

The lands that became Colorado were acquired by the United States through the Louisiana Purchase (1803) and the Treaty of Guadalupe Hidalgo (1848). The Colorado Territory was established in 1861, and statehood was finalized in 1876. Throughout the subsequent decades of westward expansion, urbanization, and ongoing trends of in-migration, many cities grew rapidly in Colorado particularly along the Front Range. The Front Range is the easternmost range of the Rocky Mountains that runs from Pikes Peak near Colorado Springs, north to the Wyoming border. Today the urban areas just to the east of the Front Range (i.e., Denver, Boulder, Fort Collins, Colorado Springs, and Pueblo) are collectively referred to as the Front Range urban corridor and are connected by the north-south Interstate 25 and U.S. Highway Route 85.

A vast majority of Colorado's population today lives in this urban corridor. And the Denver metropolitan area is the largest in the entire state. In fact, in 2015 the Denver metropolitan area contained 51 percent of the entire Colorado population, and 55 percent of all Colorado employment.[19] Today the Denver metropolitan area is defined as the Denver-Aurora-Lakewood,

Colorado, Metropolitan Statistical Area, which includes ten counties and approximately 2.7 million residents, based on 2015 U.S. Census estimates (Figure 4). The urban concentration of Denver through the mid-twentieth century was centered on the consolidated City and County of Denver as well as the surrounding counties of Adams, Arapahoe, and Jefferson. Rapid population and economic growth expanded the metropolitan area to include counties with expansive rural areas of the plains (Douglas, Elbert), several counties in the foothills of the mountains (Park, Clear Creek, Gilpin), and the newly established suburban county of Broomfield. The nearby major cities of Boulder, Greeley, Fort Collins, and Colorado Springs are all considered separate metropolitan areas.

While the topical focus of this book is on the Denver metropolitan area described here, its historic evolution is tied to a much larger hinterland area extending into both the mountains and the plains, and its regional

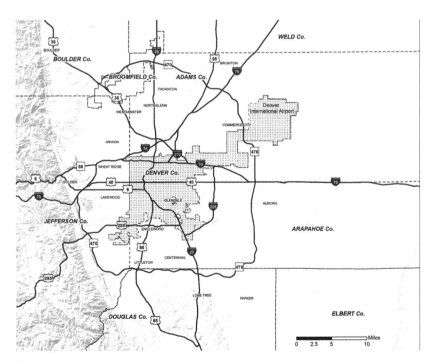

Figure 4. Map of the central portion of the Denver metropolitan area. (Map created by E. Eric Boschmann and Paul Donegan.)

prominence does connect it to the other major urban areas of Colorado. For this reason, the story of Denver today is a story inclusive of Colorado as a whole.

*   *   *

This book provides both a sweeping look at the Denver region over time, as well as many in-depth analyses of social, economic, and political processes that are central to Denver's identity. The book begins in Chapter 1 with a brief examination of key physical geographic features of the economic and social trajectory of the city, the region, and its people. First, Denver is situated within the context of Colorado's three natural regions: the eastern plains, the mountains, and the Western Slope. Then, major natural environmental issues are addressed, including Denver's climate characteristics and the perennial issues of water resources and the geographies of water distribution and consumption across Colorado. The Denver region faces natural hazards of drought, flooding, and wildfires, which are exacerbated by both increased population growth along the Front Range urban corridor as well as changes in climate patterns.

Like many cities, Denver's economic history is a story of the booming and busting cyclicality of fortunes. Chapter 2 chronicles how Denver's economic base evolved from the early mining and agricultural days, to the buildup of a large military and defense industry center during and after World War II, the rise and fall of the region's oil and gas extraction, and growth of a postindustrial economy of the late twentieth century centered on new high-tech and service industries and large public works projects. The Frontier Cities model of city growth is presented to better understand Denver's early economic and population evolution, and the development of its linkages to the larger urban system of regional and national urban centers. The construction of Denver International Airport (DIA) was a very large public works project with significant economic impacts on the region. The story of DIA's evolution is given, along with its economic benefits and political challenges, and the future proposals for "aerotropolis" developments in the surrounding areas.

With regards to population growth and diversity, at the beginning of the twenty-first century Denver is above the average for U.S. metropolitan areas.

Chapter 3 explores the trends and provides a historical overview of three key population growth eras in Denver. The "pioneering growth" occurred in the late nineteenth and early twentieth centuries when people migrated in for work in mining and agricultural industries, as well as large numbers of migrants known as health seekers—easterners suffering from tuberculosis. The post–World War II era was fueled by the military and federal buildup in Denver, and the Sun Belt city migration era began in the late twentieth century. No doubt the population growth in Denver led to outward sprawl and a changing spatial configuration of the region. Several new types of urban places emerged out of this growth, such as the Denver Tech Center edge city, or the master-planned community of Highlands Ranch. The general residential patterns are described, and emphasis is given to the history of racial discrimination and regional conflicts over school desegregation; Denver's role as a reemerging immigrant gateway is also explored. The Five Points neighborhood serves as a historical analysis of changing urban neighborhoods. One of the first suburbs of Denver, Five Points became historically prominent as the center of the African American community, a jazz music hub, and the "Harlem of the West." The neighborhood suffered decline from disinvestment in the 1960s urban crisis but today is at the center of new reurbanism trends and extensive gentrification.

With economic globalization and the rise of intercity competition, cities have needed to become more entrepreneurial in making themselves attractive to businesses, jobs, visitors, residents, and investments. Chapter 4 looks at the changing images of Denver over time, from the Old West to the New West and the emergence of Denver as the Mile High City—an urban place set apart. Furthermore, Denver is set within a larger Colorado story whereby the Rocky Mountains ushered in a new image of outdoor recreationalism, environmental consciousness, and personal attachment to place. This is firmly embedded within the development of a mountain-led tourism industry, and the selling of the American West. Denver's own tourism history is largely an effort of urban place making, with particular emphasis on the urban revitalization of downtown and the creation of "people-clustering projects," as well as the interesting cultural-led development of Denver into an art town.

With such rapid population growth and urban expansion in Denver during the latter half of the twentieth century, the region faced many challenges of political cooperation across municipalities, and competing paradigms of urban growth development strategies. The theme of regionalism is addressed in Chapter 5, which highlights the political relations between the City and

County of Denver with its neighboring counties and suburban municipalities. On one hand great conflict and fragmentation characterizes the history of Denver's growth and its processes and attempts of annexation over time. Yet successes of regional collaboration and integration are many, including regional rail transit development and a coordinated vision of long-term urban growth. Chapter 6 then outlines how the smart growth movement in Denver shifted development trends from low-density automobile-based suburban and exurban sprawl toward higher-density, mixed-use, transit-oriented urban centers. This story represents a significant effort by a relatively large U.S. metropolitan region to change its urban growth trajectory.

Chapter 1

Physical Landscape and
Natural Surroundings

Denver is an improbable city. Its origin is a bit unlikely as it lacked several of the favorable conditions from which cities typically emerge. There was no natural abundant water source to support a large, successful agricultural settlement, nor a navigable waterway. It was not located along any major trade route. In fact, the impenetrable Rocky Mountains forced the early east-west routes to traverse through Santa Fe, New Mexico, to the south, and Cheyenne, Wyoming, to the north. Nor did the region have an ideal balance of proximity to resources, markets, labor, and transportation networks central to the emergence of so many eastern U.S. industrial towns. But as it became an "instant city," Denver's founding and continuance to thrive rests on its hinterland and the inextricable economic ties to its natural surroundings. This chapter details several physical geographic characteristics central to answering the question: what is Denver today, and how did it evolve historically?

Denver's Hinterland

Understanding Denver's hinterland begins with placing the city in the larger context of the state of Colorado. A map of Colorado can generally be divided into three sections that approximate the state's primary natural regions. Each region contains distinctive topography, natural resources, vegetation, and climate, helping to create a diverse landscape (Figure 5).[1] These regions not only shaped Denver's early economic and social fortunes but also remain integral today.

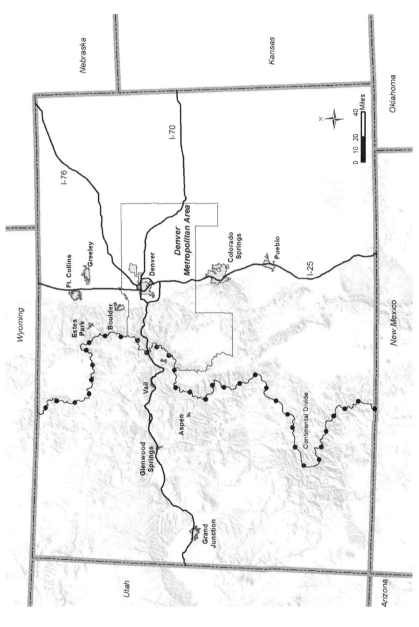

Figure 5. Colorado regional map. (Map created by E. Eric Boschmann and Court Ballinger; map data sources: Esri, NOAA, USGS.)

The Eastern Plains

The eastern section of Colorado is characterized as a large, relatively flat terrain of plains and prairie landscape, with dominant vegetation of low grasses and few trees except deciduous cottonwoods and willows that follow the paths of streams and rivers. Its elevation between four thousand and six thousand feet above sea level gradually inclines westerly toward the base of the Rocky Mountain range.[2] For contemporary travelers driving into Colorado from the east, this vast expanse is often seen as an unpleasant car ride that must be endured to reach the mountains. But while much emphasis is placed on the natural amenities of the Rocky Mountain region in Colorado, the eastern plains had significant impacts in shaping the Front Range urban corridor, of which Denver forms a part.[3]

Denver was founded much later than many West Coast and southwestern cities including Santa Fe (1610), Albuquerque (1706), San Diego (1769), Tucson (1775), San Francisco (1776), Los Angeles (1781), Seattle (1851), and Portland (1851). While the Rocky Mountains did create an impenetrable barrier during early westward expansion of the United States, it was the conditions and early perceptions of the eastern plains that made the area more likely to be avoided than explored.

The eastern plains, on which Denver is situated, was once described as "parched country," a land "almost wholly unfit for cultivation, and uninhabitable by people depending upon agriculture for their subsistence."[4] So strong was this assessment of the area as an inhospitable, arid, and barren landscape that early maps of the region labeled it the "Great American Desert."[5] No explorer in the early 1800s would have predicted that a thriving metropolitan area with over 2.6 million people would blossom in this seemingly unproductive land.

Also at that time, great fear of Native American peoples living in the eastern plains gave pause to European American pursuits in the area. The longest continuous inhabitants of Colorado are the Utes, with ancestral roots reaching back ten thousand years and extending to today's Southern Ute Indian Reservation in southwestern Colorado.[6] They are considered the only Native Americans indigenous to Colorado. Other First Coloradans were the Anasazi (Ancestral Puebloans), who resided in western Colorado from approximately 600 to 1300 c.e. Together, these First Coloradans demonstrated adaptability and resourcefulness in the sometimes harsh and changing Colorado landscape. Through creativity and pragmatism, they understood what was possible from the local environment. It is estimated that in 1100 C.E. nearly thirty thousand Ancestral Puebloans lived in a land of abundance. They learned the seasonal variations of water and used capture and conservation strategies to maintain maize, beans, and squash crops with only sixteen inches of annual rainfall. A great drought descended on the region in the mid-1200s. In this period of scarcity and fragility, the Ancestral Puebloans established cliff dwellings (preserved today at the Mesa Verde National Park) and ultimately abandoned the region by 1280.

Along the Denver Front Range the region was most likely used by a series of different tribes over time, including the Ute, Apache, Cheyenne, and Arapaho. Given the semiarid climate and the extremes in seasonal weather, it was an area best suited for nomadic existence of hunters and gatherers, often transitioning between the plains, the foothills, and the mountains. Evidence today shows that the protected alcoves created by the hogback ridges and red rock uplifts along the Front Range served as temporary shelters during times of transition. Hunting in the foothills and mountains consisted largely of elk, deer, and bighorn sheep, with more bison and black-tailed prairie dogs on the plains.[7] At the time of European contact and expansion in North America during the 1500–1600s, the Utes occupied the mountain region of Colorado, while the Apaches occupied the plains. When Denver was settled by European Americans in the 1850s, the Cheyenne and Arapaho dominated in the plains. As was true for much of the westward expansion era, fear of Native Americans often escalated into great catastrophes, losses, and forced displacement. In Colorado's history, both the 1864 Sand Creek Massacre and the 1879 Meeker Massacre represent horrific actions taken in pursuit of settling this region (see Chapter 2).

Across Colorado, place names (toponyms) reflect the local history of First Coloradans, including counties (e.g., Arapahoe), cities (e.g., Pueblo, Ouray), and street names (e.g., Zuni and Navajo in Denver). In addition to the snow-capped mountain peaks, many teepees would have dotted the plains landscape when European American settlers first arrived.[8] The historic legacy of First Coloradans remains important today for understanding regional history and reconciling with the events of domination and displacement. But also, as Coloradans today consider how to live in Colorado with changing environmental conditions, there are lessons to be learned from First Coloradans, who made hard decisions and adapted in times of scarcity.

By the 1870s, perceptions of the eastern plains as the Great American Desert changed. Southern and western Colorado regions had already utilized Spanish *acequia* irrigation techniques, a community-based system of shared building, maintenance, and management of irrigation ditches. These practices were adapted and transferred to the eastern plains where a network of ditches and canals were built along the Rocky Mountain–fed South Platte and Arkansas River valleys. Along the South Platte River in northeastern Colorado, early cattle ranchers supplemented grassland grazing with irrigated cattle crops (hay or alfalfa). This region also became important to sugar beet farming, where the Great Western Sugar Company dominated. Similarly, in the southeastern Arkansas River valley cattle feed crops were irrigated, as were melon crops and small fruit orchards. The eastern plains also developed dry-land agricultural industries, particularly in wheat and barley grains. Since the 1950s, center pivot irrigation has pumped water up from the Ogallala Aquifer, creating a new economy of water-intensive crops (soybeans, corn) that fetch higher market values. And in addition to crop cultivation and cattle ranching, these resources grown on the eastern plains were also processed for export through numerous canneries, sugar refineries, breweries, meatpacking plants, and flourmills. As discussed later (Chapter 2), this agricultural industry in Denver's hinterland of the eastern plains has long been central to the city's economy and identity.

The Mountains

Denver sits in the geologic transition zone where the eastern plains give way to the Rocky Mountains. The Rockies were formed eighty million years ago by tectonic plates sliding under the North American plate at a shallow angle of subduction, causing uplift. The mountains were further shaped by ongoing tectonic activity and erosion, resulting in a series of extraordinarily broad and high mountain ranges. The foothills are considered the higher terrain between six thousand and nine thousand feet immediately to the west of Denver and the rest of the Front Range urban corridor. This area contains many interesting geologic structures such as the Dakota Hogbacks, a ridge outcropping of steeply dipping sedimentary rock where sandstone tilts at a sixty-degree angle after millions of years of uplift and erosion. What was once a prehistoric ocean floor is today a geologic wonderland and includes dinosaur tracks and fossil segments from the Jurassic period 160 million years ago (Figure 6). Within these sandstone outcroppings humans have created many iconic parks, including the Red Rocks Amphitheater and

Figure 6. Dakota Hogback geologic formation, west of Denver. (Photo courtesy of Jeremy McCreary.)

Roxborough Park in the Denver area, or the Garden of the Gods in Colorado Springs.

This mountain region of Colorado is where the long Rocky Mountain range running the length of North America reaches its highest. It creates a diverse montane, subalpine, and alpine landscape of mountain peaks separated by river canyons and valley plains. Rather than a single range of mountains, there are several north-south-running ranges, such as the Front Range, Sangre de Cristo, Sawatch, or the San Juan Mountains. The Continental Divide runs through here separating mountain water runoff between westward flow to the Pacific Ocean and eastward flow to the Gulf of Mexico. The natural forest landscape is dominated by coniferous trees such as spruce-fir, ponderosa pine, lodgepole pine, piñon-juniper, and the deciduous aspen. With moisture fronts flowing in from the Pacific Ocean, the high country receives between twenty-five and fifty inches or more of precipitation annually, usually in the form of snowfall. This creates Colorado's snowcapped landscape, fuels the snow-based industries of skiing and snowboarding, and provides municipal water supply to millions of western U.S. residents. These mountains are the headwaters for many major rivers that flow through surrounding western, southwestern, and central plains states.

This region contains more mountain peaks (fifty-four in all) above fourteen thousand feet (referred to as "fourteeners") than anywhere else in North America, and with a relatively high average elevation throughout Colorado, it is often considered the rooftop of the continent. For tourists, residents, and adventurists alike, the picturesque mountain peaks have come to symbolize an idealized natural world (see Chapter 4). Specific physical landscape scenes, such as the oft-photographed Maroon Bells near Aspen, create iconic identities of place (Figure 7). And through time many of Colorado's peaks evolved into cultural icons for local communities (such as Mount Evans and Longs Peak as the peaks of identity for Denver), while others, such as Pikes Peak, foster a larger national identity. The majestic nature and vastness of the mountains have long inspired a sense of awe and wonder; it was atop Pikes Peak in 1893 that Katharine Lee Bates wrote a poem that would become the lyrics for *America the Beautiful*. Today, outdoor recreation including hiking, camping, biking, skiing, and water rafting establish a centrality of activity in this mountain landscape. The allure of the mountains and an ethos of recreationalism foster many urban-based adventurist subcultures. For instance, "peak baggers," who may live and work in Denver, are individuals that spend their weekends and free time aspiring to hike up every fourteener mountain for the thrill of mountaineering, skill, and endurance.[9]

Prior to the mountain landscapes' role in tourism and recreational industries of Denver and Colorado, their importance rested in the abundance of natural resources. From 1820 to 1840 the fur trade peaked in the Rocky Mountains and helped provide supply to the popular fashion of beaver fur hats in the eastern United States and across Europe. Eventually silk hats became more fashionable and decimated the fur trade. But it was the abundance of mining opportunities in the mountain region that brought about the greatest economic change, as Colorado contains over seven hundred minerals. Some of the most historically important and heavily mined have been gold, silver, lead, zinc, molybdenum, copper, and tungsten. Today's mountain landscape is dotted with both abandoned and active mines, and many old mining mountain towns live on as destinations for tourists seeking the old ghost town mystique. Across all regions of Colorado exist energy

Figure 7. The Maroon Bells, near Aspen, Colorado. (Image source: Jesse Varner, Creative Commons CC-BY-SA-2.0.)

sources of oil, natural gas, oil shale, coal, and uranium.[10] All these extractive industries in the mountains were instrumental to the economic success of the Denver region and the state as a whole. But they are also at the core of modern environmental tensions, between traditional economies of resource extraction, and the economies dependent on protecting a clean environment and ensuring the preservation of picturesque scenery.

The Western Slope

The westernmost section of the state is known as the Western Slope—where the Rocky Mountain range meets the high Colorado Plateau. Here the physical landscape transitions from the rugged mountain peak and valley system to one of more mesas, canyons, escarpments, and floodplains. Geologic time is highly evident in many colorful rock formations and visible stratigraphy. The city of Grand Junction serves as the historical regional center where uranium, molybdenum, and oil dominate the extractive resource economy. With less alpine terrain, there is limited downhill skiing in the Western Slope, but tourism exists for biking and water rafting sports, as well as visiting natural hot springs, such as at Glenwood Springs. The Grand Valley River project of 1925 diverted the Colorado River to supply water to agricultural lands in the counties surrounding Grand Junction for the sugar beet industry; today it creates a bountiful landscape of fruit tree orchards, including apples, cherries, peaches, and numerous vineyards. While geographically remote from the Denver urban area—much of it over a half day's drive away—the important agricultural, mining, and tourism economies of the Western Slope keep Denver inextricably tied to this region.

Climate

Denver's climate is influenced by three major features: the city is situated at a high elevation on the high plains, it sits along the east side of the Rocky Mountains where jet streams flow west to east, and it has a deep interior continental and midlatitude location. The regional climate is classified as a semiarid steppe (*BSk* in the Köppen system) receiving ten to twenty inches of precipitation annually. This combination of dry conditions, high elevation, and continentality results in large seasonal temperature variations, as well as large diurnal temperature swings. The thinner atmosphere allows in more intense solar energy, keeping winter days mild, but summer days hot. In the winter months this can result in frequent and numerous freeze-thaw cycles.[11]

Travel brochures have historically depicted Colorado as a snowbound landscape, resulting in a somewhat false perception of Denver as a snowy place. With the dominant west-to-east airflow pattern, the mountain ranges provide a weather-moderating rain-shadow effect that protects Denver from most major storms that blanket the high country. However, a subdominant airflow pattern brings major winter weather storms to Denver in autumn and spring that occasionally produce snow precipitation measurable in feet. This pattern occurs when warm, moist air flows up from the Texas gulf coast and meets a cold, dry Canadian air mass in the eastern plains. As the jet stream crosses the mountains a low-pressure area emerges where the contrasting temperatures between air masses creates instability, resulting in snow, hail, rain, or tornadoes.

Denver is known for pleasant weather, experiencing all four seasons, generally maintaining mild temperatures with abundant sunshine. Early on, the dry and sunny climate of Denver attracted both tourists and new residents. The migration of tuberculosis patients and their families to Colorado at the turn of the twentieth century was driven by the presumed benefits of the local climate. These health seekers arrived searching for relief and a possible cure through exposure to the cool, crisp, clean, dry air of Colorado (Figure 8). For tourism boosters, the dry and sunny climate soon became a key promotional feature. In fact, the common claim that Denver enjoys "three hundred days of sunshine a year" was a catchphrase first used in 1870 by the Colorado Promotion and Publicity Committee. It gained national attention and remains a long-standing popular myth about Denver's climate. Though an abundance of sunshine exists, there is widespread meteorological evidence contrary to this oft-cited belief.[12] For Denver to actually achieve three hun-

Figure 8. Tuberculosis patients undergoing heliotherapy at the Jewish Consumptives' Relief Society Sanatorium, Denver, Colorado, circa 1930s. (Image source: courtesy of the Beck Archives of Rocky Mountain Jewish Historical Society, Special Collections, University Libraries, University of Denver.)

dred days of sunshine would require counting all days that are sunny in the morning and cloudy in the afternoon (or vice versa), as well as days with thin clouds covering the sky.[13]

Water

"Here is a land where life is written in water," wrote Colorado poet Thomas Ferril in 1940.[14] Ferril's words underscore the scarcity of water endemic to the region. In fact, water is perhaps the defining and most critical human-environmental issue confronting Denver and all Colorado. As evidenced by First Coloradans, survival was long dictated by the availability of water resources and the practices of conservation. Today, the problems of water in Colorado emerge from three primary issues: the geographic distribution of water, downstream claims to water by surrounding states, and increased demands due to urban development and agricultural industries. This confluence of hydrologic processes, political agreements, and demographic changes is exacerbated in the era of climate destabilization and the frequency of droughts that reduce water supplies while demand grows.

Water, in the form of rain and snowfall precipitation, is unevenly distributed across Colorado. The high-country region can produce in some places more than forty inches of precipitation annually. The semiarid eastern plains, located in the rain shadow (leeward) side of the mountains, can average only ten to fifteen inches. In relationship to Colorado's human population, this creates a dramatic mismatch between locations of water resources and major urban centers. In this context, the Continental Divide is sometimes referred to as the "80–20 Line." Eighty percent of the Colorado population lives east of the divide, and 20 percent to the west. Conversely, 80 percent of available water in Colorado is *west* of the divide, and 20 percent is to the east. The abundant moisture precipitated in the Colorado Rocky Mountains creates the headwaters for numerous rivers that flow through eighteen different U.S. states and Mexico, including the Rio Grande, North Platte, South Platte, Arkansas, Cache la Poudre, and Republican Rivers flowing to the east of the divide, and the Colorado River flowing to the west.

The western side of Colorado, where most of the precipitation occurs, is dominated by the Colorado River watershed, a major source of water for the southwest region of the United States. The river begins near Lake Granby, and the entire river basin drains 243,000 square miles of land in Colorado,

Wyoming, Utah, Arizona, New Mexico, Nevada, California, and northern Mexico. Major dams include Glen Canyon Dam and Lake Powell in Utah and Arizona, and Hoover Dam and Lake Mead in Nevada and Arizona. It flows through the Sonoran Desert region along the Arizona-California border before entering Sonora and Baja California, Mexico and ending at the Sea of Cortez. More than thirty million people depend on the Colorado River for agricultural and municipal water supply. For example, diversion from the Hoover Dam supplies Las Vegas, Nevada; the Colorado River Aqueduct diverts water to Los Angeles, California; and the Central Arizona Project sends river water to the Phoenix, Arizona, area. The demand for water is so great that it is not unusual for the river to run dry before reaching the Sea of Cortez in Mexico.

Management and operation of the Colorado River is established through the Law of the River, a collection of compacts, federal laws, court decisions, contracts, regulatory guidelines, and interstate and international agreements.[15] For example, the 1922 Colorado River Compact requires that upper basin states must deliver a certain amount of annual water flow to the states of Nevada, Arizona, and California through Lake Powell. The Mexican Water Treaty of 1944 further allotted water to Mexico. As detailed below, the urban centers of eastern Colorado also draw water from the Colorado River watershed. With large and growing demand for water in the American West, the fight for water rights to meet the needs of different populations places eastern Colorado interests against western Colorado and also extends across state and international boundaries.

For the semiarid eastern portion of Colorado, the region has always struggled with the economic, social, political, and environmental implications of population and urban growth in a low-water setting. Relative to the Western Slope's water supply of the Colorado River, the east-flowing Arkansas and South Platte Rivers supply only a fraction of the water needs. Today there are three primary solutions to the water issue that defines everyday existence of life along the Front Range.

The oldest solution was the establishment of laws governing rights to use stream and river water. In Colorado the doctrine of prior appropriation, or "first in time, first in right," governs water use. Persons who were first to use water from a stream have seniority rights over newcomers, regardless of importance or economic value of water usage. In times of water shortage, the rights of the senior appropriator must be filled first, and if anything is left, it can fill the junior rights. These laws were originally established during a period of rapid homesteading, mining, and agricultural growth. But for modern-day urban residents, these laws had restricted homeowners from collecting rainwater in barrels, as the water has previously been appropriated for use downstream.[16] In 2016, the rain barrel law was changed to allow Colorado households to store up to a total of 110 gallons of rainwater to use on their lawns and gardens in one or two rain barrels.[17] So strong is the fight for water that water law remains the source of most legal battles in Colorado. While some minor changes do occur, the long-standing water laws have greatly impacted the development of urban, rural, industrial, and agricultural land uses.[18]

Though the water laws dictate who has first right to water, this solution did not solve the problem of ever-increasing demands for water that coincided with rapid population and development growth. Once Front Range urban growth began in the 1850s, demand for water outpaced the supply naturally flowing down through the Arkansas and South Platte Rivers. Thus, a second solution was to increase the volume of water flowing east by diverting water resources from the west side of the Continental Divide. Early city and territory leaders saw that high-country water supplies were essential for making the Front Range and eastern plains habitable for larger populations. By the early 1900s major transmountain diversion projects began to divert water from the upper basin of the Colorado River across the Continental Divide to the drier regions of the state. In reshaping the geography of water in Colorado today, an annual average of half a million acre feet of water is transferred to eastern Colorado through these diversion projects (for comparison, a total of 10.5 million acre feet of water leaves the entire state annually). This transmountain network includes nine ditches and seven tunnels (such as the Moffat and Roberts Tunnels) diverting water to the South Platte River basin, six ditches and four tunnels diverting water to the Arkansas River basin, and numerous reservoirs (such as Dillon on the west side of the Continental Divide, or Cheesman south of Denver). Denver Water, who supplies water to 1.3 million Denver-area residents, manages much of this system. But owing to the Law of the River, there are limits to how much water can be diverted from the Colorado River basin.

A third water supply solution is conservation. Whereas water laws and diversion projects helped address ever-expanding water demands, Denver Water began the Conservation Department in 1986 in an attempt to reduce overall consumption of water. Initially prompted by an intense drought episode, it quickly gained acceptance and popularity within the backdrop of growing environmental consciousness of the late twentieth century. Educational programs taught the public that reducing everyday water use is a personal choice with positive outcomes, using creative campaign slogans such as "Use only what you need," or "You can't make this stuff." The Conservation Department further promoted reduced usage through incentive programs, such as household installation of low-flow fixtures on toilets, sink faucets, and showers. More punitive approaches included lawn-watering restrictions and fines during drought periods and increased rates for high-volume consumers.

Denver Water also played a role in shifting public perceptions of the American lawn as cultural icon. With residential lawn irrigation consuming the largest portion of all residential water use, and as most turfgrass species are water dependent and nonnative to the region, Denver Water began promoting conservation through creative dry landscaping. In 1981 Denver Water coined the term "xeriscape" (*xeros* means dry) and developed a type of alternative landscaping for arid environments. Instead of traditional gardening or grass lawns, xeriscaping reduces irrigation needs through the use of low-water and drought-resistant plants, shrubs, and trees, along with interesting and varied landscaping of rocks, mulch, footpaths, stone washes, and patio spaces. The term is widely used today for many forms of sustainable, water-conserving landscaping. Through the years conservation of water has shifted from being a response to temporary drought conditions toward a cultural way of life for many Denver area residents—and a clearer acceptance of the importance of living within the confines of regional resource limits and climatic characteristics. As Patty Limerick argues, however, the residential lawn remains an essential factor in the water budgeting for Denver Water during drought times, as pushing residents for reductions in luxuries is less painful than cutting into necessities.[19]

Natural Hazards

Denver's deep interior continental location buffers it from coastal threats of hurricanes, tsunamis, or rising sea levels. Tornadoes in Denver can be a concern, but the risks are much greater on the nearby eastern plains. Furthermore, the region is comparatively less geologically active, containing no volcanoes or major fault lines that produce significant earthquake activity. But as the Front Range urban corridor and exurban population and housing growth encroach further into the foothill ecological systems, humans are increasingly placed in the path of some of Colorado's greatest natural disasters: drought, wildfires, and floods.

In Colorado drought is identified as a major natural hazard. Technically speaking, drought occurs when the demand for water exceeds the supply. With numerous agricultural, industrial, municipal, recreational, and hydro-electric needs pulling on scarce resources, the reality is a tenuous relationship between society and nature. While drought is a complex and varied phenomenon, there are several known characteristics within Colorado. First, drought is quite common. In most years there will be some level of drought somewhere within the state. Second, owing to topography, temperature, and precipitation trends, or persistence of dry patterns, the location of drought episodes within the state is varied. The effects of drought, therefore, can at first be quite localized before having more geographically extended impacts. Third, droughts are most commonly short in duration (about six months in length), while multiyear droughts are less common. However, with the most extreme droughts occurring in 1934, 1954, 1977, 2002, and 2012, the trends of climate change and the short duration between the two most recent episodes cause much concern. Following the short but intense droughts in 1976–77 and 1980–81, the Colorado Drought Response Plan was developed as an effective mechanism to deal with both short- and long-term droughts. It provides both assessment needs (e.g., monitoring of current water availability, economic impact assessments in different sectors) and response systems (e.g., assistance, disaster declaration).[20]

The year 2012 exemplifies one of the worst seasons of drought. This episode drew comparisons to the 1930s Dust Bowl era and had disastrous effects across the American West and Great Plains. In Colorado the year began dry, with winter snow accumulations below average. By spring, above-average temperatures and continued below-average precipitation led to an early snowpack melt and low river flows. By the month of May, all Colorado was in a state of drought, and to make matters worse, the Denver area experienced both all-time and daily high temperatures well above 100°F for many consecutive days. The impacts of such a drought were great. For instance, the 2012 wildfire season (including the High Park and Waldo Canyon fires) was one of the most destructive on record: tens of thousands of acres of agricultural and grazing lands failed, ski and summer tourism dropped by 12 percent, and declines in water storage resulted in municipal water emergencies.[21]

In direct relationship to the more intense drought episodes, wildfires are an ever-present and highly destructive disaster in the Denver and Front Range urban areas. Wildfires naturally occur in Colorado's forested landscapes. They are commonly started by lightning strikes but are exacerbated by drought conditions and some suppressive mitigation efforts that ultimately accumulate explosive tinder in the forest. Furthermore, as suburban and exurban landscapes expand into the fringes of undeveloped forested areas, this new wildland-urban interface results in increasingly destructive wildfires. The 2002 Hayman fire occurred in three of metro Denver's counties (Douglas, Jefferson, and Park), was responsible for six deaths, and is historically the largest Colorado fire, covering 138,000 acres.[22] The Black Forest fire of 2013 near Colorado Springs resulted in the greatest property damage with over five hundred homes destroyed. For the near future, ongoing population growth, extensive drought cycles, and more incidences of arson all suggest wildfires will remain the most threatening and direct hazard for thousands of Front Range residents.

The Denver and Front Range region is also prone to flash flooding, especially in the foothill communities. Rainfall on wildfire-charred slopes can lead to dangerous mudslides, but the major causes of flooding are unusually high rainfall amounts in a short period of time, or rapid mountain snow melting due to unusually high springtime temperatures. Two particular events capture the magnitude and swiftness of flooding destruction. The Big Thompson flood of 1976 occurred when a near stationary thunderstorm dumped twelve inches of rain in only three hours. In an area one hour north of Denver, campers and residents along the Big Thompson River Canyon were caught in a rushing wall of water, which killed over 140 people. More recently the northern Front Range urban areas experienced unprecedented flooding in September 2013, when a stalled cold front clashed with a warm, humid air boundary. At the center was Boulder County, which received over seventeen inches of rain in four days. The flooding affected seventeen Colorado counties, including many within metropolitan Denver, destroying fifteen hundred homes and damaging seventeen thousand others. Entire roads along stream and river valleys were washed away, leaving communities such as Lyons completely inaccessible, and greatly impacting tourism-based economies like the town of Estes Park. Given the amount of precipitation, magnitude, and scope of destruction, many considered this a flood of thousand-year epic proportions.

A much slower natural disaster looms large across the forested mountains of Denver's backyard. The current infestation of the mountain pine beetle (*Dendroctonus ponderosae*)—an insect pest that can kill millions of pine trees of varying species—is an unprecedented outbreak that began in the late 1990s, affecting many forested regions all along the Rocky Mountain range. In northern central Colorado, the lodgepole pine is most impacted, leaving thousands of acres of forest a rust-red color, particularly within the highly traveled Rocky Mountain National Park.

In all, Colorado has lost millions of trees across several hundred thousand acres. Climate conditions exacerbate this outbreak as recent droughts weaken trees, making them more vulnerable to infestation, and the insects continue thriving in the warmer winter temperatures that lack long, deep freezes. Otherwise there are few solutions. Clear cutting small regions is common, as is thinning other areas to remove susceptible trees and thwart the migration of the insect. For high-value trees in popular tourist spots pesticides can be used. But given the size of the forested landscape and scope of the infestation, costs grow rapidly.

From both a tourism economy and a natural disaster perspective, the implications are vast. Places dependent on scenery-led tourism such as state and national parks, forest reserves, ski resorts, mountain villages, and campgrounds face the risk of becoming an "ugly place" filled with dead trees or clear-cut mountain slopes. There are also safety considerations of falling trees along hiking or ski trails, at campsites, or along highways. Furthermore, the mass of dead trees in the forest is dangerous tinder for potentially enormous forest fires, the decomposition of millions of dead trees releases more carbon than the forest retains, and mudslides with sediment runoffs can be deadly and cause major damage to municipal water systems.

On the positive side, a small economy has emerged from this pine beetle kill epidemic. Some industries use felled trees to produce the renewable energy source of biomass pellets, or to manufacture shipping crates and pallets. The trees infested with pine beetles contain unusual blue streaks in the wood grain produced by the insects. Like the popularity of distressed and repurposed wood for interior design, this blue-streaked lumber is also desired for its aesthetic appeal and attention to the ideal of materials reuse. Products made with pine beetle lumber are distinctive markers of local place identity.

A cottage industry of high-end woodworking with beetle-kill lumber supplies a niche market demand for furniture (benches, chairs, tables, countertops, shelving), flooring, or wallboards and can be seen in businesses and residences across the Front Range urban corridor.

Environmental Pollution

There are numerous instances of severe environmental pollution of the air, water, and land of Denver and surrounding communities. Some of this was a consequence of rapid suburbanization during an era of automobile and fossil fuel dependency, as was true for most U.S. cities. Some of this was also due to Denver's economic growth in the industries of mineral smelting and Cold War–era weapons manufacturing (Chapter 2). Several examples highlight the worst of these conditions. But each also reflects the longer narrative central to much of Denver's civic leadership: the importance of keeping Denver beautiful. These cases rise from a broader environmental consciousness that enabled efforts to successfully mitigate and remove potential and ongoing degradation—even restoring once urban-industrial lands back to natural prairie.

If Denver once attracted thousands of health seekers to its clean air and sunshine, its reputation soured by the 1970s as the city became infamous for its ubiquitous brown cloud of pollution hanging in the air. So bad was the situation, and so widely known, it even became a national joke.[23] Particularly during winter months, smog occurs because of cold air inversions created by warmer, lighter air flowing from the mountains, and trapping heavier, colder air masses in the low-lying Denver basin. When the conditions are right this inversion can remain in place for several days, causing a buildup of microscopic particles from automobile tail pipes, industrial emissions, or wood-burning fireplaces. By the early 1970s Denver's air quality was disastrous: it continually violated federal standards for acceptable levels of carbon monoxide, ozone, nitrogen dioxide, and concentrations of suspended particulate matter. Despite the Clean Air Act (1970) and federal mandates to make measured improvements, Denver exceeded air quality limits an average of two hundred days a year throughout much of the 1980s.

Both local businesses and political communities recognized that tourism and citizen enjoyment of the Colorado landscape depended on cleaner air, and thus future economic development would be predicated on aggressive restoration and regulation of air quality.[24] Improvements were made by street dust mitigation, bans on wood-burning fireplaces on air quality "alert" days, tighter vehicle emissions standards (including catalytic converters, fuel injectors, and oxygen sensors), winter formulas for gasoline specifically to improve efficiency at higher altitudes, and reduced emissions on coal-fired power plants. Denver was able to reduce all its local pollutants through the 1990s and early 2000s despite increased suburbanization and vehicle traffic. And in the twenty-first-century movement of cities leading the way on global climate change initiatives, Denver mayor Michael Hancock pledged in 2015 to reduce Denver's carbon emissions by 80 percent (over 2005 levels) by 2050.[25]

In *preventing* potential environmental degradation, the protection of local environment for economic and social purposes was at the root of fierce opposition by local communities that resulted in Colorado rejecting its winning bid to host the 1976 Winter Olympics. The protests began as a grassroots environmentalist movement against big recreation and fears of congestion, dirty air, polluted streams and wells, unsightly developments in mountain towns and along the interstate, the loss of open space, and the attraction of even more population growth.[26] Richard Lamm, then a Colorado state legislator, furthered the fight by raising the concerns of financial feasibility. This successful public groundswell of opposition based on environmental concerns has reappeared in subsequent development projects in Colorado and the Front Range urban corridor (see Chapter 6).

Denver's buildup of military defense industries in the post–World War II era (Chapter 2) led to major toxic contaminations within the metropolitan area, affecting nearby residences and farmers and ultimately creating some of the worst environmental pollution of the region. In 1942, the U.S. Army obtained twenty thousand acres of farmland in Adams County to build the Rocky Mountain Arsenal, less than ten miles from downtown Denver. On this site, chemical weapons were manufactured, including mustard gas, white phosphorous gas, and chlorine gas, as well as napalm bombs used in Japan in March 1945. It also stockpiled sarin gas and manufactured and stored rocket fuel for Titan missiles. U.S. chemical weapons manufacturing ended at the arsenal in 1969. From 1952 to 1982 land at the arsenal was leased to Shell Chemical Company for industrial production of fourteen different herbicides and insecticides. Wastes from these chemical productions were dumped and stored on site.[27]

Not until environmental and antiwar movements beginning in the 1960s did widespread public concern emerge. In her 1962 groundbreaking book, *Silent Spring*, Rachel Carson exposed the detrimental effects of pesticides on the environment, including at the Rocky Mountain Arsenal. "Farmers several miles from the plant [reported] unexplained sickness among livestock; they complained of extensive crop damage. Foliage turned yellow, plants failed to mature, and many crops were killed outright." The holding ponds at Rocky Mountain Arsenal contained "chlorides, chlorates, salts of phosphonic acid, fluorides, and arsenic," contaminating the groundwater used for irrigation by farmers.[28] At the time, the toxic contamination at Rocky Mountain Arsenal was of such great magnitude that some considered it "the most polluted place in America."[29] Following several lawsuits against Shell and the federal government, many cleanup projects occurred, and Adams County officials and Colorado governor Roy Romer envisioned that the former chemical manufacturing site could be "transformed into a 'Central Park of the West.'"[30]

During the escalation of the Cold War, the U.S. Atomic Energy Commission opened the eleven-square-mile Rocky Flats Nuclear Weapons Plant in Arvada in 1952. Located in Jefferson County, sixteen miles northwest of downtown Denver, the Rocky Flats facility produced nearly seventy thousand plutonium triggers (used in nuclear weapons manufacturing) over a forty-year period. The facility processed highly radioactive and carcinogenic materials, including over eight thousand different chemicals. Workers were not well protected; not all had health problems, but many did. Toxic waste was buried, incinerated, or held in evaporation ponds on site. A 1957 fire released unknown amounts of radioactive and toxic material into the Denver area. After a 1969 plutonium explosion at the facility, public protests began, and throughout the 1970s and 1980s concerns were raised about regulations for public health and safety. In June 1989 the FBI raided the facility, leading to a grand jury investigation of the contamination and misrepresentation of facts to the public. The facility finally closed in 1992, leaving a divisive legacy in the community. After $7 billion was spent on remediation, demolition, and contamination removal, the cleanup effort was completed in 2005.[31]

In more recent history, both the Rocky Mountain Arsenal and Rocky Flats locations were declared Superfund sites by the Environmental Protection Agency. Remarkably, each has been transformed into community assets of wildlife refuges surrounded by urban development. In 1986 a roost of bald eagles was discovered at the arsenal. The eagles' protection under the Endangered Species Act and the Bald Eagle Act helped pave the way for Congress to pass the Rocky Mountain Arsenal National Wildlife Refuge Act in 1992.[32] The Rocky Flats National Wildlife Refuge Act was passed in 2001.

These refuges are now managed by the U.S. Fish and Wildlife Service as a network of lands set aside to restore, preserve, and conserve natural eco-logical systems of wildlife and plants across the United States. The Rocky Flats National Wildlife Refuge is described as a "home to 239 migratory and resident wildlife species, including prairie falcons, deer, elk, coyotes, song-birds, and the federally threatened Preble's meadow jumping mouse. Large areas of the Refuge have remained relatively undisturbed for the last 30 to 50 years resulting in diverse habitat and wildlife. A portion of the Refuge contains rare xeric tallgrass prairie, providing habitat for a variety of wild-life and serving as an important natural and conservation resource."[33]

The Rocky Mountain Arsenal National Wildlife Refuge has a visitor center, ten miles of hiking trails, a Wildlife Drive auto tour, and opportunities to view nearly three hundred types of animal wildlife, including bison (reintro-duced in 2007), bald eagles, black-footed ferrets, burrowing owls, deer, and coyotes.

Not only do these two spaces represent significant events of reclamation and restoration of tragic and toxic landscapes, but, of great importance, their location within the greater Denver metropolitan area enhances the quantity, quality, and accessibility of urban open space and ongoing efforts of city beautification.

Geographic Isolation

Finally, relative to other great metropolitan areas of the United States, Denver's location is one of isolation. On a nighttime satellite photograph of the United States (Figure 9), the lights vividly portray landscapes of human develop-ment: vast urban agglomerations, large and midsized cities, and small towns dotted along transportation lines. From New England to the Mississippi River and beyond a relatively dense clustering of cities is connected by a thick web of highways and interstates. However, at the Great Plains and the north-south Interstate 35 corridor in the middle of the country, the density of develop-ment, as evidenced by lights, thins out. At the West Coast a major clustering of lights again emerges—from southern California, through Oregon and Washington. Between the West Coast and the fading lights of the Great Plains, the vast expanse and emptiness of the American West is strikingly apparent. Somewhere in the middle of this dark field lies the Front Range urban corridor; a small string of lights stretching from Fort Collins to the north, to Greeley, Boulder, Denver, Colorado Springs, and Pueblo, to the south. In the middle of this narrow line of lights is the Denver metropolitan area. Seeing Denver in this way conspicuously reveals its remoteness and isolation. Denver appears as an oasis in the vast darkness of the American West. To look at it another way, the nearest metropolitan regions of comparable size—Phoenix, Arizona; Dallas, Texas; or Minneapolis, Minnesota—are all at least 550 to 700 miles away.[34]

Cities, however, rarely exist in isolation. They are nodes in larger complex networks of flows of people and migrations, ideas and communication, economies and commodities, movement and transportation. And Denver is no different. As is explored in this book, Denver is an important interregional hub, connecting the east and the west across the Great Plains and Rocky Mountains. This isolated and protected interior location was strategic to the buildup of federal, military, and research and development facilities. And likewise, Denver serves a large hinterland, acting as an intraregional

Figure 9. City lights of the United States, 2012. (Image credit: NASA Earth Observatory image by Robert Simmon, using Suomi NPP VIIRS data provided courtesy of Chris Elvidge, NOAA National Geophysical Data Center.)

center of higher-order economic functions for much of the Rocky Mountain West.

But the geographic remoteness and isolation of Denver can also be tied to its unlikely historical development and contemporary identity and functionality. It is a place founded on the frontier by people with ideals of rugged individualism, freedom, and independence. It has long been a place to escape to, away from the confines and influences of larger and older cities, and subsequently has become an amalgamation of outsiders with a broad sense of open-mindedness. This isolation with openness breeds a special mix across the social and political spectrum, creating a place to explore new landscapes, both ideological and natural.

Chapter 2

Historical Development

Denver is one of the youngest major cities in the United States, founded in 1858 as part of a gold rush in the Pikes Peak area of what was at the time western Kansas Territory. After surviving the trauma of the gold mining boom-and-bust period of the 1860s, Denver stabilized as a supply depot for the interior Rocky Mountain region. Its railroad connections, ore smelters, agricultural processing activities, and warehouses provided the basis for significant growth throughout the late 1800s and early 1900s. By 1900, Denver was ranked the twenty-fifth-largest city in the United States with a population of nearly 134,000.

Its growth in the twentieth century was even more dramatic, especially in the post-1950 period. Fueled by its continued economic growth in mining and agriculture, as well as health care (initially for tuberculosis patients), tourism, and limited manufacturing, Denver grew steadily through the first half of the twentieth century. The onset of World War II had a significant impact on Denver's fortunes as it developed into a strong military and defense industry center with heavy support from the federal government. This effect continued into the postwar era with many former servicemen and their families moving to Denver and its rapidly growing suburbs to find employment in government, military, defense, aerospace, petroleum, tourism, and recreation industries. While Denver's economy had diversified beyond its early reliance on hard-rock mining, the rapid growth of the oil and gas industry from the 1950s through the 1970s once again created a natural resource bubble that ended abruptly with the energy bust of the 1980s. Buoyed by an ambitious program of public works projects, new high-tech and service industries, and increasing population migration, however, the Denver area was once again experiencing rapid growth by the 1990s and 2000s. The Denver metropolitan area's population grew from nearly 564,000 in 1950 to over 2.8 million by 2015, making it the nineteenth-largest metropolitan area in the United States.

Early Origins

Well before Denver existed, the territory of this region was occupied by no-madic hunters more than eleven thousand years ago. Archaeological evi-dence suggests the presence of agricultural villages along the South Platte River starting about a thousand years ago. Later, various Native American hunting groups including the Apaches, Comanche, and Kiowa lived in parts of what is now eastern Colorado, but by the year 1800, they had been dis-placed by Arapaho and Cheyenne hunters. At the time of Denver's found-ing, northeastern Colorado was occupied by the Arapaho and Cheyenne nations, while western Colorado was occupied by the Ute nation. As more Euro-American settlers entered the region, conflicts with Native American groups increased, and territorial control changed. Atrocities were commit-ted on both sides, but the most infamous event was the 1864 Sand Creek Massacre, in which Colonel John Chivington of the Third Colorado regiment attacked a defenseless Native American camp, killing hundreds of men, women, and children. Based on testimony of eyewitnesses, Chivington was tried in military court for the massacre, and while his army career was ended, he otherwise went unpunished.[1] Territorial governor John Evans, who also served as superintendent of Indian Affairs, was responsible for sending Chivington's regiment to eastern Colorado and, according to a recent inves-tigative report from the University of Denver, was culpable for the Sand Creek Massacre.[2] Other less-brazen confrontations occurred, but once Den-ver and other towns in Colorado became established and more populated, incidents of violence between Native Americans and Euro-American settlers began to wane, though the "legacy of conquest" has remained.[3]

The city of Denver, at an elevation of 5,280 feet (1,609 meters) above sea level, hence the nickname Mile High City, was founded in 1858 as a supply center for miners and speculators drawn to the region in search of gold. In September 1858, a group of explorers that included gold seekers from Law-rence, Kansas, established a camp they named Saint Charles near the con-fluence of the South Platte River and Cherry Creek about seventy-five miles

north of Pikes Peak near the foothills of the Rocky Mountains in western
Kansas Territory. Shortly thereafter, another group led by William Green
Russell established a camp across Cherry Creek that they named Auraria,
in honor of Russell's hometown in Georgia. Subsequently, on November 16,
1858, a third group from Leavenworth, Kansas, led by General William H.
Larimer Jr., jumped the Saint Charles claim and renamed the settlement
Denver in honor of the governor of Kansas Territory, James W. Denver.
Reportedly, the Larimer group informed Mr. Charles Nichols, the sole
guard of the Saint Charles site, that if he objected to the claim jump, "a rope
and noose would be used on him."[4] Apparently, Nichols did not object, and
the city of Denver was born.

While significant gold deposits were not to be found at the South Platte–
Cherry Creek confluence, miners in 1859 discovered rich veins of gold
in Clear Creek canyon near the present-day towns of Black Hawk and Central
City about forty miles west of Denver. A flood of miners washed into the region, many of whom settled in Denver, which registered a population of
4,749 in the 1860 U.S. Census.[5]

Nineteenth-Century Growth

In its nascent years, Denver competed with Auraria over which would become the principal city in the region. In order not to offend either place, editor William N. Byers named the region's first newspaper the *Rocky Mountain
News* and located the *News* building in the dry bed of Cherry Creek between
the two towns.[6] It was a shrewd idea until the flood of 1864 washed out the
building and others that had been built in the dry creek bed. Both towns also
competed to become the terminus of the first stagecoach line into the area.
As an early economic development incentive, Denver town leaders in 1859
bribed the owners of the Leavenworth and Pikes Peak Express stagecoach
company to locate the stagecoach terminus in Denver by offering the firm
fifty-three lots and nine shares in the town development company, which the
owners happily accepted.[7] Soon afterward, Denver became the principal city
of the region instead of Auraria.

In 1861, the western part of the Kansas Territory became part of the
newly formed Colorado Territory. The first territorial governor of Colorado,
William J. Gilpin, was one of the staunchest promoters of Colorado and the
West. Eschewing observations by Stephen H. Long that this region was part

of a "Great American Desert," he believed in the pseudoscientific view that "rain followed the plow" and, along with the western rail barons and land promoters, did much to lure unsuspecting settlers to Denver and Colorado. Denver has experienced many colorful characters in its history, including more than its fair share of "snake oil salesmen" who have built careers based on duplicity, misleading promotionalism, and hucksterism in its most unabashed forms.[8] Gilpin's tenure as governor was short-lived. After only one year, President Abraham Lincoln replaced Gilpin with his fellow Illinois Republican John Evans.

Recognizing that the mining boom could be an ephemeral phenomenon, Evans was determined to establish Colorado, and especially Denver, as a stable settlement, based on solid institutional foundations. Together with *Rocky Mountain News* editor William Byers and town leader Amos Steck, he encouraged the establishment of financial institutions, churches, hospitals, water companies, a horse railway company, and schools.[9] Evans founded the private University of Denver in 1864, originally Colorado Seminary, a Methodist institution based on the model of Northwestern University in Evanston, Illinois, which Evans also founded. After Evans was dismissed from his post as governor owing to his involvement in the Sand Creek Massacre, he continued his town-building activities in Denver, most notably through his investments in railroads.

From its very beginning, Denver has exhibited a connectivity obsession, which helps to explain its strong historical fascination with transportation. In the debate over building Denver International Airport in the 1990s, University of Colorado at Denver history professor Tom Noel opined that "Denver suffers from 'by-pass phobia.' As one of the most isolated major cities, the Mile High City has always been afraid the world would pass by without noticing the little city in the middle of nowhere."[10] In 1866, the Union Pacific Railroad announced that it would be building its transcontinental rail line through Cheyenne, Wyoming, instead of Denver to avoid the more challenging terrain of the Colorado Rocky Mountains. Some Denver merchants began to move to Cheyenne, and Union Pacific vice president Thomas Durant infamously described Denver as "too dead to bury."[11] Very quickly thereafter, John Evans and other town leaders, including Bela Hughes, Walter Cheesman, and David Moffat, created the Denver and Pacific Railway and Telegraph Company to build a spur rail line between Denver and Cheyenne to connect to the Union Pacific tracks. Many historians and commentators have identified this single action as the most important event in the historical development of Denver: "The year was 1867. A far-sighted group of civic leaders calling themselves the Denver Board of Trade saw their city at a crossroads and prepared to take a risk. Bypassed by the transcontinental railroad which ran through Cheyenne, Denver's leading citizens feared the city of 4,000 would go the way of the ghost towns. Ignoring doubters, in a week's time they had raised the monumental sum of $300,000. The Denver-Pacific Railroad was born. Denver was on the map."[12]

While building the Denver Pacific, Denver found itself in competition with merchant William Loveland and the city of Golden, ten miles to the west, which had also announced plans to build a spur line to Cheyenne as part of the Colorado Central Railroad. With help from the Union Pacific Railroad (UP), John Evans was able to persuade Congress to provide nine hundred thousand acres of land grants to the Denver Pacific along its 106-mile right of way, and Evans's connections with the UP resulted in deals that provided trackage and rolling stock from the UP.[13] With these advantages, the Denver Pacific line was completed on June 22, 1870, while the Colorado Central rail line reached only four miles north from Golden.

After the Denver Pacific line was completed, other railroads began to connect to Denver. The Kansas Pacific Railroad reached Denver on August 15, 1870, thus providing a connection to Kansas City and St. Louis. Evans, Moffat, and Cheesman founded the Denver, South Park and Pacific narrow-gauge railway to tap into the mountains west of Denver. They brought the mineral wealth from Park, Summit, Lake (including the silver boom town of Leadville), and Gunnison Counties to Denver. Evans also started the Denver and New Orleans Railroad, which was intended to provide access to the Gulf of Mexico. Former Kansas Pacific engineer William Jackson Palmer started the Denver and Rio Grande Railway that built rail lines south and west of Denver connecting to Colorado towns including Colorado Springs (which Palmer founded), Pueblo, Leadville, Durango, Silverton, and Grand Junction. Referring to the railroads and other early town-building activities, historian Lyle Dorsett stated that "Denver's future as a great city was assured by 1870 because a diverse group of men pooled their talents and resources in a herculean effort to build a city."[14] Likewise, historians Stephen Leonard and Thomas Noel claimed, "More than any other factor, this spider web of steel explains Denver's nineteenth-century transformation from a mining camp to a regional metropolis."[15]

During the 1870s and 1880s, Denver became the most important city in Colorado, owing largely to its role as a railroad, mining, wholesaling, banking, insurance, and agricultural processing center.[16] In 1876, the state of Colorado was admitted into the United States, and Denver became its capital city in 1881. The stagnation of the 1860s (due to the Civil War and local setbacks including a major fire and flood) gave way to growth in the 1870s and 1880s, as the population of Denver expanded to 35,629 by 1880, and 106,713 by 1890, making it the twenty-sixth-largest city in the United States at that time. Many of the city's residents originated from the Northeast and Midwest, starting a pattern of migration that persisted well into the twentieth century. City boosters bragged about the growth of Denver and started referring to it as the "Queen City of the Plains." Several mining smelters were constructed in the late 1870s and 1880s at the junction of the Colorado Central and Denver Pacific railroads (the Argo Junction) about four miles north of Denver, which made smelting the largest industry in Denver by 1890. Interest in agricultural production prompted Horace Greeley, another famous promoter of the West and editor of the *New York Tribune*, to send his agricultural editor Nathan Meeker to establish a utopian farming colony fifty miles north of Denver along the South Platte River and Denver Pacific Railroad line that became the city of Greeley. Many agricultural products from the Greeley area were eventually shipped to Denver, which developed brewing, food processing, livestock, and flour-milling activities.[17] One notable example, the Coors Brewing Company, was established in 1873 in nearby Golden, as one of several beer breweries that started in the late 1800s.

Agriculture in the region was limited largely to the river valleys where irrigation water was readily accessible because precipitation in this semiarid region averaged only fifteen inches per year. Water availability proved to be a critical factor in the growth of Denver, and early entrepreneurs began to develop systems to provide water. Among the first was the City Ditch which, starting in 1867, drew water from the South Platte Canyon southwest of Denver into a twenty-four-mile-long ditch that brought water to Denver. The City Ditch allowed transplanted easterners and midwesterners to create an urban landscape with trees, lawns, and gardens that reminded them of their home towns. As the city grew, the need for a larger water supply led to the creation of the Denver City Water Company in 1872, founded by James Archer, Walter Cheesman, and David Moffat. Competitors emerged in the 1870s and 1880s resulting in numerous water wars. Eventually in 1892, the Denver Union Water Company led by Walter Cheesman emerged as the sole water provider in the city.[18] This company, today known as Denver Water, developed an elaborate water supply system of diversions, tunnels, and reservoirs that was able to bring fresh and plentiful Rocky Mountain water to Denver, thus en-suring its future growth.

Because of its linkage with the mining industry, Denver's growth histori-cally has been characterized by boom-bust cyclicality typical of a resource frontier largely dependent on external economic fortunes. The gold and silver booms of the 1870s and 1880s eventually went bust with the Depression of 1893. The high prices for silver led to significantly increased production, which eventually caused silver prices to fall precipitously. Accounting for nearly 60 percent of the nation's silver production, many Colorado silver mines were shut down, and the mining industry went into a tailspin. Other industries in Denver were negatively affected, and it is estimated that pop-ulation in Denver declined to ninety thousand by 1895. Still, owing to annexation of nearby communities connected by electric streetcars, Denver registered a 1900 population of 133,859, which was significant enough to place it as the twenty-fifth-largest city in the United States at the turn of the century. In 1902, Denver incorporated many of its outlying communities into a newly consolidated City and County of Denver, which helped to ex-pand its population to 213,381 by 1910, representing a substantial 59.4 percent increase in the first decade of the twentieth century.

The 1890 U.S. Census marked the official closing of the frontier, as orga-nized settlements had been increasingly established within the interior West, thus rendering obsolete the concept of a frontier line. The superintendent of the census for 1890 explained this occurrence as follows: "Up to and including 1880 the country had a frontier of settlement, but at present the unsettled area has been so broken into by isolated bodies of settlement that there can hardly be said to be a frontier line. In the discussion of its extent, its west-ward movement, etc., it can not, therefore, any longer have a place in the census reports."[19] Historian Frederick Jackson Turner marked the closing of the frontier in his famous essay in which he characterized the influence of the frontier in shaping American democracy and society, as well as Americans themselves.[20] In Turner's view, it was the frontier that made American soci-ety different from that of Europe, and the farther west that settlement proceeded into the frontier, the more "American" people and communities became. With westward expansion and more frequent exposure to the rigors of frontier life, Americans became more individualistic, more democratic, more intolerant of hierarchy, more distrustful of authority and institutions, and more willing to develop ad hoc organizations and solutions developed by themselves. By this logic, Denver could be considered one of the most

"American" cities owing to its relative youth and its location within the last remaining frontier region of the continental United States. The frontier theme has continued to be connected to Denver because of its close association with a vast hinterland in the Rocky Mountain West, where some of the last vestiges of the frontier remain.

The Frontier Cities Model

The growth and integration of Denver within the U.S. national urban system was the basis for the Meyer-Wyckoff Frontier Cities model.[21] In the model, a frontier city's development passes through three stages of integration. In the first stage, the principal linkages are between the newly emerging frontier city and nearby regional cities that act as gateways. In the case of Denver as a frontier city, Omaha, Nebraska; Council Bluffs, Iowa; and St. Louis, Missouri, were the nearby regional gateway cities, or jumping-off points, that had the strongest linkages with Denver because of the prevailing pattern of east-to-west settlement. In stage two, as the frontier city grows and develops, stronger linkages become established with national centers, while linkages with the nearby regional gateways are diminished. As Denver grew in size and economic importance, its linkages with national centers such as New York and Chicago became more crucial, especially in the banking and financial industries, while its linkages with regional gateways Omaha and Council Bluffs declined. There were some notable exceptions. Linkages with St. Louis remained strong, while there were increased linkages with Cheyenne, Wyoming, specifically because of the transcontinental railroad. In stage three, other regional centers may develop stronger linkages with the frontier city, based on patterns of selective growth in the national urban system and complementarity of economic specializations in each place. Linkages with the largest national centers remain strong, while linkages with the initial gateway cities stay the same as stage two. Denver's linkages with national centers New York and Chicago continue to be dominant, but growing linkages with other regional centers such as Kansas City reflect increasing transport connections and economic complementarity with Denver. Smaller linkages between Denver and other centers in the Midwest, mid-Atlantic, and southern New England regions also began to emerge for specialized trade, though they remained small in comparison to the major national linkages (Figure 10).[22]

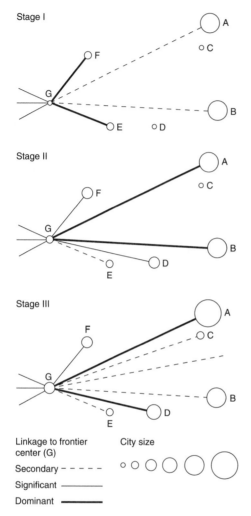

Figure 10. The dynamic geography of linkages between a frontier center and the national urban system. (Source: "Revising the Meyer Model: Denver and the National Urban System, 1859–1879," William Wyckoff, *Urban Geography* 9 (1) (1988): 14, Taylor and Francis. Reprinted by permission of Taylor and Francis.)

The Frontier Cities model illustrates the dependency that the frontier city has, first, on nearby gateway cities, and later, on major national and regional centers. The dependency of the frontier city on regional gateways and national centers is a form of frontier colonialism, whereby resource extraction dominates economic activities in the frontier city, but economic control is retained in distant command-and-control centers. In Denver's case, the mining industry was largely responsible for its early growth, but the major mining companies and banks that financed exploration activities were located in national centers such as New York and Chicago. Even though Denver benefited greatly from these investments, reliance on mining as its predominant industry placed it in a vulnerable position when the economic fortunes of mining began to wane, and distant banks were less willing to finance continued local investments. Over time, Denver's economic profile became more diverse, and somewhat less susceptible to the fluctuations of a single industry. But the legacy of frontier colonialism persisted in the form of continued economic reliance on industries and financial institutions in the largest national centers, such as New York, Chicago, and later in the twentieth century, Los Angeles, as well as larger industrial centers. By the turn of the twentieth century, a clearly defined American "core" manufacturing belt had emerged in the Northeast and Midwest regions, while Denver's resource-dependent economy and its location in the West placed it in the economic and geographic "periphery" of the country.

In the latter half of the twentieth century, the dominance of the American manufacturing belt began to decline as cities in the South and West Sunbelt region began to grow rapidly owing to numerous factors, including population migration to natural amenity locations, technological innovations (especially air-conditioning), and economic shifts away from heavy manufacturing to light manufacturing and producer services. Cities such as Los Angeles, Houston, Dallas, Atlanta, Phoenix, and Denver grew quite rapidly and contributed to a major geographic shift in population and economic activity toward the Sunbelt. With changing demographics and a more diversified economy, Denver was able to become established as a growth center, thus expanding beyond its original role as a resource-extraction frontier city.

The Early Twentieth Century

While mining and railroads still continued their importance into the twentieth century, Denver's economy started to become somewhat more diversified. Manufacturing, agriculture, health care, and tourism became more important to the local economy and helped to fuel Denver's strong growth in the early twentieth century. Denver's mining industry rebounded from the 1893 silver crash, and in the first several decades of the twentieth century, gold, silver, coal, and oil continued to be extracted in Colorado, which directly benefited Denver's smelters and refineries. After 1920, however, mining's importance declined, while other economic activities grew. Agricultural and manufacturing enterprises such as millers, meatpackers, brewers, bakers, and brick makers serving local needs thrived while a few manufacturers, such as the Gates Rubber Company and the Samsonite Luggage Company, established national markets for their products.[23] Given its isolated location and long distances to large markets, however, Denver never developed into a major manufacturing center. This economic profile was fine with Denver's leaders and residents at the time, who were quite happy to remain a smaller and cleaner town rather than a larger and dirtier industrial city, even though it meant that Denver was at an economic disadvantage during the country's industrial expansion period.

One of the direct economic benefits from its clean, dry, and relatively warm environment was that Denver became established as a major destination for patients from northeastern cities seeking treatment for respiratory ailments, especially tuberculosis (TB). A substantial segment of Denver's population from the early 1900s was related to the treatment and care of tuberculosis patients. It is known that between 1900 and 1910, 25 percent of all deaths in Denver were the result of tuberculosis,[24] while according to one report, as much as 60 percent of Colorado's population by the 1920s had migrated to the state, either directly or indirectly, for treatment of tuberculosis.[25] The early TB sanitariums and hospitals laid the foundation for Denver's development as a major medical center. Medical facilities such as National Jewish Hospital, Swedish Medical Center (in Englewood), Craig Hospital, Fitzsimons Army Hospital (in Aurora), and others were developed in the first two decades of the twentieth century, originally as centers for the treatment of TB and other respiratory ailments.

Another economic benefit of Denver's natural environment was its early development as a tourist destination. Owing to its proximity to beautiful mountain environments, western imagery, and superior railroad connections, Denver started to become a desirable tourist destination in the late 1800s and early 1900s. Tourists, including the poet Walt Whitman, were captivated by the "climatic magnetism of this curiously attractive region," while many were eager to see the last vestiges of an authentic western frontier town, complete with cowboys, Indians, and buffaloes.[26] The notion of the western frontier has been a powerful image in the history of Denver, and many people today still associate Denver with this imagery. In Jules Verne's 1873 classic *Around the World in Eighty Days*, for example, the protagonist's rail journey from San Francisco to Denver was interrupted by a massive herd of bison crossing the tracks and an attack by Sioux warriors.[27] The establishment of nearby Rocky Mountain National Park in 1915, as well as other national parks in the West, made Denver a natural gateway for tourists eager to explore the beautiful natural landscapes of the West. An extensive rail network with many tentacles emanating from Denver into the Colorado mountain regions was built for the mining industry, but later it helped to facilitate a growing tourism industry.

By the 1920s, however, new modes of transportation started to make an imprint on the urban landscape of Denver and the surrounding region. The automobile had become increasingly affordable to the general public owing to manufacturing innovations such as the moving assembly line and mass production of the Model T car introduced by Henry Ford from 1908 to 1927. Previously automobiles were quite expensive and limited only to upper-income families, but the Model T was purposely designed by Ford to be affordable for middle-class families. Together with increased road building by the City and County of Denver, as well as the newly formed Colorado Department of Highways (created in 1917), the growth of Denver began to reflect increased accessibility provided by the automobile. More streets, roads, highways, and parking spaces were built, thus expanding the city and making Denver accessible by car. While railroads and electric streetcar services were still the main forms of transportation to and from, as well as within Denver in the 1920s and 1930s, growth in the use of the automobile initiated a pattern of increasing road transport at the expense of rail. In addition, the innovation of air transport began to have increasing commercial applications in the 1920s and 1930s. In anticipation of the growth in air passenger and air mail traffic, Denver mayor Benjamin Stapleton proposed a new airport to be built northeast of the city at a then-staggering cost of $450,000. Decried by critics as "Stapleton's Folly," Denver Municipal Airport was opened on October 17, 1929, and was later renamed Stapleton Airport (in 1944) in honor of the mayor who championed the project.[28]

By 1920, the City and County of Denver's population had grown to 256,491, representing a 20.2 percent increase from 1910. But the two decades from 1920 to 1940 witnessed somewhat slower population growth in Denver, averaging only about 12 percent each decade. The decline of the mining industry in the 1920s contributed to the slower growth, as did the Great Depression in the 1930s. Just at the time when Denver's economy began to diversify slowly in the 1920s, the Depression had a devastating effect on both the city and the rest of the nation during the 1930s. Unemployment rates skyrocketed so that by 1932 only 68 percent of household heads in the city were employed, and 32 percent of banks in Colorado had failed by 1934.[29] Agriculture was severely impaired by falling prices and the Dust Bowl storms in nearby eastern Colorado, western Nebraska, Kansas, and Oklahoma. While not in the epicenter of the Dust Bowl, Denver was close enough to experience frequent dust storms and certainly felt the economic impacts from the devastated agricultural industry. Many farmers who could no longer eke out a living on the dusty plains ventured to California or into nearby cities such as Denver to start a new life. Economic conditions were quite difficult in Denver throughout the 1930s, but at least there were more opportunities in the city than in the ravaged countryside.

In response to the Great Depression, the federal government under President Franklin D. Roosevelt created numerous public works agencies as part of his New Deal programs to provide employment opportunities and put people back to work. Denver benefited from numerous projects initiated by New Deal agencies. Perhaps the most famous is Red Rocks Amphitheater, a Civilian Conservation Corps (CCC) project built in Morrison, about fifteen miles southwest of Denver, in Jefferson County. Red Rocks Park had just been acquired by Denver in 1928 as part of its Mountain Parks system. George Cranmer, Denver's manager of parks and improvements, used CCC funds to create a natural amphitheater amid the spectacular red rocks jutting out from the nearby foothills. Designed by architect Burnham Hoyt, Red Rocks Amphitheater was a highly successful project that employed thousands of workers and created a facility that was destined to become a jewel—one of Denver's most treasured entertainment/recreational facilities and scenic landmarks (Figure 11). Other New Deal projects funded by the Works Progress Administration (WPA), Public Works Administration (PWA), and the National Youth Administration (NYA) employed thousands of workers on a variety of infrastructure projects, including the construction of new schools, roads, and sewers, as well as employing many men and women as writers and artists and in other professional occupations.

While the Depression and New Deal brought a significant increase in federal government activity to Denver in the 1930s, that level of involvement

Figure 11. Red Rocks Amphitheater, a Civilian Conservation Corps (CCC) project completed in 1941. (Image source: Andrew R. Goetz.)

was dwarfed by the massive military buildup in Denver in the late 1930s and early 1940s related to World War II. In 1938, Denver purchased a tuberculosis sanitarium on the east side of the city and donated it to the U.S. Army, which converted it into an air corps training center, Lowry Air Base. Once the United States entered the war in 1941, Denver donated a tract of land just east of Lowry to the army to open another air facility named Buckley Field. Fitzsimons Army Hospital in nearby Aurora was refurbished and greatly expanded in 1941. Camp George West in Golden became a center for training military policemen, and old Fort Logan, which was established in 1888 just south of Denver, expanded in 1941 to accommodate an air corps clerical school. West of Denver in what was to become the city of Lakewood, gun manufacturer Remington opened its Denver Ordnance Plant to produce ammunition and long-range shells. In 1942, the U.S. Army acquired land near Stapleton Airport for the Rocky Mountain Arsenal, a facility that produced conventional and chemical weapons.[30] Altogether, these military bases and facilities greatly affected the local economy and society in Denver

and initiated a pattern of significant military and defense industry investment in Denver that continued well after the war.

Postwar Denver: 1945–70

While at the time it was not clear whether the economy would lapse back into
a depression after the war, the postwar era turned out to be a period of booming economic and population growth in many areas of the United States,
including Denver. Much of this growth was fueled by Sunbelt-oriented
migration, as many midwestern and northeastern residents were drawn to the
amenities of the Denver area. Many servicemen who were based in Denver
during the war decided to return to the Mile High City after the war because
of its agreeable climate and expanding job opportunities. Government, military, defense, aerospace, petroleum, tourism, and recreation were the leading
economic sectors that propelled Denver's growth in the postwar period.

The federal government continued to invest heavily in defense, especially
after the Soviet Union acquired the atomic bomb in 1949, thus leading to the
Cold War era. Denver, like other so-called Gunbelt cities in California, Washington, Texas, and Florida, benefited considerably from investments in military establishments and defense-related industries.[31] While there was no single
reason why Denver became a favored site for defense installations, its relatively isolated geographical location in the interior of the country, presumably
safer from aerial attacks, was relevant during World War II and its immediate
aftermath. In its December 11, 1950, issue, *Newsweek* magazine reported,

> If an atom bomb should wipe out Washington, or any other major
> city, what then? That grim possibility has sent top government offi-
> cials on nationwide tours. Officials of large corporations are also busy
> investigating the possibility of new plant sites.
>
> Recently, the search for safety has centered on one largely unde-
> veloped region—the Denver metropolitan area. Its advantages are
> obvious: A thousand miles of mountain protect it on the west, great
> distances separate it from the Canadian border, the Atlantic Ocean
> and the Gulf of Mexico.[32]

Later, as intercontinental ballistic missiles rendered all locations unsafe,
other factors such as climatic amenities, pioneering entrepreneurs, a favor-

able business climate, civic boosterism, and political lobbying efforts played a more important role in Denver's favor. Geographers Ann Markusen, Peter Hall, and their coauthors do not discount a possible connection between the nineteenth-century frontier mentality and the twentieth-century enthusiasm for winning military contracts: "Long after the closing of the agrarian-settlement frontier in 1890, the expansive 'can do,' tall tale–telling western culture engendered a continuing frontier of urban-real estate development, coupled with intense civic boosterism, that has provided a welcome to all kinds of new activities, including military installations and defense industries."[33]

In Denver, Lowry and Buckley Air Force bases, Fitzsimons Army Hospital, and the Rocky Mountain Arsenal continued operations after the war, while a nuclear weapons facility called Rocky Flats was opened in 1952 northwest of Denver in Jefferson County. Nearby Colorado Springs was selected as the site for the North American Aerospace Defense Command (NORAD) headquarters, the Cheyenne Mountain nuclear bunker, and the U.S. Air Force Academy. In addition, numerous defense-related companies in aerospace, research, engineering, precision tools, and electronic equipment were established in Denver and the surrounding region during the 1950s, including Martin Marietta Aerospace, Honeywell, Ball Aerospace, and Hewlett Packard.[34]

The federal government's role in the economic growth of postwar Denver extended beyond the military-industrial complex. As civilian agencies of the federal government expanded in the 1950s and 1960s, Denver was a favored location representing the western Great Plains/Rocky Mountain region. The Denver Ordnance Plant in the western suburb of Lakewood was converted into the Denver Federal Center, which housed regional offices for a number of federal civilian agencies, including the Department of Interior's Bureau of Reclamation, Bureau of Land Management, and U.S. Geological Survey. The federally funded National Center for Atmospheric Research (NCAR) was established in Boulder in 1960. In 1948, ten thousand federal civilian employees worked in the Denver metro area, a figure that grew to twenty-three thousand by 1961, and 31,500 by 1975.[35] Denver became such a favored site for federal agencies that its federal government workforce was eclipsed by only Washington, D.C., and Denver became known for a time as the nation's "second capital." In the 1950s, President Dwight D. Eisenhower's frequent visits to Denver (where the family of his wife, Mamie, lived) enhanced Denver's national profile.

While the oil industry had been established in Colorado well before the war, it expanded considerably during the late 1940s and 1950s. In 1923, the state produced only eighty-six thousand barrels of oil, rising to nine hundred thousand barrels by 1933. In 1945, the state produced five million barrels, which expanded to twenty-three million barrels by 1950, and fifty-eight million by 1956.[36] Most of the oil was pumped from wells in northeastern and northwestern Colorado, as well as from fields in the nearby states of Wyoming, Nebraska, and Kansas. Because of its proximity to these fields, Denver became a regional center for oil exploration, drilling, and refining, and a home for over one hundred oil companies by 1964, including Philip Anschutz's Circle A Drilling Company, Marvin Davis's Davis Oil Company, and Jerome Lewis's Petro-Lewis Company.[37]

The postwar era was also a time when the tourism and recreation industries, especially the skiing industry, expanded greatly in Colorado, which benefited Denver and the nearby mountain communities. While some ski areas, such as Monarch, Winter Park, and Wolf Creek, were started in the 1930s partly through federal New Deal programs, it was not until after 1945 that skiing in Colorado became a recreational industry.[38] Several army veterans from the Tenth Mountain Division, which trained at Camp Hale near Leadville during the war, returned to become pioneers in establishing the recreational skiing industry in Colorado. Early ski resorts based in Aspen, Vail, and Arapahoe Basin were started by veterans of the Tenth Mountain Division, and many other of these veterans were instrumental in popularizing skiing throughout Colorado and the rest of the country.[39] The Aspen Skiing Corporation financed and constructed Aspen's first chairlift in the 1946–47 season, which at the time was the world's longest and fastest lift, and led to Aspen's tremendous growth as a ski resort. By the 1956–57 season, Aspen had 83,000 skier visits, which was more than any other U.S. ski resort except for Sun Valley, Idaho, and by 1965–66, the number had grown to 143,000.[40] Arapahoe Basin grew from 33,000 to 90,000 skier visits, and Winter Park from 70,000 to 213,000 during the same time period, while Vail, which opened in 1962–63, had reached 189,000 visits only three years later.[41] Statewide, skier visits rose from 801,000 in 1963–64 to 5,194,000 by 1974–75.[42] As a gateway to many of Colorado's ski resorts, Denver benefited from the increasing flow of tourists traveling by rail, road, and air. The construction of Interstate Highway 70 west from Denver greatly improved accessibility to the mountain ski resorts and allowed both Denver area residents and visitors flying into Denver Stapleton Airport quicker access to the mountains.[43] The manufacturing and retailing of ski equipment and clothing also benefited the economy of Denver and nearby mountain communities.

Skiing was not the only tourist activity that expanded in the postwar era, as other outdoor recreational activities and convention business grew as well. The postwar prosperity of American households provided increasing opportunities for travel and tourism throughout the United States, and because of its outstanding scenic beauty and promotional focus, Colorado was a favored destination. Visits to Colorado's national parks, such as Rocky Mountain National Park near Estes Park, as well as visits to numerous camping, fishing, hiking, and rafting locations grew substantially. Visits were made easier from increasing rates of automobile ownership among the growing middle class, and construction of the Interstate Highway System. The string of motels, motor lodges, restaurants, and diners lining U.S. Route 40 (Colfax Avenue) in Denver in the 1950s and 1960s, some of which still remain today, represent tangible evidence of tourism's economic impact on Denver in the postwar era (Figure 12). The Denver Chamber of Commerce actively promoted Denver as a convention destination, which, together with the construction of the Thomas G. Currigan Convention Center and Exhibition Hall in the 1960s, as well as several downtown hotels, contributed to growth in convention activity.[44] Denver has been the home to the National Western Stock Show, Rodeo, and Horse Show every year since 1906, and the Chamber of Commerce was eager to build on this foundation and expand Denver's convention and tourism profile.

Altogether, Denver's role as a tourist destination and gateway to the nearby mountains had a significant impact on its desirability as a residential location, as more people chose to live in the Denver area based on its amenities of climate, scenery, and lifestyle. While new migrants to the area still relied on a strong employment base for their livelihoods, many were drawn to the area simply because of the amenities that Denver and the surrounding region had to offer. In his book *Vacationland*, historian William Philpott emphasized this connection between tourism, leisure lifestyles, and residential growth: "Homes sat close to famous tourist destinations, and residents enjoyed easy access to some of the nation's most popular playgrounds. That, as much as anything, was what made western metropolises like Denver, Phoenix, and Los Angeles so different—at least in the popular imagination—from older eastern cities. Here, like nowhere else, work seemed to blur with play, vacation time with everyday life, and with them the settings where each took place."[45]

Figure 12. Davies' Chuck Wagon Diner, one of the classic 1950s-era stops along U.S. Route 40 (Colfax Avenue) on the way to the mountains. (Image source: Andrew R. Goetz.)

Boom and Bust: 1970–90

By the 1970s, Denver was once again a boomtown. But instead of gold and silver mining, development of energy resources, especially oil, drove economic growth. The Arab oil embargo of 1973 began a period of sharply increasing oil prices that led to greater investment in energy exploration. Interest focused on large estimates of petroleum embedded in shale rock on Colorado's western slope near Grand Junction as well as in the Overthrust belt in western Wyoming, eastern Utah, and Idaho.[46] Major oil companies, such as Gulf, Mobil, Chevron, and Phillips, established regional offices in Denver, from which exploration activities were directed. Many new office buildings were built in downtown Denver during the 1970s and early 1980s as a result of this demand as well as the formation of the Skyline Urban Renewal District, which facilitated downtown redevelopment. Restrictions on skyscraper development in Denver dating to the City Beautiful era (for the purpose of maintaining views of the mountains) were lifted in the postwar era as opportunities for growth in the office real estate market were too lucrative for city officials and business leaders to ignore.[47]

Interest in energy development expanded beyond petroleum exploration to include alternative energy sources, such as solar and nuclear power. In 1977, the federal government started the Solar Energy Research Institute (SERI) in Golden, Colorado, which later became the National Renewable Energy Laboratory (NREL). A nuclear power plant was built in the 1970s at Fort Saint Vrain north of Denver along the Cache La Poudre River but was plagued by cost overruns and increasing concerns about the safety of nuclear power, eventually closing in 1988.

Denver, which started as a frontier mining boomtown and grew steadily through the twentieth century as a provincial city, was becoming a major U.S. metropolis, joining the ranks of other rapidly growing Sunbelt cities such as Los Angeles, Houston, Dallas, Miami, Atlanta, Phoenix, and San Diego. As a symbol of its rising status, Denver acquired its first major league professional sports franchise with the Denver Broncos football team, which started in the American Football League (AFL) in 1960 and then joined the National Football League (NFL) as part of the NFL-AFL merger in 1970. In 1967, Denver acquired an American Basketball Association (ABA) franchise initially called the Denver Rockets, later becoming the Denver Nuggets, which joined the National Basketball Association (NBA) in 1976 as part of the NBA-ABA merger.[48] Owing to its emerging metropolitan profile and the growing status of its nearby ski resorts, Denver was chosen by the International Olympic Committee (IOC) in 1970 to host the 1976 Winter Olympic Games. But in 1972, an opposition group, led by Colorado state representative Richard Lamm, questioned the environmental and financial impacts from the proposed Olympics. In a statewide referendum, Colorado voters rejected hosting the Winter Olympic Games by a 60–40 margin, the first and only time in history that a community already selected by the IOC had rejected hosting the Olympics. So, while Denver's profile as a major metropolitan center was being established, concerns about its limits to growth began to appear, a theme that returned again in the 1990s and 2000s.[49]

Much of the economic growth in the 1970s was fueled by the high oil prices of the energy boom and the increased investment in energy exploration within Colorado and the Rocky Mountain region.[50] Denver became the regional headquarters for many energy companies, which expanded oil, gas, and oil shale production throughout the region. But by the early 1980s, oil prices had started to decline, and in 1982, Exxon announced that it was pulling out of its western Colorado oil shale project and its Denver regional headquarters. This led to a stampede of other energy companies announcing similar pullouts. By the mid-1980s, office vacancy rates in downtown Denver exceeded 30 percent, and both the City and County of Denver and the state of Colorado were pursuing vigorous economic development strategies to combat the energy bust. A concerted effort to invigorate the state and city economies featured the construction of large public projects such as Denver International Airport, the Colorado Convention Center in downtown Denver, upgraded scientific and cultural facilities including museums and a performing arts center, and Coors Field in the Lower Downtown (LoDo) area, each of which benefited from strong business support.[51] Coors Field was built to house the Colorado Rockies Major League Baseball team, which started playing in 1993, showing that Denver still considered itself very much a major league sports city, twenty years after the rejection of the Winter Olympics.[52]

Denver International Airport

The largest public project that the City and County of Denver has ever built is Denver International Airport (DIA). Because of its massive size, distinctive architecture, and notoriety for problems encountered in its construction, it is one of Denver's most familiar and recognizable landmarks (Figure 13). It serves as the gateway for people entering Denver, and the extensive route networks of airlines operating there connect Denver directly with major U.S. cities, as well as an increasing number of international destinations. But the story of DIA's evolution is anything but smooth, as it was bedeviled by numerous obstacles and setbacks throughout its planning, construction, and operation.

During the 1980s, Denver decided to build a new airport to replace the overburdened Stapleton International (located seven miles from Denver's central business district [CBD]), which was experiencing rapid passenger growth but faced expansion constraints because it had become nearly surrounded by urban development. At that time, Denver Stapleton was one of the busiest airports in the world as it served as a hub for three airlines (United, Continental, and Frontier) in the early years of U.S. airline deregulation. Passenger projections indicated that Stapleton would soon exceed its

Figure 13. Denver International Airport Jeppesen Terminal and its distinctive white, multipeaked roof. Photograph provided courtesy of Denver International Airport.

capacity, resulting in congestion and delays that would stunt air transport growth and economic development in Denver and the surrounding region. The new Denver International Airport (DIA) would be located twenty-three miles away from Denver's CBD on a fifty-three-square-mile site that had a full build-out capacity for twelve runways and two hundred million passengers per year, thus allowing economic development opportunities to expand greatly.[53] DIA's projected size dwarfed nearly every other airport in the world. By comparison, London's Heathrow Airport, the busiest airport in the world for international passengers, occupies less than five square miles and accommodated over seventy-two million passengers in 2013 using only two runways.

The site selected for the new airport was located in nearby Adams County. So that the City and County of Denver could still remain the owners and operators of the airport, it was necessary for Denver to annex the land from Adams County. While Denver had previously found it relatively easy to annex land from suburban counties, the 1974 Poundstone Amendment to the Colorado Constitution changed the procedures for counties (and city-counties such as Denver) to annex land by requiring a majority vote of residents from the *entire* county from which any land would be annexed. Previously, a majority vote of residents in only the targeted territory was required to approve the annexation. This change severely restricted the City and County of Denver's ability to annex land because the suburban counties were largely opposed to Denver's annexation policies. After plans for the new airport were announced, a referendum was scheduled for May 1988 in which Adams County voters were asked to allow the City and County of Denver to annex land for the purpose of constructing a new airport. This led to a vigorous campaign in which Colorado governor Roy Romer intensely lobbied voters as part of his so-called breakfast oatmeal circuit at Adams County diners and restaurants. Denver mayor Federico Peña also lobbied intensely for the annexation and negotiated several intergovernmental agreements with Adams County officials, including noise ordinances to ensure that aircraft noise would not be a problem for Adams County residents, and an agreement that the airport land to be annexed would be used for aviation purposes only and not for spinoff economic development projects. Adams County officials wanted to ensure that airport-related economic development would be located in nearby areas of Adams County (and not in Denver). With these agreements in place, Adams County voters passed the annexation referendum with 56 percent approval. The following year, even though it was not legally required, voters in the City and County of Denver were allowed the opportunity to vote on the airport plan, which they passed with 63 percent approval.[54] The two referenda, federal funding support, and lease agreements signed by Continental Airlines in 1990 and United Airlines in 1991 paved the way for the new airport's construction.

The construction of DIA was beset by numerous problems, but the new airport eventually opened in 1995, and Stapleton was closed to aviation activity. The largest construction problem was the ill-fated effort to build a fully automated baggage system throughout the airport, which resulted in several years of delay and significant cost overruns.[55] Originally estimated in 1988 to cost a total of $1.7 billion, the final cost for the airport grew to over $5 billion. DIA faced other problems in its first few years such as slower-than-expected passenger growth due in part to the acquisition of Frontier by Continental Airlines (via People Express) in the late 1980s, and the decision by Continental in 1994 to dismantle its hub operations in Denver, as well as overall higher airline fares because of higher rental and landing fees at the new airport. These initial setbacks limited passenger growth and the economic benefits of the new airport in its early years, though the airport itself has remained profitable.[56]

Since it opened, DIA has steadily increased its total passenger activity from thirty-eight million in 1997 to fifty-four million by 2015, currently ranking as the fifth-busiest airport in the United States and nineteenth-busiest in the world. DIA has grown largely owing to its role as a domestic hub airport for United Airlines and for the reconstituted low-cost Frontier Airlines, as well as being a focus city for Southwest Airlines since it restarted service to Denver in 2006. Denver is well suited to be a domestic hub because of its geographical situation as a relatively large city in the interior United States that possesses the characteristics of both centrality and intermediacy between the West Coast and the Midwest, South, and East.[57] Cost per passenger enplanement is down 31 percent from 2001, from $15.28 to $10.59, which has improved DIA's competitiveness with other airports.[58] DIA currently operates six runways, including one sixteen-thousand-foot runway that was specially designed for heavily laden aircraft embarking on long international flights to take off in Denver's thinner high-altitude air. Owing in part to Denver's interior location, international service has thus far been limited to nonstop flights only to Canada, Mexico, Central America, a few destinations in Europe (London, Frankfurt, Munich, Reykjavik), and Tokyo.[59] It is expected that the nonstop flight to Tokyo will help to recruit new companies and generate more than $130 million in annual economic benefits to Denver and the surrounding region.[60] New nonstop flights to Paris and Zurich are scheduled to begin in 2018.

The economic benefits from DIA have grown in conjunction with increasing air traffic. A 2008 study estimated direct, indirect, and induced economic impacts from DIA in the form of 217,000 jobs generating over $7 billion in payroll, resulting in a total annual economic output of $22 billion, which was a substantial increase over previous estimates in 1998 and 2003.[61] The same study found through a survey of businesses in Colorado that 72 percent of respondents indicated that proximity to a major commercial service airport was important to their decision to locate in Colorado. DaVita Incorporated, a Fortune 500 company, relocated its corporate headquarters to downtown Denver in 2009, and one of their primary reasons was high-quality air service and future rail transit access from downtown to DIA.[62]

The local area land use around DIA has also started to become more developed since the airport opened, and recently announced plans for a new "airport city" aim to develop the area around DIA into an emerging "aerotropolis." Because DIA was located twenty-three miles northeast from downtown Denver in a quadrant of the metropolitan area that had not experienced much development, most of the land in and around DIA's fifty-three-square-mile site remained open prairie after the new airport opened. The most active land development has since occurred in the Gateway area at the junction of Interstate Highway 70 and Peña Boulevard, the main access road into the airport. Several mixed-use developments, offices, hotels, industrial parks, retail, and residential activities have been built in the Gateway corridor, resulting in significant population growth for the adjacent Montbello and Green Valley Ranch neighborhoods of Denver. Airport-related development has also occurred along the E-470 beltway corridor in the nearby jurisdictions of Aurora, Brighton, Commerce City, and Adams County, including new office parks, new medical centers, a justice center, and a stadium for the Colorado Rapids professional soccer team.[63] More recently, a new smart city transit-oriented development called Peña Station Next at Sixty-First and Peña Boulevard along the commuter rail line is being developed through a partnership between the City and County of Denver and Panasonic. And the Gaylord Rockies Resort and Convention Center in Aurora just south of the airport is due to open in 2018.

Development plans at the airport site itself have also been moving forward. The $598 million South Terminal project at DIA includes a 519-room Westin Hotel (opened in November 2015) and a new commuter rail station (opened in April 2016). In April 2012, new areas for future development were identified by the City and County of Denver as part of the ambitious Airport City Denver plan. Organized into Aero, Agro, Center, Logistics, and Tech clusters, the plan called for hotels, retail, renewable-energy research sites, power-generating systems, agricultural sites, manufacturing, and logistics activities to flank airport runways and access roads. City officials estimated the full development of the projects proposed in the plan could create twenty-five thousand construction jobs, followed by some thirty thousand jobs within the Airport City development and forty thousand elsewhere in metro Denver.[64] Shortly after the Airport City Denver plan was announced, however, officials from Adams County, Aurora, Brighton, and Commerce City objected to the plan because they contended it violated the 1988 intergovernmental agreement that originally allowed Denver to annex the land for the airport from Adams County and that limited potential development on the airport site.[65] Adams County and the nearby municipalities wanted to ensure that airport-related development would be located in their jurisdictions, and not on the City and County of Denver airport site.[66] After several years of contentious negotiations, a revenue-sharing agreement was reached in June 2015 to allow Denver to proceed with economic development opportunities on fifteen hundred acres of land at DIA. Denver agreed to pay $10 million up front to Adams County, and to split property tax revenues from new development on airport land with Adams County and its affected cities.[67] Voters in both Denver and Adams County approved the agreement in a November 2015 referendum.

While city officials and consultants have been characteristically ebullient about the economic development impacts from DIA, there is nevertheless some negative fallout from the financial costs of building the airport, as well as questions about the long-term sustainability of air transport and the sprawling urban development that the airport has exacerbated. The $5 billion price tag for DIA was three times higher than original estimates, which represented a drag on the local economy especially in the airport's early years of operation. There are also concerns about the trajectory of urban growth in the Denver area wherein current regional plans call for higher-density, infill development and less reliance on single-occupant vehicle use. The location of DIA on the urban fringe has contributed to the outward extension of the urbanized area as businesses and residences have been developed at locations near the airport. Most of this development is low density and automobile oriented, which has not contributed to the goals of current smart growth planning in the Denver area (see Chapter 6).[68] A considerable amount of urban development has moved further out in the direction toward the airport, so much so that the perceived distance from the city to the airport seems to have decreased over time.

_____

Growth Since 1990

The Denver region rebounded from the 1980s energy bust to experience very strong growth during the 1990s. As of the 2000 U.S. Census, the newly designated Denver-Boulder-Greeley Consolidated Metropolitan Statistical

Area (CMSA) grew by 30.7 percent from 1990 to 2000. The area was paced by strong growth across all counties including a phenomenal 191 percent growth rate in Douglas County, making it the fastest growing metropolitan county in the United States during the 1990s. Responsible for much of that growth was the unincorporated community of Highlands Ranch, started by the Mission Viejo Company in 1981, that grew to over ninety thousand residents by 2000 (see Chapter 3). Adams, Boulder, Arapahoe, and Jefferson Counties each had growth rates over 20 percent, with strong growth in the suburbs of Aurora, Thornton, Westminster, Longmont, and Lakewood. Interestingly, the City and County of Denver reversed its declining population of the previous twenty years by adding eighty-seven thousand residents (18.6 percent increase) during the 1990s. Aggressive economic development strategies of the 1980s as well as increased in-fill and new urbanist development in several Denver neighborhoods helped to spur the revitalization of the central city.

Growth in the 2000–2010 decade has continued but at a slower pace. Most of the growth occurred in Douglas, Adams, and Arapahoe Counties, with the cities of Aurora, Thornton, Commerce City (Adams), Castle Rock (Douglas), and Parker (Douglas) having strong growth. The City and County of Denver continued to grow as well, adding over forty-five thousand residents between 2000 and 2010. The newly incorporated city of Centennial in Arapahoe County became the seventh-largest city in the metropolitan area with a population of 100,377 by 2010. In 2003, the U.S. Census created new metropolitan area definitions, no longer designating CMSAs. The newly named Denver-Aurora-Broomfield Metropolitan Statistical Area (MSA) (Boulder and Greeley were designated as separate MSAs) grew by 15 percent from 2000 to 2010 and was expanded to include Broomfield, Elbert, Gilpin, Clear Creek, and Park Counties.[69] In 2013, the U.S. Census renamed the MSA again to the Denver-Aurora-Lakewood MSA.

By the 1990s, the Denver metropolitan area was able to diversify its economic base so that it became less reliant on oil development. In fact, high-tech industries such as broadcasting and telecommunications, aerospace, and information technology expanded substantially and became increasingly important mainstays of the Denver economy. The broadcasting and telecommunications industry expanded from humble beginnings owing to technological innovations and geographic factors that favored Denver's site and situation (Figure 14). Because of Denver's elevation at one mile (1.6 kilometers) above sea level, commercial transmitters and receivers experience less interference with communications satellites. Furthermore, Denver's location at 105° west longitude places it equidistant between telecommunications satellites that are in geosynchronous orbit above the Atlantic and Pacific Oceans. This locational advantage allows telecommunication and broadcasting companies in Denver to avoid "double-hop" transmissions in which a signal goes up to a satellite and then down and up again before reaching its destination, a process that increases costs and reduces transmission quality.[70] Denver is the largest city in the United States to offer so-called one-bounce satellite uplinks that provide companies with real-time connections to every continent except Antarctica in one business day.[71] The broadcasting and telecommunications industry today includes landline and wireless telephone communications companies, radio and television communications services, and cable and Internet service providers. As of 2015, the nine-county metro Denver and northern Colorado region[72] ranked sixth out of the fifty largest metro areas in the United States for broadcasting and telecommunications employment concentration with over forty thousand employees in this industry.

The aerospace industry in Denver has grown steadily from its roots in the early postwar era to become a significant industry cluster in the region.

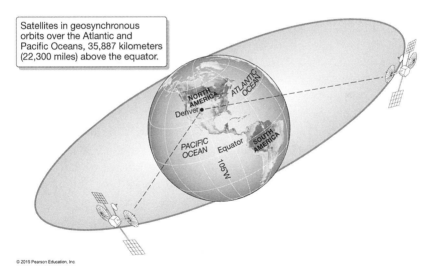

Satellites in geosynchronous orbits over the Atlantic and Pacific Oceans, 35,887 kilometers (22,300 miles) above the equator.

© 2016 Pearson Education, Inc.

Figure 14. Denver's advantageous site and situation have been instrumental in the growth of its telecommunication activities. (Source: Knox, Paul L., and Marston, Sallie A., *Human Geography: Places and Regions in Global Context*, 1st ed. ©1998. Reprinted by permission of Pearson Education, Inc., New York, New York.)

Aerospace contractors support the U.S. Department of Defense (DoD) to procure, place, and manage national space assets for the military. They also provide manned and unmanned spacecraft, instrumentation, and ground control services for the National Aeronautics and Space Administration (NASA) and other federal agencies. Several elements of NASA's Orion Project, which seeks to reestablish manned space flights to the moon and perhaps to Mars, were built by Denver-based aerospace companies. With direct employment of 19,520 aerospace workers, the nine-county metro Denver and northern Colorado region ranked second in private aerospace employment concentration out of the fifty largest metro areas in 2015.[73] Major aerospace companies with operations in the Denver area include Lockheed Martin, United Launch Alliance, Raytheon, Boeing, Northrop Grumman, and Ball Aerospace.

Information technology (IT) has also grown to become an important industry in the Denver region. Combining software, Internet, hardware, telecommunications, and related technology companies, the Colorado Technology Association estimates that the entire state of Colorado has over 146,000 IT workers employed in over ten thousand companies.[74] A narrower focus just on the software industry would include activities such as software reproduction, software publishing, custom computer programming, data processing and hosting, computer facilities management services, and computer systems design services. The Denver region ranked among the top ten out of the fifty largest U.S. metro areas in software employment concentration and had direct employment of 48,610 software employees in 2015.[75]

Other industries that today employ sizable numbers of people in the Denver region include health care and wellness (over 180,000 employees), financial services (over 90,000 employees), energy (over 46,000 employees) including both traditional fossil fuels (oil and gas) and cleantech (wind and solar), aviation (over 16,000 employees) and bioscience (over 15,000 employees).[76] While several of these industries have built on historical foundations in Denver, such as health care, energy, and aviation, the mix of industries today is much more diverse and illustrates the broader-based strength of the regional economy as compared to previous resource-based booms and busts. One indication of Denver's economic strength has been its ability to withstand and recover more quickly from the Great Recession of 2008–9 than many other U.S. metropolitan areas. The unemployment rate in the Denver metro area has generally stayed 1–2 percentage points below the national average since 2008.

*   *   *

Owing to its origins as a resource-based frontier town, Denver has experienced a number of booms and busts in its historical development. Yet despite the cyclicality of its economic fortunes, Denver's population has continued to grow strongly throughout its relatively short history. In comparison to other major cities in the Northeast and Midwest, Denver did not develop as a manufacturing center but has relied instead on mining and natural resource extraction, agriculture, health care, tourism, military, defense, government, tourism, recreation, telecommunications, aerospace, and information technology industries to propel its growth. Denver has become a classic example of a Sunbelt metropolis, similar to other western cities such as Los Angeles, San Diego, Phoenix, Dallas, Seattle, and Portland, which have each experienced very strong growth during the twentieth century, especially in the post-1950 period. By 2015, the Denver-Aurora-Lakewood MSA had a total population of 2.8 million, ranking it as the nineteenth-largest metropolitan area in the United States.

Chapter 3

Demographics and Culture

At the beginning of the twenty-first century Denver is considered a "next frontier" city, a place experiencing population growth and levels of social diversity above the average for metropolitan areas in the United States.[1] This is also characteristic of Denver's past. An urban oasis in the wild frontier, the city has long attracted opportunists, tireless workers, and adventurists alike. Denver has experienced several distinct historic periods of rapid population growth. It is also a place that over the decades became home to many immigrants and ethnic minorities, experiencing periods of tension that socially fractured the city. Accommodating growth has meant changes to the spatial configuration of Denver, pushing outward from the original downtown to the many regional suburbs and mountain community exurbs. Today there is even a mini-trend of reurbanism back to the urban core. Thus, part of understanding Denver today is to understand its historic growth of people and changing spatial geographies.

Three Periods of Rapid Growth

Since its founding, the population of Denver and the surrounding region has grown rapidly (Table 1). Undoubtedly the periods of economic downturns negatively affected population size, but over the long view these times were short-lived. There are three distinct periods of exceptional population growth. First, the era of "pioneering growth" in the late nineteenth and early twentieth centuries was crucial to establishing the city of Denver beyond merely a mining camp and into a hub for the Rocky Mountain region. Denver built its strength through the challenges of many economic boom-and-bust

Table 1. Population Growth Trends in Denver and the Metropolitan Area,
1870–2010

	Denver			Metropolitan Area	
	Population	*% Growth*	*Population as a Percentage of Metropolitan Area Population*	*Population*	*% Growth*
1870	4,759				
1880	35,629	648.7%			
1890	106,713	199.5%			
1900	133,859	25.4%			
1910	213,381	59.4%		219,314	
1920	256,491	20.2%	*97%*	264,232	20.5%
1930	287,861	12.2%	*87%*	330,761	25.2%
1940	322,412	12.0%	*84%*	384,372	16.2%
1950	415,786	29.0%	*74%*	563,832	46.7%
1960	493,887	18.8%	*53%*	929,383	64.8%
1970	514,678	4.2%	*40%*	1,277,529	37.5%
1980	492,365	−4.5%	*30%*	1,619,921	26.8%
1990	467,610	−4.8%	*25%*	1,848,319	14.1%
2000	554,636	18.6%	*26%*	2,157,756	16.7%
2010	600,158	8.2%	*24%*	2,543,482	17.9%

Sources: 1870–2000 U.S. Census data as compiled by C. Abbott, S. J. Leonard, and T. J. Noel,
Colorado: A History of the Centennial State. 4th ed. (Boulder: University Press of Colorado,
2005); 2010 U.S. Census.

cycles. Second, the era of post–World War II growth in Denver was similar to the freeway and suburban expansion that occurred across U.S. cities. This era changed the spatial scope of the city, as the balance of
metropolitan population shifted toward the suburbs. Denver's role in federal and military build-up accelerated the pace of regional decentralization. Finally, the Sun Belt city–style amenity-led and tech-boom growth of
the late twentieth and early twenty-first centuries further expanded the regional extent of the metropolitan area with even greater outward growth.
More recently, revitalization in central Denver has brought a resurgence
of population growth, social vitality, and economic stability to the urban
core.

Pioneering Growth

Like San Francisco, a gold rush and population boom in the wilderness created the "instant city" of Denver.[2] After the initial discovery of gold, Denver
quickly became a frontier supply camp for mining operations. Though a
series of economic swings challenged the city's survival, it did not take
long for Denver to become a well-established, bustling service city. Moti-
vated by economic opportunities in westward expansion, gold and mineral
rushes, the Homestead Act (1862), agricultural prosperity, and even health
migrants, rapid population growth in the region helped Denver become
one of the largest cities west of the Mississippi River during its pioneering
days. While many mining towns became ghost towns soon after a mineral
market crash, Denver survived this fate by establishing a diverse economic
base and eventually becoming the dominant city for the Rocky Mountain
region.

The 1860s to early twentieth century was a period when Denver saw its
most spectacular population growth. Between 1870 and 1880, the city expanded by nearly 650 percent, and nearly 200 percent the following decade (Table 1). This pace of population increase was not uncommon for
frontier cities during the pioneering era of westward expansion. Heavy
streams of people flowed to the region with dreams of easy wealth in the
gold and silver rushes. While the get-rich fairy tale was a reality to relatively few individuals, the fast growth of the city of Denver provided economic opportunities for most. Modest prosperity occurred through land
ownership, business ventures in a booming supply town, or laboring for
railroad and mineral smelting industries. Well into the 1920s, another
major source of population growth were health seekers (and their families) who moved to Colorado in search of relief from the symptoms of
tuberculosis.

As in the rest of the United States, the ethnic composition of the early
population of Denver was diverse. Pioneers were primarily European American migrants from midwestern and East Coast states, including Germans,
Irish, English, Polish, Swedes, and Italians.[3] African Americans migrated from
the South, via Kansas, Texas, or New Mexico, and sought the same opportunities available in the Homestead Act, through laboring jobs, or establishing
themselves as business owners and professionals. In the 1890 U.S. Census,
6,000 blacks lived in Colorado, with 3,254 in Denver.[4] Prior to in-migrations

during the 1920s, most Mexican Americans in Colorado were of Spanish Mexican, Hispano, or Chicano origins living in the Colorado territory when the U.S.-Mexico border changed under the Treaty of Guadalupe Hidalgo (1848). There were also smaller populations of West Coast Chinese immigrants in the region.

As Denver grew in population, so did its spatial extent. Starting from the small river confluence settlement, the city grew by annexing other pioneer towns, such as Auraria and Highland. Denver entrepreneurs started horse-drawn railway services in the 1870s, and later, electrified streetcars. The Denver Tramway Company served the city until 1950, covering 260 miles of track across thirty-one lines.[5] Many streetcar neighborhoods emerged in the open prairie, including the smelter towns of Argo, Swansea, Elyria, and Globeville, as well as suburban enclaves such as Five Points (see end of this chapter), Park Hill, Capitol Hill, Montclair, Barnum, Valverde, Berkeley, and South Denver. All these protosuburbs and other built-up areas nearby were incorporated into Denver by 1902, when the consolidated City and County of Denver was created.[6] The city of Denver grew to fifty-nine square miles but remained relatively unchanged in size until the World War II era. During this era of pioneering growth Mayor Speer's commitment to the City Beautiful movement transformed the city with fountains, lights, city parks, wide tree-lined boulevards, and the grand neoclassical structures seen today in the Civic Center complex of government offices, library, museums, and public promenades.

Surrounding communities resisted annexation by Denver and incorporated as separate municipalities, including Littleton, Englewood, Glendale, and Sheridan in Arapahoe County; Golden, Wheat Ridge, and Arvada in Jefferson County; and Aurora and Westminster in Adams County.[7] Town leaders and residents believed the benefits of separate incorporation to be greater than the benefits of joining the central city. Outsiders perceived Denver as congested, dirty, unhealthy, and politically corrupt, with too much immoral activity of drinking, gambling, and prostitution. Even though significant economic, political, and service benefits in joining the central city existed, many suburban towns chose to remain separate. The suburban municipalities grew more steadily in the 1920–50 period owing in part to the popularity of automobile transportation, initiating a pattern whereby the City and County of Denver became hemmed in from future growth through annexation.

After World War II: The Second Capital of the United States

The period just before and after World War II was a decisive turning point for Denver's urban form. The city's spatial growth had been occurring in a more centralized and concentrated pattern, with a focus on the downtown region, the surrounding neighborhoods, and first-tier suburbs. This period saw moderate growth relative to the pioneering era, but remarkable absolute population increases (Table 1). The region's diverse service-based economy and employment opportunities expanded, including thousands of military and federal jobs. Boundaries of urban development pushed outward, and Denver quickly became a more sprawling and decentralized region.

In *Crabgrass Frontier*, Kenneth Jackson details the history of suburbanization in U.S. cities that gained momentum in the years immediately following World War II.[8] Even before the end of the war, population was growing, and urban areas began to claim a larger share of the U.S. population, as more people migrated out of rural communities. Further, the postwar euphoric baby boom effect saw families growing rapidly. Desire grew for spacious housing, quiet neighborhoods, and the benefits of country life within reach of a city's amenities. Here emerged the "home as a haven" suburban ideal.

Other factors also propelled suburbanization. Rising fears associated with racial prejudices led to the out-migration of residents, ultimately reinforcing race and class segregations. Homeownership became more widely available to the middle class through cheaper production processes and federally subsidized home mortgage loans (e.g., FHA, VA). And the 1956 Federal Aid Highway Act helped states and cities obtain subsidies to build highways that both radiated outward from the downtown core and encircled cities with beltways, making movement around the city in a personal automobile easier, particularly to new homes in the urban periphery.

The rapid rise of suburban growth caused the U.S. Census to begin recording population statistics based on newly designated metropolitan area units, as defined by the Office of Management and Budget. Metropolitan areas were defined by a central city, a central county, and any nearby suburban counties. The inclusion/exclusion of counties helped establish boundaries of urban and suburban areas with a high degree of social and economic integration—usually measured by commuting-to-work patterns. This was a clear reflection of the changing political geography of U.S. cities whereby urban growth was no longer confined just to the central city or county.

This national trend of postwar suburbanization was no exception in the Denver region. In 1950, the Denver Standard Metropolitan Area (SMA) had a total population of 563,832, while the City and County of Denver, with a population of 415,786, accounted for 73.7 percent of the metropolitan total (Table 1). The other components of the Denver SMA—Adams, Arapahoe, and Jefferson Counties—each experienced a higher rate of population growth than Denver (Table 2). As post-war suburbanization movement heightened by 1960, the City and County of Denver represented only 53 percent of the metropolitan area total of 929,383 (Table 1), as each of the outer counties— Adams, Arapahoe, and Jefferson—experienced much stronger growth (Table 2). By the 1970s the growth trends clearly shifted: central Denver lost the majority share of the metropolitan area, and its slow growth was greatly outpaced by the suburban municipalities (Table 3). Aurora, Englewood, Arvada, and Littleton are four of the oldest and largest suburban communities situated directly adjacent to Denver. These first-tier suburbs had their golden era of growth in the late 1940s and onward. Lakewood, which in 1969 incorporated some of the already urbanized portions of Jefferson County just west of Denver, became the second-largest city in the metro area and the fourth-largest city in the state by 1970 with a population of 92,787. Aurora, straddling both Adams and Arapahoe counties just east of Denver, grew from 11,421 in 1950 to 74,974 by 1970, ranking it as the fifth-largest city in Colorado. Further away, the city of Boulder, the county seat of Boulder County and site of the University of Colorado, ranked sixth with a 1970 population of 66,870, while Arvada in Jefferson County was the seventh most populous city in Colorado with 46,814 residents. Such suburban growth was typical of most major U.S. urban areas during this period.

Denver's suburbanization process and outward expansion during this period was accelerated by the development of numerous military and federal installations. With a federal payroll that grew to become second in size only to Washington, D.C., Denver was quickly referred to as the "Second (or Little) Capital of the United States." The growth as a minicapital for the federal government and defense industry was part of a strategic plan by city leaders during the early twentieth century. Mayor Speer's beautification vision of Denver as a "Paris on the Platte" was not going to occur by promoting industrial production growth. Instead, he—and also Mayor Stapleton in later decades—led administrations premised on improving the quality of life for city residents, maintaining a clean and healthy city appreciative of its natural setting, and preserving the attractiveness of the locale. While

Table 2. Population of Denver Metropolitan Area Counties, 1950–2010

County	1950	1960	1970	1980	1990	2000	% change 1970–2000	% change 1990–2000	2010	% change 2000–2010
Denver	415,786	493,887	514,678	492,365	467,610	554,636	7.8%	18.6%	600,158	8.3%
Arapahoe	52,125	113,426	162,142	293,621	391,511	487,967	200.9%	24.6%	572,003	17.5%
Jefferson	55,687	127,520	233,031	371,753	438,430	527,056	126.2%	20.2%	534,543	1.3%
Adams	40,234	120,296	185,789	245,944	265,038	363,857	95.8%	37.3%	441,603	17.7%
Boulder	48,296*	74,254	131,889	189,625	225,339*	291,288*	120.9%	29.3%	294,567	1.0%
Douglas	*	*	*	25,153	60,391	175,766	598.8%**	191.0%	285,465	62.9%
Broomfield	*	*	*	*	*	*	*	*	55,889	
Gilpin	*	*	*	*	*	*	*	*	5,441	
Clear Creek	*	*	*	*	*	*	*	*	9,088	
Park	*	*	*	*	*	*	*	*	16,206	
Elbert	*	*	*	*	*	*	*	*	23,086	

Sources: U.S. Census decennial data.

*Not a part of OMB designation of Denver MSA during these years.

**Percent change, 1980–2000.

Table 3. Population of Cities over Ten Thousand in the Denver Metropolitan Area, 1950–2010

City	1950	1960	1970	1980	1990	2000	2010
Denver (1)	415,786	493,887	524,678	492,365	467,610	554,636	600,158
Boulder* (11)	19,999	37,718	66,870	76,685	83,312	94,673	97,385
Englewood	16,869	33,398	33,695	30,021	29,387	31,727	30,225
Aurora (3)	11,421	48,548	74,974	158,588	222,103	276,393	325,078
Arvada (8)		19,242	46,814	84,576	89,235	102,153	106,433
Westminster (9)		13,850	19,432	50,211	74,625	100,940	106,114
Littleton (20)		13,670	26,466	28,631	33,685	40,340	41,737
Longmont* (13)		11,489	23,209	42,942	51,555	71,093	86,270
Thornton (6)		11,353	13,326	40,343	55,031	82,384	118,772
Lakewood (5)			92,787	112,860	126,481	144,126	142,980
Wheat Ridge			29,795	30,293	29,419	32,913	30,166
Northglenn			27,937	29,847	27,195	31,575	35,789
Commerce City (18)			17,407	16,234	16,466	20,991	45,913
Broomfield (16)				20,730	24,638	38,272	55,889
Brighton				12,773	14,203	20,905	33,352
Golden				12,237	13,116	17,159	18,867
Lafayette					14,548	23,197	24,453
Louisville					12,361	18,937	18,376
Parker (19)						23,558	45,297
Castle Rock (17)						20,224	48,231
Federal Heights						12,065	11,467
Greenwood Village						11,035	13,925
Centennial (10)							100,377
Erie							18,135
Lone Tree							10,218
Castle Pines North							10,360

Sources: U.S. Census decennial data.
Note: Numbers in parentheses indicate statewide rank of city size by population, 2010. Other largest cities in Colorado include: Colorado Springs (2), Fort Collins (4), Pueblo (7), Greeley (12), and Grand Junction (15).
*Cities included with Denver MSA only during 1960–80 census years.

both mayors valued growth as good for the city, they took a position of controlled growth. For example, while some boosters sought to expand the industrial economy in Denver, the mayors thought otherwise: why bring in more factories that pollute the air and spoil the surrounding landscape? One area of aggressive growth they promoted was tourism. Another was to attract well-paying office jobs—seen as a clean enterprise that didn't despoil the landscape. Toward this end, city leaders courted Washington, D.C., to assemble Denver into a protected interior hub for the U.S. government.[9] By the late 1930s, the federal government spent millions of dollars on major military installations in the metropolitan Denver area, adding fifty thousand direct jobs and numerous indirect jobs.[10] Even today the federal presence remains strong. Across 125 federal facilities there are nearly forty thousand employees in the Denver area with an average annual salary of $59,000.[11]

All the new facilities associated with the military and federal growth were constructed along the metropolitan periphery, hastening the deconcentration and decentralization of Denver's jobs and housing. Lowry Field was built in 1937 on the site of a former tuberculosis sanatorium along the Denver-Aurora boundary and served as an army training school, an airfield, and a bombing range. Near Lowry was Buckley Field, a naval airbase. The Denver Ordnance Plant, built in 1941 on two thousand acres just west of downtown, later became the Denver Federal Center, which continues to operate as a governmental office park employing over five thousand today. To the northeast of Denver, the twenty-thousand-acre Rocky Mountain Arsenal complex served as a chemical weapons plant and repository during World War II, the Korean War, and the Vietnam War. The old Fitzsimons Army Hospital in Aurora was originally built to serve tuberculosis patients, then expanded and was repurposed to treat World War II casualties. In each case, these major military and federal installations consumed large swaths of prime land in outlying suburban areas. In later decades the subsequent decommissioning and reconfiguring of these military facilities provided many brownfield and in-fill redevelopment opportunities in the metropolitan area.

The Suburban Dominance of Late Twentieth-Century Growth

Growth in the late twentieth century was characterized by the suburban dominance in population expansion. Starting in 1970 the metropolitan population doubled, with nearly all the growth occurring in Denver's suburban areas (Table 1). In the 1970s the metropolitan area population grew by 29.8 percent, with almost all the growth occurring in Jefferson, Arapahoe, and Adams Counties (Table 2). Strong growth occurred in suburban municipalities such as Aurora, Arvada, Westminster, Thornton, Lakewood, Longmont, and Broomfield (Table 3). By contrast, Denver actually lost population in the 1970s, shrinking from a previous high of 514,678 in 1970 to 492,365 in 1980, to represent only 30.9 percent of the metropolitan population by 1980. Despite the economic slowdown during the 1980s, the metropolitan population continued to grow at a slower, but still substantial 16 percent rate. Suburban Arapahoe, Jefferson, Boulder, and Adams Counties again led the growth. Aurora, Westminster, Lakewood, and Thornton were among the fastest growing suburbs, as were Lafayette and Louisville, two places that absorbed some of the growth pressures in Boulder. It was at this time that rapidly growing Douglas County was added to the Denver MSA. Denver's population declined again to 467,610 by 1990 and accounted for only 25 percent of the metropolitan area population.

This rapid population growth due to in-migration gave rise to the social phenomena of the Denver metropolitan area being a city of transplants. As of 2010, only 43.3 percent of Denver area residents were born in the state of Colorado. Among the twenty-five largest U.S. metropolitan areas and the rates of birth within their respective states, Denver ranks sixth, behind Washington, D.C. (31.3 percent), Miami (32.3 percent), Tampa (35.3 percent), Phoenix (37.4 percent), and Portland (43.2 percent). This transplant pattern also extends across the urban areas of the Front Range. In Boulder and Colorado Springs approximately 30 percent of the residents were born in Colorado, while the rates are higher in Fort Collins (39 percent), Greeley (51 percent), and Pueblo (66 percent).[12]

The last few decades of the twentieth century and early 2000s saw some of the most significant suburban population growth that further changed the regional extent of Denver's metropolitan area. Boulder County, with the major cities of Boulder and Longmont, was previously included in the 1960, 1970, and 1980 definitions of the Denver MSA but was categorized in 1990 as a separate independent metropolitan area.[13] Most of the counties in the metro area experienced substantial growth, especially Douglas County, registering a 191 percent increase from 1990 to 2000 (it was one of the fastest-growing counties in the United States that decade) and 62.9 percent growth since 2000 (Table 2). Other counties also grew significantly, including Adams and Arapahoe, and after two decades of decline, Denver has experienced significant growth since 1990.

In response to such rapid growth and changing geographies of the metropolitan region identified in the 2000 U.S. Census, several key changes altered the Denver metropolitan designation. First, new formulations by the Office of Management and Budget favored the Metropolitan Statistical Area (MSA) terminology over previous designations of Consolidated Metropolitan Statistical Areas (CMSA) and Primary Metropolitan Statistical Areas (PMSA). Thus, the Boulder and Greeley areas were removed from Denver's consolidated statistical unit, each established as their own MSA. The Denver MSA was officially named the Denver-Aurora MSA. In addition to the Colorado Springs MSA and Pueblo MSA immediately south, and the Fort Collins–Loveland MSA and Cheyenne, Wyoming, MSA to the north, the overall concentration of seven contiguous metropolitan areas illustrates the ongoing urban growth corridor along the Colorado Front Range. Second, in November 2001, Broomfield became the newest (sixty-fourth) and smallest (in land area) county in the State of Colorado. Originally part of Boulder County, the city of Broomfield's rapid growth stretched its municipal boundaries into three neighboring counties, including Adams, Jefferson, and Weld. Crossing too many governmental jurisdictions for administering courts, sales taxes, and county seat duties, the decision was made to consolidate Broomfield into a single county, which was added to the Denver MSA. Third, four other counties were newly added to the Denver MSA, including the mountain counties of Clear Creek, Gilpin, and Park, as well as Elbert County in the rural eastern plains. These county additions resulted from the rise of exurban development, the increases of longer-distance commuters to Denver area jobs, and the growing economic integration of these mountain and plains communities with Denver. The metropolitan area was again renamed the Denver-Aurora-Lakewood MSA to include both Aurora and Lakewood as principal cities.

Beyond the suburban periphery, significant exurban growth in the late twentieth century was the reason for the addition of new outlying counties to the Denver region. With the majestic Rocky Mountains such a prominent feature located directly west of the city, it was inevitable that residential development would extend into the nearby foothills and Front Range region. The construction of Interstate 70 west of Denver into the mountains opened up a major access corridor, allowing residents the ability to live in the mountains and still commute to the Denver area. Numerous exurban communities in Jefferson, Boulder, Clear Creek, Gilpin, and Park counties, located up to thirty to fifty miles away from Denver, started to experience substantial growth. Particularly popular are the one- to forty-acre "ranchettes" that give residents a "home on the range" within driving distance of metropolitan Denver. Despite now being included in the Denver metropolitan designation, this ultralow density exurban sprawl is not usually included in statistical analyses of urbanized land expansion, thus many studies tend to underestimate the extent of residential development in the hinterlands of metropolitan areas.[14]

Denver area job growth was similarly explosive during the late twentieth century. From 1980 to 2005 the region expanded jobs by 71 percent. Denver County, including the central business district, saw a rise of only 8 percent during that time. But Adams County jobs grew by 98 percent, Arapahoe County 152 percent, and Douglas County increased jobs by 1,685 percent.[15] Undoubtedly such wild growth of population and jobs altered the spatial landscape of Denver, particularly in the suburban periphery. Two suburban places that characterize this outward growth are the Denver Technological Center (DTC or Tech Center) and Highlands Ranch. These commercial and residential developments on the southern periphery of the Denver region reflect the decentralizing trend of both jobs and housing developments.

The Denver Tech Center

The Denver Technological Center (DTC) is a classic example of an "edge city,"[16] a location on the urban periphery containing high concentrations of decentralized urban activities, including a large supply of leasable office and retail space. Edge cities typically contain more jobs than bedrooms and are essentially places that "have it all." They are also marked by their relatively recent emergence into the urban landscape.

In the mid-1950s, a notoriously arrogant and intolerant developer, George MacKenzie Wallace, began his dream to relocate his downtown office far away from the perceived troubles of the city. As he explained it, "some goddam [ethnic slur deleted] left a scratch in my shiny new black Lincoln sedan. That's when I decided to find a place—with 14 foot wide parking spaces—where my people could have some room to work."[17] At that time, suburban office parks were virtually nonexistent. Seeing advantages in the newly constructed Valley Highway (Interstate 25) heading south out of Denver, Wallace envisioned a tranquil place for his office building. He began with the purchase of a forty-acre farm adjacent to a Valley Highway exit, eleven miles from downtown. By 1968 Wallace had acquired seven hundred additional acres, and Hewlett-Packard became the first major firm to locate in the new office park.

The master plan for the Denver Technological Center sought to create an urban setting in a suburban context by using a balanced mixture of land uses. And Wallace's vision of a peaceful natural setting for an office park is quite evident today: clusters of modern midrise office buildings are nestled amid large open spaces and well-manicured lawns and parks, with gently curving tree-lined streets, all in relative proximity to other urban amenities of banks, shops, grocers, restaurants, and entertainment. By 1994, when Wallace retired, his DTC had grown to cover one thousand acres, with nine hundred firms and 165 office buildings, including twelve glass-and-steel towers.[18] Early on the complex attracted many corporate giants including Diner's Club International, Kodak, and United Airlines. Similar office park developments emerged nearby along the I-25 corridor—including Meridien International Business Center (1,692 acres), Greenwood Plaza (400 acres), and Inverness (1,000 acres)—all contributing to a concentration of office-based employment southeast of downtown Denver. Within a ten-minute drive is Centennial Airport, the region's largest airport for private and general aviation and a major strategic asset for the nearby corporations. Numerous convention-style and all-suite hotels (including Marriott, Hilton, Hyatt, and Sheraton) serve a wide variety of guests as well as the surrounding corporate office community. The Denver Broncos football team corporate offices and practice facilities are located at Dove Valley in the Tech Center area.

Significantly, this agglomeration is a major employment center of the Denver area with the second-highest concentration of jobs. Denver's central business district (CBD) has approximately 126,000 employees (16 percent of the urban area employment) in 1.53 square miles (an average of 82,253 workers per square mile). The entire Denver Tech Center area (including Meridien, Greenwood Plaza, and Inverness) has approximately 86,500 employees (11 percent of urban area employment) in a 10.5 square mile area (an average of 8,238 workers per square mile).[19] The corporate headquarters of several Fortune 500 companies are located within the DTC area, including: CH2M, Arrow Electronics, Western Union, DISH Network, Liberty Interactive, Newmont Mining, and Envision Healthcare, as are the headquarters of two aerospace companies, United Launch Alliance and Jeppesen. Other major companies with regional offices located here include Sprint, Clear Channel, Time Warner Cable, XO Communications, Comcast (cable and telecommunications); Morgan Stanley, Merrill Lynch (banking and finance); and Oracle, Agilent, and HP (high-tech industries).

The DTC also contains extensive retail and entertainment development. Movie theaters and higher-end restaurants sit scattered among the office towers, providing both proximity to amenities, the spaciousness of suburbia, and an appeal of pseudonatural landscaping aesthetics. Larger strip mall developments on either side of the I-25 corridor serve the nearby residential populations. In 1996 one of Denver's largest and most palatial regional shopping malls opened at the I-25 and C-470 intersection, just between the Tech Center and Highlands Ranch. The Park Meadows Mall, with over three million square feet, is a prime example of retail space constructed to create a fantasy experience in the otherwise mundane act of shopping. Described more as a "retail resort,"[20] the mall was built to resemble a mountain lodge. The interior utilizes exposed wooden beams from lodgepole pines and Douglas fir trees; the seating areas are situated around active fireplaces; several water features resemble flowing mountain streams; and wall murals depict scenery from the surrounding mountains and plains landscapes. The lyrics for "America the Beautiful," based on a poem Katharine Lee Bates wrote after summiting Pikes Peak in 1893, appear in a central rotunda mural. From an outside vantage point with the Rocky Mountains as a backdrop, the mall's earth-toned wood-and-brick façade with red steel roof reflects images of a ski lodge setting. Several golf courses sit adjacent to the Tech Center, and the massive Cherry Creek Reservoir and Cherry Creek State Park offer extensive water- and trail-related activities. And in the recent trend of building suburban area entertainment venues, the original Fiddler's Green Amphitheater opened in 1988 in the Greenwood Plaza area of the DTC. It has a capacity for eighteen thousand people and is the largest outdoor amphitheater in the metropolitan area consistently running a summer concert series featuring national-level traveling acts.

The long string of midrise office towers of the DTC is an unmistakable imprint on the metropolitan skyline at its southern edge. The Tech Center activity concentration stretches for nearly eight miles along I-25 beginning at the junction with I-225 (a spur highway through Aurora), straddling the border between Denver and Arapahoe Counties and continuing southward along I-25 past the C-470 intersection into Douglas County, where new growth and development on open prairie continues, including in the Lone Tree and RidgeGate areas.

Highlands Ranch

Just to the south and west of the Denver Tech Center is the Highlands Ranch residential community in Douglas County. In the 1990s and 2000s Douglas

County experienced very rapid population growth especially in an area concentrated on the northern edge bordering Arapahoe County, Jefferson County, and the C-470 highway. With some exception given to recent growth in the Castle Rock community, much of Douglas County's growth can be attributed to the development of Highlands Ranch, a prototypical greenfield development of sprawling suburban residential communities.

Highlands Ranch is a twenty-two-hundred-acre master-planned community, approximately twenty miles from downtown Denver. Originally a large ranch far outside the city, ownership changed hands numerous times throughout the twentieth century, from John Springer, to Lawrence C. Phipps Jr., to Marvin Davis, until the California-based Mission Viejo Company purchased it in 1979. That developer built the first homes by 1981, and it was acquired by Shea Homes in 1997. In just thirty years the development has grown to 93,477 residents, 29,040 single-family homes, and 3,305 apartments.[21] By 2020 the community is expected to have over 100,000 residents in over 36,700 homes.

Antisuburbia critics have chided Highlands Ranch as the "ugliest and most embarrassing feature of the Front Range," a "big smush of beige puke," and representative of all that is "soulless and evil in the world." But despite the oft-levied critiques of cookie-cutter-style suburban landscapes that occur across the United States, Highlands Ranch is increasingly praised for utilizing smart growth principles of density, housing variety, mixed land uses, and nearby access to light rail—all alongside greenbelts and preserved natural landscapes.[22]

The master plan of the development included small office parks and retail and commercial centers developed as "town centers" and commercial corridors. There are over one thousand acres of business and industrial parks, including the Santa Fe Distribution Center on the western edge of Highlands Ranch with several light manufacturing or warehousing and distribution operations, as well as Lockheed Martin and W. R. Grace. The business parks originally included corporate research and development (R&D) offices for firms such as Lucent, Avaya, Qwest, and Visa. And Highlands Ranch is located near existing light rail stations. The planned extensions of both the Southeast and Southwest RTD lines will provide the community with even greater access to this public transit amenity.

Beyond its sheer size and rapid pace of development, Highlands Ranch is also noteworthy for both its intentional interface with nature and its unusual political structure. The master plan for Highlands Ranch calls for land use heavily balanced toward the natural environment. Only 31 percent is designated for residential development and 8 percent for business development. The remaining 61 percent is dedicated to nonurban uses, including large open spaces, golf courses, parks, and trails. This access and proximity to the natural environment is a major marketing point and helps meet the increased residential desire of living the Colorado "tourist way of life" (see Chapter 4). And as Highlands Ranch and other residential developments encroach further on open prairie space or the mountain forests, suburban and exurban homes become the sites of more human-wildlife encounters, including with coyotes, wildcats, elk, mountain lions, and black bears— interactions that are on the rise as food shortages force wildlife further into the urban landscape.

Politically, Highlands Ranch is in unincorporated Douglas County. The Highlands Ranch Metropolitan District (HRMD), a seven-member board of directors, is responsible for providing certain municipal services, such as overseeing the construction and maintenance of major roads, the adjacent landscaping, traffic signals, and construction of storm drainage facilities. Beyond these built infrastructure duties, the HRMD is also responsible for managing the extensive nonurban-use lands, including all the open-space areas and the parks and trails. Further, the district organizes an extensive outdoor recreation and sports program for youth, adults, and senior citizens of the community. There is also an emphasis on environmental education programs. The major services not provided by the HRMD are contracted from nearby municipalities. For example, law enforcement is provided by the Douglas County Sheriff's Office, fire and emergency service is established through an intergovernmental agreement with the neighboring Littleton community, and water supply and wastewater treatment is contracted with nearby Centennial Water and Sanitary District.

Is Denver a Sprawling Region?

Given the suburban and exurban growth that has occurred around Denver since the 1940s, and more rapidly in the past twenty to thirty years, it is fair to assume that Denver suffers from the ubiquitous problems of suburban sprawl. In a special report examining the unique challenges facing Denver, David Rusk posed the question, "Does Denver have a sprawl problem?"[23]

Interestingly he concludes the answer is both yes and no: while most residents *perceive* and *experience* the area as having a sprawling problem (especially regarding traffic congestion), national comparisons suggest otherwise.

By observation and experience, Denver feels like a very sprawling place. The region extends over a very large area: stretching thirty-three driving miles north to south between Broomfield and Highlands Ranch, and twenty-eight driving miles east to west from Aurora to Golden. The fivefold growth of urbanized land from 105 square miles in 1950 to 499 square miles in 2000 was primarily onto greenfields (agricultural and prairie lands) surrounding the region. New peripheral development since the 1950s and 1960s has segregated the land uses of housing (e.g., Highlands Ranch), retail, and employment (e.g., DTC), reducing the walkability to access these spaces of everyday life. Recent residential growth in the exurban realm, especially in the foothill mountain communities, creates even lower density sprawl.

Indicative of Denver's sense of sprawl is the traffic congestion and automobile dependence. In terms of per capita gasoline consumption (relative to urban density), one comparative study[24] of U.S. and global cities placed Denver very high—in a cohort similar to Houston, Phoenix, and Los Angeles. In 2000, Denver households owned 1.79 cars on average, 87.2 percent of commuters traveled to work by car, either alone (76.1 percent) or carpooling (11.1 percent), and Denverites spent on average 26.5 minutes commuting to work.[25]

Though Denver certainly looks and feels like a sprawling place, relative to other cities in the United States, its development is more compact than perceived. Based on one standard sprawl measure, Denver's *population per square mile of urbanized land* fell only 16 percent, from 4,741 in 1950 to 3,979 in 2000. This rate of change since the era of rapid suburbanization is low compared to Portland, Oregon (−26 percent), Rochester, New York (−63 percent), or the national average (−45 percent). As an example, during the tech-boom growth of the 1990s, Denver's urbanized land expanded by 8 percent, while population grew 30 percent.[26] Thus, while Denver experienced rapid population growth and outward expansion since the mid-twentieth century, its growth is in a more compact or dense fashion relative to other U.S. cities. And future Denver growth is expected to follow this trend (see Chapter 6).

Why has Denver's growth been more dense than many other locations? In a region with abundant room for expansion—wide-open plains to the east, north, and south—why hasn't Denver sprawled similarly to the national averages? One key reason, as argued by Rusk, is *water*. In the Denver region, leapfrog development of isolated communities occurs less frequently as groundwater is insufficient to supply large residential areas. Instead, new residential developments occur adjacent to existing urbanized areas where water service can be tapped from existing supply systems (such as Denver Water). Another reason for the lower-than-expected rates of sprawl is the trend toward smart growth initiatives favoring compact developments, especially mixed-use high-density urban centers (see Chapter 6).

The Reurbanism Trend

At the beginning of the twenty-first century many U.S. cities are beginning to experience a new urban migration of *reurbanism*. Somewhat reversing the trend of central city population decline, individuals are rethinking the benefits of living in the city and opting out of the suburban lifestyle.[27] While suburban living remains strong in Denver, a new residential settlement trend is spurring a revival of population growth in the central urban core.

By the late 1990s significant population growth in central Denver occurred, reflecting national trends of increased downtown living.[28] Such a return to the city can be attributed to many causes. For one, desirability of a postindustrial downtown live-work-play lifestyle has skyrocketed, especially among young single adults and older childfree couples. Second, the remarkable urban revitalization of downtown Denver (see Chapter 4) since the 1990s has created the place for this urban lifestyle to become a reality. The transformative redevelopment established abundant new living opportunities in lofts, apartments, or rehabbed historic homes. New bars, coffee shops, restaurants, nightclubs, sporting venues, and art galleries created a giant playground in the heart of the city. Furthermore, the economic stability of job opportunities in Denver enabled the viability of this trend. Resurgent city population growth is not confined to just downtown Denver, but has occurred throughout the central city. The City and County of Denver grew by 8.2 percent between 2000 and 2010, aided in part by new in-fill housing construction projects in Stapleton and LoDo, and has continued at that pace, resulting in a 2015 U.S. Census population estimate of nearly 683,000. Other principal cities with a similar growth rate over this period

include: Miami, Phoenix, Seattle, Houston, San Diego, Tucson, San Jose, and
Washington, D.C.

Social Diversity of Denver:
Demographics and Discrimination

As noted earlier, a Brookings Institution study characterized Denver today as
a "high diversity" region—having above the national metropolitan average
of nonwhite and nonblack population. Using census classifications of race
and ethnicity, in 2010 the entire Denver metropolitan area population was
65.8 percent white alone, 22.5 percent Hispanic or Latino, 5.3 percent black
or African American alone, and 3.6 percent Asian alone (Table 4). Those who
identify with two or more races constitute 2.1 percent of the population; all
other categories are below 1 percent. The City and County of Denver contains larger measures of diversity: white alone accounts for about half the
population (52.2 percent) followed by 31.8 percent Hispanic or Latino,
9.7 percent black or African American alone, and 3.3 percent Asian alone.
Aurora is one of the most diverse municipalities, where white alone was
47.3 percent, Hispanic or Latino 28.7 percent, and African American
15.1 percent. Hispanics and Latinos reside in Denver, Thornton, Aurora, and
Lakewood at rates at or above the regional population rate of 22.5 percent.
While these current statistics reflect an overall diverse city, it is important to
understand some of the social complexities in Denver's fractured past and
present.

Originating as a city of immigrants, Denver has never been culturally
homogenous.[29] When the city was founded in 1858, several Native American
groups populated the mountain and plains regions around Denver. Today
approximately twenty thousand Native Americans live in the Denver region,
descendants of Cheyenne, Lakota, Kiowa, Navajo, and many other groups.
Among the early European American pioneers who settled in Denver, exact
origins within Europe were distinct cultural dividing lines of distrust and
strife, establishing segregated neighborhoods. For instance eastern European Jews settled in the West Colfax area, Italians in the Highlands neighborhood, and Poles and other eastern Europeans in Globeville. But early
economic opportunists also included thousands of African Americans mi-
grating from the South, and Chinese workers from the West Coast. Anti-
Japanese sentiment during World War II resulted in Japanese internment

Table 4. Race and Ethnicity Composition of the Denver-Aurora-Lakewood Metropolitan Statistical Area (MSA) and Six of the Largest Municipalities (as % of Total Population)

	White alone	Black / African American	Hispanic	Asian	Two or more races
MSA	65.8%	5.3%	22.5%	3.6%	2.1%
Denver	52.2%	9.7%	31.8%	3.3%	2.1%
Aurora	47.3%	15.1%	28.7%	4.8%	3.2%
Lakewood	71.8%	1.4%	22.0%	3.0%	1.7%
Thornton	59.9%	1.6%	31.7%	4.3%	1.9%
Centennial	82.4%	3.1%	7.4%	4.3%	2.3%
Arvada	81.3%	0.8%	13.7%	2.1%	1.6%

Source: 2010 U.S. Census.
Notes: Rows do not equal 100 percent as not all race/ethnicity categories are included.
See Table 3 for total population counts of each municipality.

camps across the United States, including the relocation of many West Coast Japanese to the Amache camp in southeastern Colorado. In 1942, Colorado governor Ralph Carr articulated a more tolerant attitude toward Japanese Americans, and in the post–internment camp era many Japanese Americans migrated to Denver and Colorado to establish new livelihoods. To commemorate Governor Carr's welcoming efforts, Colorado's Japanese American community established a memorial plaza in Sakura Square in downtown Denver. The entire block at Larimer and Nineteenth Streets remains a cultural enclave for those seeking Japanese goods and services, including a grocery market, the Tri-State Denver Buddhist Temple, and a residential complex for elderly. There are over fifteen thousand Japanese Americans in the region today.[30]

Hispanics and Latinos are the largest ethnic minority group in Denver, and their early origins and migrations to the region occurred in three distinct phases. First, there were many Spanish Mexican residents in the area who predated the existence of Colorado. When the territory was ceded to the United States in 1846 these residents were granted U.S. citizenship and became "charter members" of Colorado upon statehood in 1876. Second, as did thousands of others, many Mexican Americans migrated to Denver during the gold and silver rushes of the late 1800s. And third, people migrated for work in the sugar beet industry in the eastern plains during the 1920s, and many ultimately settled in the Denver area. By the late twentieth century Latinos and Hispanics constituted the largest minority population in Denver. The state of Colorado has the eighth-largest (absolute) and seventh-largest (relative) Hispanic/Latino population among U.S. states.[31] While approximately 1,165,000 Hispanic/Latinos live in the state, 56.4 percent (657,000) live in the Denver MSA.

From the outside it might seem that Denver has not been as racially segregated or socially polarized as has occurred in other large U.S. cities. Perhaps perceptions of tolerance reflect the libertarian attitudes of individual freedoms or the spirit of openness that came with the common endeavor of pursuing individual prosperity in the city's origins as a melting pot of economic opportunists. But in reality, Denver has at times been a socially fractured city.[32]

In the early 1920s the Ku Klux Klan was strong in Denver. There were over fifty thousand members in Colorado, second only to the state of Indiana. The Klan wielded political power that included a mayor, a governor, and a U.S. senator.[33] And white supremacist dogmas ran deep. As one restaurant sign in Denver read, "No Dogs, Negros, Mexicans"; it was a time and place where both blacks *and* Hispanics/Latinos faced prejudice and bigotry. Both experienced employment discrimination and business segregation and received old and outdated school facilities, and school curriculum generally ignored black and Hispanic/Latino heritage.[34] The Chicano movement in the 1960s, led by Corky Gonzalez, a political activist and early pioneer for equal rights of Mexican Americans, arose after the city's west-side Hispanic/Latino population suffered decades of discrimination, racism, poverty, and clashes with police.[35] The movement focused on the lack of acceptance into society through relevant jobs and education. It raised political consciousness and activism to bring about pride and dignity, and a rebellion against injustices. It also revived cultural pride in being Spanish, Mexican, or Indian, rather than experiencing loss of culture through assimilation. New opportunities for the Chicano movement from the 1990s onward included efforts toward rights to find work, rights to citizenship, and advocating for immigration as an opportunity to make America better.

During the era of racial tension and urban riots across the United States in the 1960s and onward, there was a false sense of racial ease in Denver. Denver was seemingly unburdened "with the sins of the biracial South, [and] color-blindness made racial difference for the majority of those living in insulated, insular, and unconnected suburban communities a relic of the past."[36] But the reality of Denver's racial tension was revealed in the 1973 U.S. Supreme Court case *Keyes v. Denver School District No. 1* and the Poundstone Amendment (1974) to the Constitution of the State of Colorado.

In 1969, several black residents of the Park Hill neighborhood, led by Wilfred Keyes, filed suit against the Denver school district claiming violation of constitutional rights to equal education for their children. A federal district court ruling found school apartheid and unequal education occurring owing to neighborhood residential patterns and called for integration through busing. The firestorm between pro-integrationists and the antibusing majority escalated and revealed festering racism in the city. While largely nonviolent, the depth of division was exposed in February 1970 when forty-six school busses were bombed in their parking facility.[37]

The case was taken to the U.S. Supreme Court in 1973; it was the first school desegregation case heard by the court from outside the deeply segregated South. The court ruled that gerrymandering of school enrollments had created segregated and unequal schools; that proof of de jure segregation in one area of the district was enough to assume the entire district was affected; and that blacks and Hispanics should not be considered as desegregating each other, as they suffered similar inequities of inferior education. The directive of the court was that Denver must desegregate its entire school system, "root and branch." For the entire nation, this ruling extended desegregation mandates to schools in the North, and that desegregation applied to entire districts, not just a few schools within them. Furthermore, it recognized Denver's triracial and multiracial complexity (and across the United States), and the ruling provided Hispanics the same rights that had been given to blacks in earlier rulings.

The ruling of forced busing to achieve integration of schools further exposed the racially fragmented Denver metropolis. The suburbs of Denver differed widely in their composition of white and nonwhite populations. And as Denver sought to expand its boundaries through annexation, many white suburban communities feared the possibilities of school integration as fallout from the Supreme Court case. In response, suburban residents called for the Poundstone Amendment to the state constitution, which would require any annexation bid to receive majority approval of residents from the entire county, not just from the area to be annexed. The amendment passed in 1974 and effectively ended Denver's ability to annex (Denver International Airport's expansion into Adams County is one exception). It also allowed the metropolitan suburbs to permanently split from Denver, escaping the social and economic problems of the city, or any possible broader school busing programs. Despite goals for social and economic equality, a 1988 study by the *Rocky Mountain News* regarding the African American community of Denver found that "racism still festered, housing discrimination persisted, and economic progress fell short of Black hopes."[38]

Residential Patterns and Segregation

With over half a million Hispanics and Latinos in the Denver area, nearly one-third live in Denver. The Denver city neighborhoods with a majority of Hispanic/Latino residents are primarily located along the South Platte River valley, and directly surrounding the downtown district. Along the river corridor is a major railroad line with large rail yards, U.S. Highway 85 (Santa Fe Boulevard), the I-25 Valley Highway, and light manufacturing, industrial, and warehousing businesses. Adjacent to this corridor are some of the highest residential concentrations of Hispanic populations, including the neighborhoods of Valverde, Barnum, Villa Park, and Westwood, each with over 75 percent Hispanic/Latino population. In this area of southwest Denver is the Federal Boulevard ethnic enclave, which contains the greatest concentration of Hispanic businesses, as well as Vietnamese and Chinese businesses.

Many Hispanic and Latino neighborhoods also existed directly adjacent to the downtown district. Southwest of downtown the neighborhoods of Auraria, Sun Valley, and Jefferson Park have long been part of the Hispanic west side, although displacement occurred with the redevelopment of Auraria into a downtown college campus (Community College of Denver, Metropolitan State University of Denver, and University of Colorado at Denver all share this same complex). The Highland neighborhood west of Union Station was historically home to southern and western Europeans, particularly Italians, and later became a Hispanic-infused neighborhood. Today its proximity to downtown and the revitalized LoDo district is causing gentrification of the Highland neighborhood, and it is no longer affordable to working-class families. North of downtown Denver, the Sunnyside, Globeville, and Elyria/Swansea neighborhoods are also dominated by Hispanics. Historically they were home to many eastern Europeans, but the neighborhoods suffered when construction of two major interstates (the confluence of I-25 and I-70) negatively impacted the community fabric. These neighborhoods also experienced environmental injustices from the nearby industrial smelters (see Chapter 5).

African American neighborhoods are to the east of downtown, along the I-70 corridor and Martin Luther King Drive. A small minority in the entire metropolitan area (5.3 percent), African Americans constitute 9.7 percent of the Denver population. Similar to the Hispanic population, less than half (44 percent) reside in Denver, with the balance in surrounding suburban counties. The historic center of the African American community is the Five Points neighborhood (see end of this chapter), but today it is only 25 percent black. Since the 1960s many families have migrated to east-side neighborhoods of Whittier, Skyland, and some sections of Park Hill.

As seen in Table 4, residential diversity extends into Denver's suburban areas, especially some of the older first-tier suburbs. For example, Aurora has evolved into one of Denver's most diverse suburbs, with 15.1 percent African American and 28.7 percent Hispanic/Latino populations. While most African American population is concentrated in Denver and Aurora, the Hispanic/Latino residential pattern is more dispersed across many different suburban municipalities. More Hispanics live in the suburban counties than in Denver. In fact, while Denver County is 32 percent Hispanic, Adams County to the north is 36 percent (which includes Thornton, 31.7 percent, Westminster, 20.7 percent, and Commerce City, 46.8 percent), and Jefferson County is 15.2 percent (including Lakewood, 22.0 percent, and Arvada, 13.7 percent).

Immigration Patterns

The Denver region also contains a significant population of foreign-born persons. In fact, Denver is considered a *reemerging immigrant gateway city*: in the early twentieth century its foreign-born percentage exceeded national averages, then lagged in the middle decades, and again accelerated rapidly at the end of the century. Other U.S. metropolitan areas with similar foreign-born immigration trends include: Minneapolis, Oakland, Phoenix, Portland, Sacramento, San Jose, Seattle, and Tampa.[39]

In 2010 there were over 314,000 foreign-born persons living in the Denver metropolitan area, or 12.3 percent of the population, which was a

34 percent increase over 2000 (234,121 foreign born). The percent of population that is foreign born in some of the largest municipalities are: Denver (15.8 percent), Aurora (20.4 percent), Thornton (11.2 percent), Centennial (8.3 percent), Lakewood (8.2 percent), Littleton (6.8 percent), and Arvada (4.9 percent).[40] Regionally, most individuals were born in Latin America (55.2 percent), nearly one-fourth from Asia (23.1 percent), 13 percent from Europe, and 6 percent from Africa. One-third (32.7 percent) entered the United States between 1990 and 1999, and 36.8 percent since 2000. Only 15 percent of Denver's foreign-born residents entered the United States during the 1980s, and the remaining 15.4 percent arrived before 1980.[41]

The cultural landscape of Denver is richly diverse, as migrants and refugees have settled in Denver from a multitude of countries. Nearly half of all foreign-born persons living in the Denver region were born in Mexico (46.6 percent). The next single largest countries of origin are Vietnam (4.2 percent), China (3.1 percent) and Korea (2.9 percent). Beyond these core countries of origin, immigrant residents of Denver come from all regions of the world. There are an estimated thirty thousand East Africans from Ethiopia, Eritrea, Somalia, and Sudan who began arriving thirty years ago and primarily reside in Aurora. Many refugee service providers, such as the African Community Center of Denver, play an important role in refugee resettlement that assists newcomers. Recent migrations from North Africa and the Middle East include large clusters from Turkey, Morocco, Iran, Iraq, Afghanistan, and Israel. From South and Southeast Asia there are sizable immigrant groups from India, Cambodia, Laos, Thailand, Vietnam, Nepal, Burma, and Bhutan. From Laos approximately sixty-five hundred Hmong have lived in northwest Denver suburbs since arriving in the 1970s. The Jewish Russian American community in Denver has burgeoned since the 1970s, to nearly eighty thousand today, with a very high residential concentration around Cherry Creek in southeast Denver, near the Jewish Community Center and the Russian Plaza at Oneida Square. Overall immigration from Russia increased in the late twentieth century.

Undoubtedly the variety of immigrant groups in Denver has created a rich array of ethnic enclave neighborhoods that reflect both traditional cultural heritages, as well as continued global transnational linkages through markets and groceries, restaurants and local businesses, outreach groups and houses of worship. In Aurora, along East Colfax Avenue there is an East African enclave, and at Parker Road and Peoria, there is a confluence of South Asian, Middle Eastern/North Africa enclaves. Hispanic enclaves occur throughout the city, with the highest concentrations along the Federal Boulevard corridor and on Colfax Avenue.

Denver's Five Points Neighborhood

One neighborhood at the center of the reurbanism trend in Denver is Five Points, which has experienced rapid neighborhood change particularly since the 2000s. Five Points is also one of Denver's oldest neighborhoods, located directly northeast of the central business district and the emerging Ball Park neighborhood near Union Station. Once known as the Harlem of the West for its jazz history and thriving African American residential and commercial community, it exists today as a gentrifying milieu of social and economic diversity. The changes are occurring rapidly, and today one can observe three distinct historical eras within the neighborhood: its origins as a thriving community and vibrant neighborhood through the 1950s, the period of urban decay of the 1960s and 1970s, and the current trend of gentrification of the early 2000s.

In the 1860s and 1870s Five Points emerged as one of Denver's first residential neighborhoods far away from town on the wide open prairie. It was an obvious direction for city residential expansion, as existing downtown streets easily extended northeasterly parallel to the South Platte River without the need to construct bridges and viaducts. By 1871 horse-drawn streetcar service to the neighborhood, and later trolleys from the Denver Tramway Company, rolled through the peaceful tree-lined neighborhood. This streetcar suburb was an attractive place to live, becoming one of the premier residential neighborhoods of the city. It offered elegant and large Victorian homes and the city's first public park (Curtis Park), and it was removed from the noise and filth of the city. Many immigrants built their family communities in Five Points. Temple Emanuel, established in 1874 to serve early eastern Europeans, became the oldest Jewish congregation in Colorado; the congregation still exists today, but in a different location. And Sacred Heart Church, built in 1879 to serve Italian and Irish immigrants, continues offering services today in English and Spanish. Two of Denver's oldest African American churches were also established here at that time, Shorter AME (1868) and Zion Baptist (1867). But by the 1900s many of the European groups had moved out to the Capitol Hill neighborhood and elsewhere, and Five Points evolved into a socially and economically diverse place.

With streetcar access to downtown, and proximity to nearby industrial plants, smelters, and rail yards, the neighborhood attracted many families who wished to be near their places of employment. In the late 1890s more blacks lived here than any other neighborhood of the city. By the early 1900s, residential segregation practices of housing covenants and mortgage lending "redlining" had begun and forced African Americans to remain in the Five Points neighborhood until the 1960s. For much of the twentieth century, Five Points was not only the primary residential neighborhood for African Americans in the city; it became the historic and symbolic heart of Denver's African American community.

The forced segregation created a city within a city, a place of self-sufficiency where a strong community of "entrepreneurial, creative, and persevering spirits" emerged.[42] Welton Street was the thriving commercial district with opportunities for jobs, education, and retail. The corridor bustled with drugstores, restaurants, soda shops, barbers, beauty parlors, hotels, jazz venues, billiard halls, tailors, cleaners, and the first all-black firehouse in Denver. Several professionals not only provided their basic services in Five Points but also emerged as community leaders. Dr. Clarence Holmes, a local dentist, and Sonny Lawson, a pharmacist, became local leaders of human and civil rights through political action. Dr. Justina "Lady Doctor" Ford, who was not allowed to practice in public hospitals, delivered over seven thousand babies from her in-home practice and pioneered health care for Denver's low-income women and children. Banker McKinley Harris worked to provide home mortgages for neighborhood families. Many local residents had well-paid occupations as porters, waiters, and maids on Pullman railroad cars. The Local 465 porter union simultaneously served as a center for civil rights activism and community pride. The great entrepreneurial spirit in Five Points helped many get their start, including Madame C. J. Walker (America's first self-made female millionaire). In spite of the segregation, it was a prosperous time for the community, where people took great pride in their homes, and classy style in dress and cars mattered.

Culturally, the Five Points neighborhood developed a significant jazz music heritage. Through much of the 1930s, 1940s, and 1950s big band and bebop jazz eras, Five Points was a major stopover for musicians traveling through from eastern cities to the West Coast. Big-name musicians such as Duke Ellington, Ella Fitzgerald, Dinah Washington, Count Basie, Lionel Hampton, Nat King Cole, Louis Armstrong, and Billie Holliday performed in Denver but were not welcome to stay in downtown hotels. Instead, they found a safe haven in Five Points, where they performed late into the night at renowned venues such as the Rossonian Hotel and Lounge—which became the single greatest jazz hotspot of the Rocky Mountain West. The fever of the jazz scene earned Five Points the identity of the Harlem of the West. The Casino Ballroom was the area's best dance hall, with a hardwood floor and forty-foot bar, capturing the best African American musicians of the day, including George Morrison. Nearby, the Roxy Theater was the only venue in Denver where blacks could watch movies from the regular seats, not just the balcony. Many of these and other venues still stand today and have wandered through various phases of disinvestment. The Five Points jazz legacy lives on through the annual Five Points Jazz Festival, and KUVO, one of the nation's only all-jazz public radio stations, operated locally by the Five Points Media Corporation. Plans have been approved to redevelop the Rossonian into a mixed-use building with a hotel, jazz club, restaurants, fitness center, and collaborative office space.

As the historic and symbolic center of Denver's African American community, Five Points today celebrates the culture of African Americans in Denver and more broadly in the American West. In 1971 the Black American West Heritage Museum opened as a place to showcase the many contributions of blacks in the Old West, from "cowboys, to miners, soldiers, homesteaders, ranchers, blacksmiths, schoolteachers, lawmen, and every other profession needed to build up the West."[43] Taking a broader scope of the African American legacy, in 1999 Denver mayor Wellington Webb established the Denver Public Library's Blair-Caldwell African American Research Library, focusing on the history, literature, art, music, religion, and politics of African Americans in Colorado and throughout the Rocky Mountain West. The library remains the only one of its kind between Detroit and Oakland. While much of today's African American community in Denver is dispersed from Five Points, the important legacy of this Harlem of the West community lives on.

The late 1960s saw an urban crisis spread across U.S. cities. During this period many central-city neighborhoods suffered ongoing racialized residential segregation, increased fiscal problems and disinvestment, decreased tax revenues and local service provisions, disruptive urban renewal projects, high unemployment, social unrest, and concentrated poverty—culminating in the wave of urban riots. Although Denver's experience was more muted than what occurred in the large cities of the Northeast or the West Coast,[44] it was the period when national debates over school desegregation played out in Denver, along with metropolitan-wide fragmentation over the ruling of the *Keyes v. School District No. 1* case.[45]

After Five Points' era of vitality and prosperity through the 1950s, the face of the neighborhood changed in the 1960s. Once residential barriers fell with Denver's 1959 Fair Housing Act, many middle-class black families migrated east of Five Points to the Park Hill neighborhood or suburban communities, such as Aurora. At the same time, in response to the urban crisis and issues of abandoned buildings, urban renewal projects by the Denver Housing Renewal Authority leveled large swaths of land to provide public housing and parking lots. For example, the lots between Arapahoe, Lawrence, Twenty-Fifth, and Twenty-Fourth streets in Five Points were demolished and replaced with public housing projects.

The legacy of the urban decay era's fiscal disinvestment, social isolation, and middle-class out-migration remains evident today. Abandoned buildings, empty storefronts, and empty lots are common. The local public schools face challenges in meeting performance standards, with both elementary schools and one of the high schools serving the Five Points neighborhood having received either a "low" or "unsatisfactory" rating in the most recent overall academic performance on state assessments. The neighborhood experiences a crime rate (146 per 1,000 persons) more than double the Denver city average (68 per 1,000 persons). Five Points has remained one of the more impoverished neighborhoods in Denver, as neighborhood averages in low household incomes, public assistance, and poverty rates exceed the citywide averages.[46] Furthermore, the homeless population in Five Points is high, as most resource providers for Denver's homeless are located along the Ball Park–Five Points boundary, at the intersection of Broadway and Park Avenue.

Five Points is now experiencing rapid gentrification, as new investment is developing many new housing opportunities and businesses, and the residential population is growing and changing. The historic character of Five Points, close proximity to downtown Denver, and inner-city urban feel is fueling this modern resurgence. The process of change began as early as the 1970s, and today it is considered one of the hot real estate neighborhoods with some of the fastest-rising housing values in the area. This neighborhood change, however, is controversial. While reinvestment is seen as having a positive revitalization effect, rising costs displace longtime residents from their homes and threaten the neighborhood heterogeneity.

Between 2000 and 2010 the population of Five Points increased 45 percent,[47] a phenomenal growth trend for any inner neighborhood of a central city. The only other neighborhoods in the immediate vicinity of downtown Denver that experienced as much growth over this period were

Highland (up by 18 percent) and Union Station (a 56 percent increase).[48] In either of these neighborhoods, the housing construction boom in and around Union Station and the LoDo area accounts for much of the residential growth, while Highland has also seen similar gentrification as Five Points. The boom has driven up real estate values, as the July 2015 median home sale price in Five Points of $416,000 was well above the Denver city median sale price of $330,000. This reflects an 80 percent price growth over five years in Five Points, relative to a 38 percent growth in all Denver, and illustrates the real estate financial pressures of local residents. Despite this period of residential growth, Denver public schools K–12 enrollment within Five Points *decreased* by 46 percent,[49] likely owing to a growth in childfree households, and increased use of private and charter schools. With the out-migration of African Americans since the 1960s, historical in-migration of Hispanic/Latinos, and the more recent in-migration of whites, Five Points now is one of the city's more racially diverse neighborhoods. But the changing racial composition between 2000 and 2010 reflects the migratory effects of gentrification: a 23.9 percent Latino/Hispanic decrease, a 13.3 percent black decrease, and a 200 percent white increase.[50]

There are many factors that led to this dramatic transition of Five Points. For one, potential residents became attracted to the historic architectural value of some of Denver's oldest and grandest homes. In the 1970s the Curtis Park district was listed on the National Register of Historic Places, and residents arrived seeking new urban thrills and the investment potential of rehabbing the stock of Victorian homes. Yet still reeling from the trend of urban decay of the 1960s and 1970s, local residents at the time proclaimed to the newcomers: "This isn't a neighborhood you move into, it's one you move out of!"[51]

The trend of buying fixer-upper homes in Five Points continues today. However, with a limited stock of Victorian homes, the early 2000s market speculation for living space in the area prompted a rush of new-build housing in abandoned in-fill spaces. In contrast to the existing historic homes, these developments use contemporary postmodern architectural styles, with eclectic colors and materials, an abundance of glass, organic sightlines, and limited connection to the streetscape with very small porches or balconies. They come in a variety of options from multidwelling buildings with one-, two-, and three-bedroom residences or new modern townhomes. In the context of place historicity, these structures emote a sense of fleeting trends, and perhaps a tone of separation from the neighborhood's authentic identity.

Centrality and proximity with convenient transportation access for work commutes is another driver of change in Five Points. Five Points historically emerged as a residential neighborhood because it was removed from downtown Denver. But today its location is attractive because of quick access to the central business district job centers. The nearby confluence of major interstates and highways provides easy access to driving routes toward the mountains, Boulder, Greeley, and Fort Collins. The Central Corridor line of the RTD's light rail system built along Welton Street in the 1990s was originally intended to stimulate economic development of the area (Figure 15) and has become an alluring feature for new residents seeking alternative forms of transportation. Furthermore, Five Points also experiences a spillover growth effect from the entertainment redevelopment occurring in the nearby Ballpark neighborhood.

The availability of abandoned industrial spaces has also driven the Five Points neighborhood transition. The area that parallels the freight rail line and the South Platte River contained a historically vibrant cluster of warehouses, smelters, and light manufacturing buildings but experienced serious economic downturns and abandonment since the 1970s. Low rent values and opportunities of spacious indoor facilities attracted working artist

Figure 15. Welton Street corridor in the Five Points neighborhood. (Image source: E. Eric Boschmann.)

communities to these buildings in the late 1990s. The vitality grew over time, and to commercially capture redevelopment potential the area became a branded place in 2005, known as the River North Art District, or more collectively, RiNo. Concentrated on Walnut and Larimer Streets, today the area contains numerous art galleries, cooperatives, and studio spaces; creative business, including designers and furniture makers; small-scale craft breweries; and food markets that sell locally produced sustainable consumables. And building on Denver's visions for sustainable transportation in the city, a new bicycle- and pedestrian-friendly corridor was constructed along Larimer Street. Undoubtedly the proximity to this new amenity puts further pressure on housing values in the Five Points residential areas. The contentiousness of gentrification reached a boiling point in late November 2017 when a RiNo-area coffee shop posted an advertisement outside their establishment. One side of the board read, "Happily gentrifying the neighborhood since 2014," while the other side read, "Nothing says gentrification like being able to order a cortado." The uproar on social media for the coffee shop's insensitivity and disrespectfulness of the very real downsides of gentrification was immediate. The establishment was boycotted, people sprayed graffiti on the building, and local protesters carried posters outside with the words: "Gentrification = Urban Colonialism," or, "Black Lives Matter. White Coffee Doesn't." The shop owner later apologized for not fully appreciating the real and troubling issues of gentrification.[52]

The social and economic changes occurring in Five Points have placed great pressures on preserving the historical legacy of the neighborhood. Along the Welton Street corridor, businesses have appeared that reflect the new influx of more hip and trendy commercial development, including a New York–style bagel shop, an espresso coffee shop, a microbrewery, and a bilingual yoga studio. Also, as of late 2015 there were four new high-density mixed-use residential developments under construction scattered within the historic commercial corridor. Seeing the brisk tide of gentrification redevelopment, the city has articulated its desire to illuminate and preserve the special importance of Five Points in Denver's history. New plans were established to protect the cultural and historical significance of Five Points, including architectural guidelines to maintain congruence with historic buildings. And in 2015 the Denver City Council renamed the Welton Street corridor the Five Points Historic Cultural District as an effort to keep eyes on the past while the neighborhood develops into the future.

Chapter 4

Image and Place Making

In April 2013 the new West Line of the RTD light rail system opened and began rail service from downtown Denver to Golden, Colorado. The advertising campaign promoting this new light rail line used a variety of western-themed motifs, with images of cowboy boots and hats, longhorn cattle, a sheriff's badge, and dancing cowboys and cowgirls. The tagline of one advertisement was simple and direct: "This cowtown's all grown up" (Figure 16). These advertisements connected Denver's Old West heritage to its pursuits of a more cosmopolitan and global identity. But there is also a bit of irony in this advertisement, as the region spent decades of place promotion to move beyond its "cow town" image that originated from its agricultural and mining roots. This part of Denver's identity has now come full circle, proudly reclaiming its historic origins.

In an era of global competition for scarce and mobile capital, cities and urban regions pay a lot of attention to making themselves into attractive places. In doing so, cities identify what is unique about their location, what gives it personality, and how is it distinguished from other places. Place identity often capitalizes on community assets and natural amenities that give meaning to a location emerging from collective human experiences. But there is an acute awareness that outside perception of a city is critical to local economic success. Thus, "place" is purposefully rebuilt, repackaged, marketed, and promoted. Images of a city are created, or a city brand is established. These images are most often deliberately constructed by local elites but can be shaped by the routine everyday actions and interactions of local individuals. Place making, therefore, is the act of promoting specific images of place in an effort to make it attractive and desirable to a broad range of audiences, including tourists, businesses, or potential residents. Objec-

Figure 16. RTD light rail advertisement. (Image source: RTD.)

tives often include being ranked on a "best places to live" list; creating diverse and appealing tourists destinations; building iconic and recognizable structures such as buildings, bridges, or monuments; or establishing a business-friendly environment.

This chapter chronicles both the images of Denver and several of its key place-making strategies. As a diverse place with a storied past, Denver may be aptly characterized by scores of images today. The focus here is on the more enduring and prominent yet evolving images of Denver including its identity as an Old West cow town, a New West urban center, and the Mile High City in the twenty-first century. This chapter emphasizes place making that has occurred through state and local tourism promotion, downtown urban revitalization, and culture-led urban economic development.

From Old West to New West

Denver's origins as a mining town and long relationship with an expansive cattle-based agricultural hinterland gave the city an indelible Old West image that remains today. The nineteenth-century gold and silver rushes gave rise to a landscape of numerous get-rich-quick mountain mining towns, many with grand hotels, saloons, opera houses, and gambling halls. Similarly the surrounding agriculture and cattle industry, with open ranges, cattle drives, and cowboys, adorned Denver with a sleepy and dusty cow town identity. Legacies of this historic era were made famous by colorful characters, including the "Unsinkable" Molly Brown, a Denver socialite, or Baby Doe Tabor's tragic tale of attaining a flamboyant mining-wealth lifestyle only to fall victim to a mining bust and die destitute in the Matchless Mine in Leadville, Colorado.

But even today the Old West remains evident across the Denver landscape. There are many not-so-out-of-place sightings of cowboy hats and boots, and traditional western wear shops such as the legendary Rockmount in Lower Downtown Denver. The Buckhorn Exchange restaurant, an iconic Old West steakhouse in operation since 1893, is now a national historic landmark and western museum where traditional western music can be heard live most nights of the week. The gravesite and museum of "Buffalo Bill" Cody, made famous for his Wild West Show tours, is located on nearby Lookout Mountain. And each January the annual National Western Stock Show and Rodeo is held in Denver, a two-week event bringing in over six hundred thousand visitors, complete with a livestock parade through the streets of downtown Denver (Figure 17), and the Grand Champion steer's entrance to the Brown Palace Hotel lobby during afternoon tea.

For early tourism promotion of Colorado, the Old West had an alluring mystique to people with a western romance appeal in search of the mythic cowboy, or some living ghost town such as Central City or Idaho Springs.[1] Later, however, this Old West image became a drag on Denver's identity, particularly in the late twentieth-century rise of globalization and the necessity

Figure 17. National Western Stock Show opening parade in downtown Denver. (Image source: E. Eric Boschmann.)

to attract jobs, talented workers, and discriminating tourists in a competitive global economy. City leaders feared Denver had a less-than-cosmopolitan image as a backward cow town, a problematic and negative connotation particularly when seeking to be a more world-class destination. Thus rose the need to shake Denver of its cow town image, and create a new, modern, international identity.

The post-1980s influx of new residents to the city and the greater Colorado region helped transition Denver into an urban place of the New West—a conversion repeated throughout many western Sun Belt cities experiencing rapid growth, urban sprawl, and new economy jobs. In the New West, the search for Old West mystique became mixed with the urban and high tech: where SUVs replace pickup trucks, espresso shops replace diners, and microbreweries replace watering holes: as one author describes it, a place for "cappuccino cowboys."[2]

In the escape from urban rat races elsewhere, cities of the New West became a place to seek a rugged landscape with ideal suburban lifestyles, resulting in a locale where walled estates, golf courses, and factory outlet malls weave through vast open spaces and old mining or ranching towns. It became a place to live out the "live-work-play" mantra, with a good job in one of many new economy industries and weekend excursions in mountain biking, river kayaking, or skiing and snowboarding. Or where the ghosts of mining town opera houses are replaced with contemporary ballet, symphony, and traveling Broadway musicals. In the high country, emergence of the New West gave rise to the ultrarich jet-set second- and third-home communities of Aspen, Vail, and Telluride, and various ski and summer vacation resort towns, as well as numerous hardscrabble workaday towns.[3]

There is an irony to this new development of the "recreational West." People bring with them particular proenvironmental attitudes, yet facilitating the growth occurs at the cost of burgeoning sprawl, pollution, traffic congestion, and disruption of views and wildlife habitat. And differing ideologies of Old West versus New West have resulted in a war zone over the land, a culture clash of "cattlemen versus granola bars," or "corrals versus country clubs."[4]

The Mile High City

During its Old West days, Denver was referred to as the Queen City of the Plains—an urban oasis in the wild western frontier. Today Denver is more widely known as the Mile High City. This nickname refers to the city's elevation at exactly 5,280 feet (one mile) above sea level and has become a clear signature of the region's attachment to an elevation-centered identity. Indicators of, and references to, elevation can be seen throughout the city. On the steps of the Colorado state capitol building in downtown is a marker indicating a precise elevation of 5,280 feet (Figure 18), and at the Coors Field baseball stadium one row of purple-colored seats marks this elevation in the upper deck. The professional football stadium is colloquially known as Mile High Stadium, regardless of changing corporate naming sponsorship. And scores of businesses, local and tourist advertisements, and even a city magazine use "5280" or "Mile High" as a place-specific branding scheme. This sense of hyperattention to elevation is captured at one local hotel where a change in visitors' elevation is indicated as they travel up or down the hotel elevator. One might begin to think such an emphasis suggests Denver is among the *highest* of cities. Yet in reality, many international cities of similar or larger size have much higher elevations, such as Mexico City, Mexico

Figure 18. Marker of mile-high elevation at the Colorado state capitol steps. (Image source: E. Eric Boschmann.)

(8,000 feet); Bogotá, Colombia (8,500 feet); Quito, Ecuador (9,500 feet); or even El Alto, Bolivia (13,000 feet plus). Closer to Denver, both Santa Fe, New Mexico, and Flagstaff, Arizona, climb over 7,000 feet, and even nearby Colorado Springs, Colorado, reaches upward to 6,300 feet.

Rather, like its geographic isolation, the elevation suggests for Denver an image and sense of a city set apart from all others, and an urban place with a distinctive set of natural amenities of enviable climate and close proximity to a scenic mountain landscape. In fact, the thin, dry air and abundant sunshine was precisely the force behind the swell of health tourism between the 1890s and 1920s. In the more geographically footloose economy of the late twentieth century, Denver's proximity to the Rocky Mountains ushered a new image of outdoor recreationalism, environmental consciousness, and personal attachment to place—prompting a greater consumption of, and identity with, the natural surrounding landscapes. In the 1970s, the popularity of John Denver's songs about the Rocky Mountains, soaring eagles, a quaint town of Aspen, and campfires in the high country all addressed a wider desire to escape the city and return to nature, and "crystallized Colorado's outdoor mystique" in people's imaginations.[5]

William Philpott makes the compelling argument that, as with many advertising schemes of the twentieth century, Colorado boosters similarly sought to create a personal bond between consumers and a branded product. "The high country became a land where you could realize yourself in your own eyes and the eyes of others, by indulging your adventurous side, achieving inner peace, discovering your inner pioneer, showing yourself to be sophisticated, and strengthening family bonds. The overarching message [was] that you could achieve self-fulfillment and social definition by consuming" Colorado. And this blending of consumer culture with the shopping for places has ultimately led to the search for locales that best fit "the reputations we hope to cultivate and the self-image we want to project."[6]

Not only did this personal attachment to place boost state tourism; it also created an outdoors/recreation image of Denver that attracted an in-migration of residents seeking the "allure of living where tourists play," resulting in a rapid development, growth, and sprawl of Front Range cities and mountain resort towns.[7] Thus today Denver's proximity to the Rocky Mountains is central to its image, often seen in pictures of a snow-capped backdrop to a modern city skyline (Figure 19). But it also illuminates the promise of easy access to the many mountain ski resorts, hiking among the rugged terrains of pine and juniper forests, and swift-flowing creeks and rivers of "pure Rocky Mountain spring water."[8] Denver's identity is therefore quite tied to its ability to facilitate diverse outdoors lifestyle pursuits, to be an amenity-rich place fit for recreational consumerism. It is not uncommon during sporting events nationally televised from downtown Denver to feature commercial break transitions of live images of action on ski slopes occurring more than one hundred miles away from the city. It fosters the notion of a vast recreational backyard inextricably linked to Denver. Some smaller communities such as Boulder have earned the satirical nickname of the "Gore-Tex Vortex," parodying the idea of a geographic clustering of like-minded individuals with moisture-wicking gear and all-wheel-drive vehicles, coupled with equal parts over-the-top liberalism, extreme fitness, and health-food consciousness.[9]

While the images of Old West–turned–New West, or the identity of the Mile High City's favorable access to natural amenities encapsulate mere slices of Denver's diverse social identity, they have an impact in shaping external perceptions of Denver. A recent public opinion poll showed that the Denver metropolitan area tops the list of Americans' favorite big cities to potentially live in, followed by San Diego, Seattle, Orlando, and Tampa.[10] As

Figure 19. Promotional view of Denver skyline and the Rocky Mountains; City Park boat pavilion in the foreground. (Image source: E. Eric Boschmann.)

David Brooks opined, this survey suggests that the American Dream circa 2009 was having it all: living in a place with natural scenery and abundant outdoor activities, with medium density of both sprawl and urban centers, a slower pace, strong service economies, and relative social equity.[11] Perhaps the survey also revealed lingering wanderlust among Americans. But as the next section chronicles, the place making of Denver and its identity is not just an early twenty-first-century phenomena, but one long embedded in the history of the region's tourism industry that really did shape feelings of wanderlust.

Selling the American West in Denver

Tourism is one of Colorado's most important economies. In 2014, 33.6 million visitors came to Colorado for overnight leisure and business trips. The tourism industry employs over 155,000 persons, resulting in an estimated $18.6 billion in total direct spending, and generates over $1.1 billion in state and local taxes.[12] As the metropolis of the Rocky Mountain West region,

Denver's role in area tourism has been ever changing. Though Denver was once seen as merely a gateway or "locker room" to the mountains, civic leaders have consistently worked not only to attract visitors at least for a stopover in Denver, but also to make Denver a primary destination. Today nearly 50 percent of Colorado overnight travel spending occurs in the Denver metro area. But how the region captured this sizable share is a long story of active place promotion and urban revitalization, embedded within the larger narrative of statewide outdoor recreational tourism.

If the first modern settlers to the Denver region were speculators, entrepreneurs, and health seekers, the first tourists were those who came to witness the splendor of a landscape once compared to the European Alps—calling it the "Switzerland of America."[13] The romanticized notion of encountering the natural world was an American cultural pursuit, and people sought to experience the sublime scenery and natural settings offered in Colorado.[14] The new railroads converging in Denver in the 1870s established the city's position as a transportation gateway to the mountains and thus formed a new identity of Denver as tourism entrepôt to its hinterland of scenery and recreation. Narrow-gauge railroad lines connected the mountain mining towns to Denver, also giving some access for visitors to consume the mountain landscapes. Yet until Interstate 70 opened the mountains for the masses, Colorado mountain tourism remained limited to elite classes with expendable time and money or dedicated adventurists.

In the decades after the silver crash of 1893, Denver leaders decided the future survival of the city could not rely on the mining industry alone. While cities in the East were expanding through industrial growth and some local boosters sought to do the same in Denver, more visionary leaders were cautious toward such industrial expansion. Mayor Speer's City Beautiful movement was premised on improving citizens' quality of life and preserving the natural surroundings. It took a more controlled approach to growth and focused on more clean industries, such as tourism. By the early twentieth century, city leaders sought to capitalize on the natural amenities of Denver's nearby landscape and aggressively promoted tourism expansion to attract more visitors to come experience the dry climate, pure air, and mountain scenery.[15]

One approach was to create attractive destinations out of large forested lands preserved under federal laws. After the Forest Reserve Act of 1891, President Benjamin Harrison set aside 3.1 million acres of forested land in

Colorado, and President Theodore Roosevelt set aside another 9 million acres. Many became national forests (e.g., Roosevelt National Forest, San Juan National Forest, or the Grand Mesa National Forest) or national monuments (e.g., Dinosaur National Monument in the Uinta Mountains, or Colorado National Monument near Grand Junction). The Denver Chamber of Commerce lobbied the federal government to also create national parks within Colorado, as the designation was certain to attract visitors. Mesa Verde in southwest Colorado, containing the Ancestral Puebloan (Anasazi) cliff dwellings, became a U.S. national park in 1906. Thousands of dollars were also spent to establish a tourist playground at Estes Park, a much closer drive from Denver. In 1915 the Rocky Mountain National Park was created there and remains today the crown jewel of tourism attraction in the state. This early aggressive campaigning and development of place identity proved successful: annual visitors to Colorado grew from twenty thousand in the late 1880s to three million by 1941.[16]

Today there are nearly twenty-four million acres of federal land in Colorado, covering nearly 35 percent of the state.[17] This includes four national parks, eight national monuments, two national recreation areas, two national historic sites, four national historic trails, eleven national forests, and forty-two national wilderness areas. There are also numerous national grasslands, conservation areas, wildlife refuges, recreation trails, and scenic trails.

The rise of the automobile in the early decades of the twentieth century provided city leaders another opportunity for growth in Denver's tourism. On the heels of Mayor Speer's construction of wide boulevards and motorways, one Denver-based forest service worker noted, "auto tourism could become Denver's greatest manufacturing plant"[18] without all the ill effects of actual industrial production. And thus began a "manufacturing of recreation" campaign that started with the creation of the Denver Mountain Parks system.

Frederick Olmsted Jr. was commissioned in 1912 to design a series of mountain parks with scenic drives that preserved and protected some of the region's greatest scenery and picturesque settings. But most crucially, the development ensured the parks were easily accessible by automobile from Denver. Genesee Park was the first project completed in 1913, and the entire system was finished in the 1930s with the help of many New Deal programs, including the Works Progress Administration (WPA) and the Civilian Conservation Corps (CCC). As America's automobile culture flourished, more people across the country took to the highways in the spirit of exploration. And to capture mountain-bound tourists, Denver developed several "motor camps" in these city parks; in 1923 as many as fifty-nine thousand people stayed in the Overland Park camp alone. Across the state over six hundred thousand people stayed in 250 camps. By 1940, tourism became the state's third-largest source of income, after mining and agriculture.[19]

The Denver Mountain Park system now covers 14,141 acres across forty-six separate mountain parks and conservation areas. While managed by the City of Denver, all these parks are entirely outside its municipal boundary, spread across the foothills and mountains in the counties of Jefferson, Clear Creek, Douglas, and Grand. Some of the region's most iconic landscapes that draw millions of annual visitors are within this century-old park system. This includes Mount Evans, a fourteener[20] overlooking the Denver region accessible by a high-altitude paved road; the iconic Red Rocks Amphitheater, an open-air amphitheater created by natural rock outcroppings with a view of the city and plains below; the bison herd at Genesee Park; and initially Winter Park, a family-oriented ski resort originally built with rail service from Denver through the Moffat Tunnel.

Development of Denver's mountain park system was not only meant to attract tourists; it also was designed to enhance the quality of life for local residents. Spending leisure time in the mountains in general became a common pastime for Denverites. For African Americans, much of the twentieth century was a time of bigotry, hatred, and racial tension in the city, and the Lincoln Hills Country Club in Gilpin County was a mountain wilderness resort that gave African Americans an escape from both city life and the oppressive Jim Crow laws. A family-oriented resort that contained numerous lodges and cottages, it provided many opportunities for fishing and hiking, and Camp Nizhoni was a YWCA camp for black girls. At the time it was the only such place west of the Mississippi River. Jazz musicians traveling through Denver often stopped here, as did literary greats such as Langston Hughes and Zora Neale Hurston. While the mountains were a playground for many, Lincoln Hills not only provided summer fun for African American families; it was a safe haven and shelter from the storms of oppression in Denver.[21]

Skiing and mountain recreation soon became a major feature of place identity and the wider consumption of the Rocky Mountain West. Prior to the 1940s, downhill skiing was not big business in Colorado. It remained largely a pursuit of amateur enthusiasts who established small recreational ski clubs. The modern ski tourism industry blossomed after World War II, as highway construction made distant slopes more accessible, as small ski clubs developed into large corporations, and as skiing grew into a pursuit of the middle class.[22] Mountain sports became one of Colorado's steadiest growth industries, attracting millions of people per year. And unlike mining or oil and gas, snow proved less volatile as a renewable resource with potentials for enhancement through cloud seeding and artificial snowmaking. It remains an industry highly vulnerable to trends in global climate destabilization. Today nearly 40 percent of all nonbusiness travelers to Colorado visit the mountains, with skiing being a top recreational purpose for visiting. On the whole, Colorado ranks only twenty-third nationally in its share of overnight pleasure trips. But it remains first for skiing trips, where the state holds 18.3 percent of the national market share. Close behind are California, New York, and Utah. In 2002, statewide ski revenues were over $2 billion.[23] Colorado ski resorts annually count about twelve million visits—which includes repeat visitors, and a high portion of Colorado residents. In 2008 there were about 1.7 million overnight skiing visitors from out of state.[24]

Despite the importance of the ski industry, summer tourism remains the larger, more significant component of the mountain tourist economy. Summer is the true peak travel time as people come to the state on driving touring trips. In terms of sports and recreation among overnight pleasure trippers, 17 percent of visitors participate in hiking and backpacking and 10 percent in skiing. With the historic mining towns, gambling towns, and national parks, Colorado tourism is more dependent on pleasure travelers and recreationalists who come for the sights, than on skiing alone.[25]

Getting to the mountain recreation communities was not always easy, and arguably much of this tourism could not occur without Interstate 70. Begun in the 1960s, the I-70 corridor west of Denver is celebrated for great engineering feats of roadway construction across the rugged Rocky Mountains, including cutting through the Dakota Hogbacks, blasting the Eisenhower-Johnson Memorial Tunnel (at 11,158 feet, it is the highest point, and at 1.7 miles, the longest mountain tunnel in all the U.S. Interstate system), summiting Vail Pass, and traversing through the narrow Glenwood Canyon alongside the Colorado River. Many resorts and recreational destinations did not exist prior to the interstate construction, as its opening ushered in a new era of mass consumption of the Rocky Mountain high country. Once the mountains became more easily accessible and open to the middle class, resort and outdoor-led entertainment development occurred. Soon ski resorts spread throughout the Rockies, including all-inclusive resorts such as Vail, Beaver Creek, Breckinridge, Copper Mountain, Keystone, and Arapahoe Basin as well as scores of low-frills ski slopes, giving birth to a lucrative industry and becoming a linchpin to the state's economy. Today the relative proximity to Denver and easy interstate access creates a large-scale weekend commuting trend, linking the city's residential communities with recreation in Denver's "backyard."

Aspen is perhaps Colorado's most exclusive mountain resort town today and has become situated within a wider popular collective consciousness as a playground of the rich and famous. Having become a dilapidated mining town, a resort economy began there with Chicago industrialist Walter Paepcke and the Tenth Mountain Division in the 1930s and the creation of the Aspen Ski Company. Over the past several decades, the development of the surrounding landscape has changed with greater influxes of wealth. Across many mountain communities, condominium and time-share markets exist because of the skiing and recreation industry. Aspen too has spawned an economy of second-, third-, or fourth-home markets, where billionaire homes displace millionaire homes further down the Roaring Fork Valley away from Aspen. It is both a place of conspicuous consumption, and a place where environmental greenness happens with a "self-congratulatory air."[26] Like other mountain resort towns, the very lifestyle of Aspen is dependent on a large supply of global immigrant labor to work in service industries such as hospitality and maintenance. But the scarcity of housing driven by exclusivity of consuming scenic views and protecting landscapes from development creates a sharp spatial inequality that forces most workers to live in geographically distant towns. Ironically there exists a great contradiction between the dependency on immigrant labor and the push for strict immigration reform in an effort to preserve Aspen's environmental privilege.[27]

Access to the elite resorts of Aspen and Vail increased with the growth of both the Eagle-Vail and Aspen-Pitkin County airports. As a consequence, Denver's role as regional gateway to these exclusive high-country resort communities has been downgraded. Both airports have seasonal and year-round commercial airline service from major airports in Los Angeles, San Francisco, New York, Chicago, Washington, Dallas, Miami, and Atlanta. Similarly the line-up of private jets along the tarmac indicates an increased ability of many to bypass Denver completely. While these places developed as part of Denver's broader hinterland, they now exemplify locales more connected to economies and networks beyond the sphere of Denver. They also developed their own place identity independent of the Front Range urban corridor.

A more lasting imprint on the cities in Colorado, including Denver, is how the tourism and recreational consumerism of high-country landscapes reshaped the environmental and place consumption value systems of people living, working, and vacationing there.[28] In the creation of this twentieth-century "vacationland," places themselves became products "manufactured, packaged, branded, and marketed like so many consumer goods," where locations of leisure are "sold" for their climate, scenery, and other environmental qualities. At the same time, the more spatially footloose new economies allowed for the seduction of permanent residential living in such a vacationland, manifesting in amenity- and lifestyle-led migrations to desirable places. And Colorado suburban lifestyle was well suited to deliver a more permanent enjoyment of otherwise fleeting Colorado vacations—the "tourist way of life." In the newly developed suburbs around Denver, residents "could soak in Colorado's sunshine and crisp air and find inspiration in its celebrated mountain views from their picture windows, patios, and backyards. Every weekend, if they wanted, they could take paved highways up to the high country for some fishing, hiking, or skiing." From this consumption of place, a particular environmental attitude emerged, one that focused more on landscapes depicted in travel brochures, and less on the untamed rawness of nature, but the "thrilling and unthreatening kinds of settings that promised easy enjoyment for car dependent leisure seekers."

It is clear that environmental, recreational, and tourism place-making schemes of Colorado have impacted Denver's identity, both as the regional gateway to the Rocky Mountain West and as a city nestled in an amenity-filled natural environment. But on another front, Denver itself emerged into a destination city, one that could be enjoyed even without the experiences of the mountains.

Downtown as a Destination in the Twenty-First Century

A common discourse among entrepreneurial city leaders around the turn of the twenty-first century has been the goal of becoming a world-class city. This typically suggests a place with a strong, globally linked economy; a reputation for sophistication and cultural vibrancy; a level of exciting entertainment that comes from restaurants, nightlife, and art galleries; the presence of recognizable architecture and sleek new skyscrapers; and perhaps sports stadiums with winning professional teams. These are markers of what city leaders and developers pursue today. Making a place attractive to international visitors and businesses through intentional branding and marketing is a core mission of today's entrepreneurial city.

In this competitive pursuit for mobile capital, jobs, residents, and visitors, Denver is no different than many other cities. But where does Denver's quest in becoming a world-class city begin? When did the city first enter a more global consciousness, if it has? Was it with the first hosting of the Democratic National Convention in 1908 (the second being in 2008)? Or with Colorado's winning bid to host the 1976 Winter Olympics?[29] Perhaps it was Pope John Paul II's decision to have World Youth Day in Denver in 1993, an event attended by over 750,000 persons. There are numerous events leading the way to the creation of today's external image of Denver. And part of the effort of branding itself included a strong need to overcome the burdensome weight of its cow town character. Arguably, the greatest turning point for Denver was a longer-term urban revitalization effort that has reshaped the character, look, atmosphere, functionality, and appeal of the entire downtown area. By re-creating downtown into a vibrant center, Denver positioned itself *as a destination*, a place people sought for its own urbane offerings.

Since the 1990s, downtown Denver has experienced a great renaissance of vitality due to a popular rediscovery of urban amenities and significant investments in redevelopment. This resurgence began with the Lower Downtown (LoDo) neighborhood, a prime example of urban revitalization that combines the urban chic with western heritage and historic brick buildings, in an era of postindustrial loft living and downtown entertainment, restaurants, bars, art galleries, and sporting events. It is here where scores of new residential high-rise developments today market themselves for their "unmatched views of the mountains and city"—a place offering the best of both worlds.

From the 1870s, LoDo served as the economic center of Denver. With Union Station receiving more than eighty trains per day at its peak, this was where the comings and goings of Denver happened. It was the gateway to the world beyond Denver. The surrounding warehousing district provided storage and processing of goods that traveled through Denver's rail hub. By the 1950s train travel began a decline as competition from automobiles and airplanes increased. The "Travel by Train" neon lights were added to the Union Station signage in hopes of retaining rail passengers. But the ultimate demise of rail travel and the no-longer-relevant Union Station and surrounding warehouses led to a great downturn in the Lower Downtown neighborhood.

The disappearance of economic activity caused this area to become Denver's skid row. New investments in downtown building construction had shifted to the central business district, many blocks to the southeast. This left the old dilapidated buildings of LoDo to become a magnet for society's down-and-out individuals. Larimer Street in particular became infamous for its flophouses, saloons, cheap liquor stores, seedy hotels, pawnshops, loan shops, and the stench of urine. The place even appeared in Jack Kerouac's classic novel *On the Road*. The narrator, Sal Paradise, found his way to Denver and said, "Here I was in Denver. . . . I stumbled along with the most wicked grin of joy in the world, among the bums and beat cowboys of Larimer Street."[30] From the 1960s through the early 1990s the area suffered from high vacancy rates, blighted conditions, vagrancy, and violence. Some historic buildings were demolished to create parking lots for downtown office workers.

Across the United States, many cities had similar experiences of massive disinvestment, decay, and blight in central downtown areas, as development and population growth focused on decentralized suburban areas. At that time, two ideologies in urban planning offered opposing visions of how to fix the derelict and blighted neighborhoods of America's central cities, and both were influential in the evolution of downtown Denver.

In New York City, Robert Moses championed urban renewal as a solution for modernizing the city. His approach called for "slum clearance": the demolition and removal of large sections of cities that contained old, blighted, and abandoned buildings. In its place developers could build highways and bridges for greater efficiency in moving cars in and around cities. Following this model, in 1964 the Denver Urban Renewal Authority (DURA) designated twenty-two square blocks in and around the LoDo area as blighted and slated them for demolition. In fact, plans were established to tear down Union Station and all buildings along Wynkoop Street in order to build the Skyline Freeway through Lower Downtown.

On the other hand, the approaches of urban revival, most influentially voiced by the urban theorist and writer Jane Jacobs, focused on city design for people, not automobiles. This included creating livable streets and neighborhoods through the creation of mixed-use, high-density, and walkable urban spaces. In many ways this meant retaining existing historic buildings and streetscapes, rather than demolition. This was the vision held by Dana Crawford, the most important pioneering figure in downtown Denver's urban revitalization.

In 1954, the Radcliffe-educated Dana Crawford (née Hudkins) arrived in Denver. She brought a vision for place making and "urban revitalization that centered on people and their times spent together, . . . [making] a gathering spot for people, where they could eat, drink, and mingle."[31] Her influences of successful examples included Ghirardelli Square (San Francisco), Gaslight Square (Saint Louis), and Country Club Plaza (Kansas City), and she focused on finding an ideal location to bring this about in Denver.

By 1965 she began assembling properties on the 1400 block of Larimer Street, historically Denver's first commercial strip. It contained nearly a complete block of two- to four-story stone and brick buildings constructed in the 1870s and 1880s with Italianate and high Victorian architectural styles. Most original structures were destroyed in an 1863 fire. Her vision was to create an "authentic setting . . . on a Denver street . . . to recapture the gaiety and excitement of the early days (1860s and 1870s). . . . Larimer Square will transform a shabby district into a handsome and useful one. . . . It will contain the nucleus of Denver's nightlife—restaurants, coffee houses, bars, nightclubs, off broadway [sic] theater, and jazz."[32] Not only did her tireless work transform a single shabby district; it set the stage for even more transformations in historic downtown Denver neighborhoods. The success of Larimer Square (Figure 20), which was placed on the National Register of Historic Places in 1973, drew national attention to Denver and to Crawford herself. She subsequently founded Historic Denver Incorporated in 1970 to save other historic buildings in Denver. And in 1987, Mayor Peña's Downtown Area Plan focused on Lower Downtown as an anchor for wider downtown revitalization. This led to the 1988 Lower Downtown Historic District city ordinance, which protected the twenty-three-block historic warehouse neighborhood from demolition.

The Larimer Square success did not deliver immediate spillover effects in the LoDo area surrounding Union Station, many blocks away. But Crawford's proven vision of rehabilitating old buildings and repurposing them for new uses stimulated the actions of both city leaders and private entrepreneurs alike. In the 1980s Mayor Peña began cleaning up the four thousand acres of underutilized land in the Central Platte River valley west of Union Station, and in the 1990s Mayor Webb established large areas of green space

Figure 20. Refurbished buildings in Larimer Square, downtown Denver. (Image source: E. Eric Boschmann.)

along the rivers by developing Confluence Park, Commons Park, and City of Cuernavaca Park. Two pioneering entrepreneurs, John Hickenlooper,[33] who founded the Wynkoop Brewing Company (1988), and Joyce Meskis, founder of the local independent bookstore the Tattered Cover (1990), made the daring investment to place their businesses in LoDo, which still retained the skid row vibe. As Meskis noted, "the properties in LoDo were so sad, there were more pigeons than people, but you could just feel that something was going to happen."[34] Crawford was also involved in this LoDo area by developing several of Denver's first warehouse-turned-loft projects, including the Edbrooke Lofts (1990), the Acme Lofts (1992), and initial efforts at the Ice House.

Today Larimer Square and LoDo are emblematic of the centrality of old preserved historic buildings with architectural appeal to heritage-led consumption of place.[35] Many new in-fill developments seek to retain the local brick warehouse architectural motif, such as Coors Field baseball stadium or the U.S. EPA Region 8 Headquarters office building. Here Denver's Old West identity is remembered yet overlaid and updated with more hip and contemporary amenities of bars and brewpubs, coffee shops and restaurants, retail shops and nearby entertainment. Numerous viaducts that once allowed cars to bypass parts of LoDo altogether were removed to enhance car and pedestrian accessibility within LoDo. A 2014 letter to the *Denver Post* poignantly conveys the value of this historic preservation: "On my first visit to Denver in the late 1960s, Larimer Square was the one point of interest in what was otherwise an old cow town. This was the beginning of what has become Denver's amazing transformation into a world-class city, one in which people actually want to spend time, with room for the Western tradition along with groundbreaking developments in sustainable ecology and the arts."[36] In July 2014 the renovated Union Station reopened as the centerpiece of a new multimodal transit hub and a gathering spot for people—similar to Crawford's initial vision of Larimer Square. Union Station now contains locally based restaurants, shops, cafes, and lounges. Dana Crawford has referred to Union Station's Great Hall as "Denver's living room"—a central meeting place for the extended community, complete with couches, tables, wi-fi, and table shuffleboard.[37] Just as it did in the early twentieth century, Union Station again bustles with great energy of people. To honor her unparalleled contribution to the revitalization of Denver, the new 112-room luxury hotel in Union Station was named the Crawford Hotel.

The transformation of Lower Downtown simultaneously resulted in a dramatic population boom of residents in the neighborhood. From 2010 to 2015, fifty-five hundred new mixed-use high-density residential units were built in LoDo, including the Highlands neighborhood. The combined population growth in the Union Station, Ball Park, and central business district neighborhoods grew from 3,230 in 2000 to 7,414 in 2013. The possibility of a live-work-play-without-a-car-lifestyle has appealed to millennial and baby boomer generations alike. And the 2013 opening of a new elementary school and full-service grocery store in 2015 further signaled the transition of this once-skid-row area into a "real" neighborhood. A middle school, dog park, playgrounds, and additional retailers are further amenities to come.[38]

Outside of LoDo, Denver's urban revitalization can also be linked to the development of numerous large projects. In 1969 the Currigan Hall convention center opened along Fourteenth Street in downtown. Because the long-standing Auditorium Arena (built 1908, and refurbished into the Ellie Caulkins Opera House in 2005) no longer filled the capacity and technology needs for more modern conventions, the Denver Urban Renewal's Skyline Redevelopment Project called for a new facility that provided one hundred thousand square feet of unobstructed exhibit space. Part of the building's design included a metal exterior façade that would weather into a rust color, and architecturally blend with surrounding brick building styles. The life of Currigan Hall was short, however. Throughout the 1970s it hosted no more than twenty conventions annually, and capacity expansion was needed. Also, the facility influenced visitors' negative experiences and perceptions of Denver. The building had a very dark, boxy interior with a depressive feeling, and the rusting exterior façade failed in its attempt to blend in and quickly earned the unlucky nickname of the Rust Barn. Such an experience did not create a desire among visitors to return to Denver, and city leaders quickly took note.[39] In the 1980s, Mayor Peña's "Imagine a Great City" campaign called for the construction of a new sunlight-filled open facility, and by 1990 the first phase of the Colorado Convention Center (with over one million square feet) opened. This began a frenzy of large-scale construction projects that has further shaped the flavor of downtown Denver today.

Much like Philpott's arguments of the broader tourism industry across Colorado, Murray contends that the development of downtown Denver was predicated on the view of consumerism as the defining element in contemporary society, and that people will be attracted to interactive spaces where there are lots of other people. Thus, one may look at downtown Denver through the rise of many people-clustering projects.[40] Table 5 outlines the wide scope of such projects that occurred at the turn of the twenty-first century. These many destination-oriented projects, along with regional transportation development (Chapter 6) that brought more rail transit into the city, have collectively transformed downtown Denver into an active round-the-clock city.

One early downtown Denver project was the Sixteenth Street Mall, a mile-long outdoor pedestrian-friendly promenade that serves both daytime office workers and visitors alike. Designed by famed architect I. M. Pei in the early 1980s, the colored granite paving tiles originally gave it an appearance of a western diamondback rattlesnake. The mall functions to create a central focusing "spine" of downtown, an activity corridor from which everything else is oriented. With free clean-energy shuttle buses, today the Mall connects Lower Downtown and Union Station on one end to the central business district, government centers, Civic Center Park, and the Golden Triangle on the other end. While the Sixteenth Street Mall has struggled to keep major anchoring department stores, it does host a particular niche of themed chain

Table 5. The Building Frenzy in Downtown Denver

Project	Function	Date of opening	Estimated cost
Sports Authority Field at Mile High	Football stadium	2001	$400 million
Pepsi Center	Multipurpose indoor arena	1999	$180 million
Downtown Aquarium	Aquarium	1999	$93 million
Coors Field	Baseball stadium	1995	$215 million
Denver Public Library	Library (main branch)	Expanded 1995	$65 million
Elitch Gardens	Amusement park	1995	$118 million
Denver Performing Arts Complex	9 theaters and concert halls	Expanded 1991	$34 million
Colorado Convention Center	Exhibitions, meeting hall, ballrooms, Bellco Theater		
Phase I		1990	$126 million
Phase II		2004	$308 million
Denver Art Museum	Art museum		
North Building		Renovated 1990	$9.3 million
Hamilton Building		2006	$110 million
Museum of Contemporary Art	Art museum	2007	$15.9 million
Denver Zoo	Zoological park	Renovations 1999	$125 million
Denver Botanic Gardens	Botanical garden	Renovations 2007	$32 million

Source: Michael Murray, "City Profile: Denver," *Cities* 19, no. 4 (2002.): 283–294, table 1, with some updates.

restaurants and retail outlets attractive to tourists (e.g., Hard Rock Café), along with smaller retail chain stores, theaters, and a vibrant outdoors pedestrian culture with street performers.

Keeping in line with competitive city trends across the United States, Denver also worked feverishly to identify itself as a major and viable professional sports entertainment town. This included the construction of several new sports stadiums and arenas and the rapid acquisition of franchises (Table 6) to give Denver a more robust professional sports profile. Prior to the early 1990s, Denver was home to only two major professional sports teams: the Denver Broncos of the National Football League (NFL), and the Denver Nuggets of the National Basketball Association (NBA). By 2005, the roster of professional teams grew to eight, including the expansion of the Colorado Rockies to Major League Baseball (MLB) in 1993, and the acquisition of the Colorado Avalanche of the National Hockey League (NHL) in 1995 from Quebec. Today Denver is one of thirteen U.S. cities to have teams from four major leagues (NFL, MLB, NBA, and NHL), and one of only nine cities to have teams from five major leagues (including Major League Soccer).[41] To accommodate the sporting growth and define itself as a city with modern sporting venues, Denver underwent an aggressive campaign to upgrade its major sports stadiums. A six-year period saw the opening of the new Coors Field (1995) for baseball, Pepsi Center (1999) for basketball, hockey, and indoor concerts, and Sports Authority Field at Mile High (2001) for football.[42] All three of these new facilities are located within the downtown frame instead of in suburban locations, further emphasizing the focus on

Table 6. Growth in Professional Sports in Denver

Team	Sport	First Game	League	Venue
Denver Broncos	Football	Sept. 9, 1960	National Football League	Sports Authority Field at Mile High
Denver Nuggets	Basketball	Sept. 27, 1967	National Basketball Association	Pepsi Center
Colorado Rockies	Baseball	Apr. 5, 1993	Major League Baseball	Coors Field
Colorado Avalanche	Hockey	Oct. 6, 1995	National Hockey League	Pepsi Center
Colorado Rapids	Soccer	Apr. 13, 1996	Major League Soccer	Dick's Sporting Goods Park
Colorado Mammoth	Lacrosse	Jan. 3, 2003	National Lacrosse League	Pepsi Center
Denver Outlaws	Lacrosse	May 20, 2006	Major League Lacrosse	Sports Authority Field at Mile High

centralizing new developments downtown. Each stadium was constructed with high accessibility via the new light rail system, and in the case of Coors Field, right in the heart of LoDo nightlife.

Denver's "Camping Ban"

By the early twenty-first century, downtown Denver's revitalization was prospering. The city center was an attractive focal point for people to visit restaurants, museums, shops, sporting events, and theaters. Offering a place to sit, stroll, or mingle among the many locals and out-of-towners, downtown became a vibrant place, full of life and social activity—something that was once nonexistent outside the rhythm of nine-to-five office schedules. But the growing homeless population, particularly along the Sixteenth Street Mall, began to cause concern for many and resulted in a highly controversial ban on camping in the city.

Much of the downtown Denver business community argued that homelessness was a matter of health and safety for the city, and was driving away businesses and visitors, ultimately reducing tax dollars. A strong contingent sought a new camping ban city ordinance to address homelessness in Denver that would both improve the business climate and appearance in downtown, and improve the life of homeless individuals by connecting them to area resources and social services.

For the homeless facing shortages of available shelter beds, sleeping on the Sixteenth Street Mall offered the best alternative: the many buildings' door corridors provided protection from the weather elements, while the lighting, foot traffic, and police presence offered a greater level of personal safety and security. Opponents of the proposed ordinance argued that it would criminalize homelessness and poverty and would push individuals into an even more dangerous and precarious existence, and that instead, more resources for homelessness were needed in the city.

On May 14, 2012, the Denver City Council voted 9–4 in support of the "unauthorized camping on public or private property prohibited" ordinance, otherwise referred to as the camping ban. The new ordinance states that it is unlawful to "camp" on any private or public property without permission. More specifically, "camping" in the ordinance refers to temporarily dwelling in a place with "shelter," including "any tent, tarpaulin, lean-to, sleeping bag, bedroll, blankets, or any form of cover or protection from the elements other than clothing."[43]

One year after the camping ban was implemented, a study conducted to understand its effects on the homeless found that they felt less safe under the new law.[44] Many individuals were forced into hiding to avoid police (in alleyways, along rivers, or under bridges). Others chose to remain exposed to the elements (i.e., to sleep without the use of a blanket or cardboard for coverage) so as to not officially violate the law. The study also found no evidence that homeless people's access to social services improved. In fact, some downtown businesses stopped supporting the camping ban for its failure to provide homelessness assistance originally articulated as a goal of the ordinance.[45] After several years the ordinance remains in effect. More effort is being given, from multiple directions, to improve the availability of resources such as increasing the number of shelter beds in the city. But the delivery of resources to the homeless population in Denver remains publically controversial.

Cultural-Led Development

Cultural-led policies are another approach to urban economic development that can make cities more attractive and competitive, stimulate growth and diversify the economy, or revitalize distressed neighborhoods. Such efforts not only attract tourism through images of fun, leisure, and sophistication; they can also attract creative-class workers by promoting an amenity-rich high quality of life that is enabled by a live-work-play lifestyle in a central downtown location. Oftentimes cultural-led development policies include creating an iconic identity of a place through the construction of stunning and spectacular buildings, or hosting international events. A premier example is the wild success of Bilbao, Spain. In an otherwise economically depressed deindustrialized town, Bilbao re-created its image and gained international recognition by franchising a global name in museums (Guggenheim), and building an iconic structure designed by a star architect (Frank Gehry). The Guggenheim Museum created a surge of tourism to Bilbao, and the visitor economy stimulated other elements of the city. Since then, scores of cities have followed this so-called Bilbao effect of cultural-led economic development schemes premised on tourism and a "build it and they will come" model. In many ways Denver is no different.

Denver is not known historically as an art town. Clark Richert—one of Denver's most internationally known contemporary artists—referred to Denver in the 1960s as a "cultural wasteland" for its lack of contemporary and modern art at that time.[46] Even the City of Denver's 1989 cultural plan Cultural Denver admitted the city lacked a self-image and that arts remained elitist and was not well linked to tourism.[47] The goal was set for Denver to become the cultural capital of the Rocky Mountain region. And today national newspaper headlines, such as "A Cow Town That Acquired High Culture" or "Denver's Art Scene Soars," capture the growth and attention the city has acquired for its identity as an art destination.[48] In a city beleaguered with the weight of a dusty cow town image, how and why did Denver's contemporary and modern art scene emerge so rapidly?

There are many characteristics that led to the aggressive growth of Denver's art scene today. First, much can be attributed to the numerous civically minded philanthropists—the fortunes made in Denver's many industries—whose strong support for the arts made an art museum building frenzy possible. Second, the landscape of art museums in Denver was remade in the 2000s. For instance, in 2006 the Denver Art Museum's Hamilton Building addition was completed. Designed by the star architect Daniel Libeskind, the building's angular titanium structure offered the "wow" effect and became an instant icon with potential for global recognition (Figure 21). But the same criticism leveled against Bilbao's Guggenheim museum—that the architecture was more of a draw for international tourists than the stature of the artwork housed inside—is sometimes directed at the Denver Art Museum (DAM) today. However, the growth of three new museums and one important collection in the 2000s work together to increase the overall profile of contemporary art in Denver, helping make the city more of an international destination for art fans. The Kirkland Museum of Fine and Decorative Art opened in 2003, as did the Dikeou Collection. In 2007 the Museum of Contemporary Art (MCA) opened in LoDo, and the Clyfford Still Museum opened in 2011 adjacent to DAM. Together this clustering of contemporary art offerings represents a clear distinction from Denver's image as a place with only western-themed historic art. Further, the city has a large public arts program that helps foster new, fresh, and iconic images of the city. This includes the Art-n-Transit program—intended to enhance the design, aesthetic quality, and user-friendliness of transit projects, and foster transit-

Figure 21. The Denver Art Museum (DAM) Hamilton Building. (Image source: E. Eric Boschmann.)

oriented *community* development. There is also a thriving art community, as evidenced by nearly one hundred art galleries and artist co-operatives with the First Friday Art Walks throughout several gallery districts, consistently luring thousands of visitors.

But these qualities of philanthropic support, diverse art offerings, vibrant local artist communities, iconic art museum architecture, and monthly art walks are really not unique to Denver. They exemplify cultural planning practices replicated in scores of U.S. cities. If the rapid rise of Denver's art scene can be explained in the context of cultural-led urban economic redevelopment, is there anything that makes its art scene different than other cities? Through conversations with several key figures in the city, it seems two broad themes characterize the distinctiveness of Denver's art scene: a spirit of openness, and progressive politics.[49]

First, Denver's art scene today thrives within a context where there is a great spirit of openness. Consider Denver's site and situation. It is situated as a place relatively isolated from most other major metropolitan areas of comparable size, creating a kind of buffer from the influences of other urban art scenes. It is the type of place where individuals escape to when seeking refuge from the confines of coastal art centers. Also, with the city's relatively young origins and dramatic population influxes not occurring until after World War II, some argue that as an art town Denver has less established tradition, and fewer historical dominating institutions that commonly drive local thought and practice. Given the site characteristics luring new residents for decades, the art scene too experiences the city as full of transplants; it is a young place, with a strong counterculture to what exists in coastal cities, and a great milieu of ideas. This coalesces with the legacy of American western and libertarian ideals of a "leave me alone" philosophy of individualism, self-reliance, and generally not following the lead of others. For the art community this appears to translate into an openness to new people and ideas and an anything-goes mentality. It was and remains a place to be a pioneer.

All this suggests that in Denver's art scene there is less tradition, less hierarchy, and greater acceptance of unconventionality. For example, in this context it is okay to be an "art jock"—where the artist identity can gel with an outdoorsy lifestyle. Such a combination may not be socially permissible in other cities. The Lab@Belmar was another example of this radical openness. In the mid-2000s the old Villa Italia regional shopping mall in the suburb of Lakewood was refashioned into a mixed-use new urbanism development. Adam Lerner successfully took his vision of bringing prestigious contemporary art to the most unlikely of places: the sprawling suburbs of Denver. And in this context of radical openness, it worked. The Lab@Belmar was an intentional act of looking for authenticity in the city through invention—creating a space for a democratic public sphere and enriched civic life, a combination not typical for a suburban shopping center.

For many of the artist transplants, Denver has a very strong artist community with an above-average cooperative gallery scene. These are nonprofit art galleries dedicated to artists offering a different domain from commercial art venues. In these co-ops they are less dependent on sales, giving artists more freedom to pursue personal interests and ideas, and to celebrate individuality and uniqueness. Artists run their own gallery and studio space, do it cheaply, and have autonomy. Two of Denver's oldest such co-ops include Pirate formerly located in the Navajo Street art district, and Spark in the art district on Santa Fe. The openness of Denver particularly allows for these types of galleries to flourish abundantly.

This openness also translates into broad support from local residents. Local Denverites are more active in consuming the arts than many other cities. To be clear, Denver's offerings are modest in comparison to the world's major art centers. But Denver residents participate in the arts at a rate far higher than national averages. Across the United States, 21 percent of adults report visiting an art museum or gallery in the past twelve months. For Denver area residents, 65 percent have visited a museum and 56 percent a gallery in the past twelve months.[50] And while monthly art walks are central to any city's recipe for cultural-led urban economic development, Denver's First Friday has very strong public patronage. With the event regularly attracting five thousand people or more, one gallery owner quipped, "in other cities I've worked in, the only time you can get at least 5,000 people together is for a football game."[51]

Second, Denver's progressive policies provide strong public support for the arts. When state funding for major museums was cut in 1982 during an economic crisis, residents across a six-county region voted in 1988 to enact landmark legislation that created the Scientific and Cultural Facilities District (SCFD). This new tax district established a one-tenth of 1 percent sales tax to ensure the future of regional cultural institutions. Over three hundred facilities receive funding through the SCFD, with 65 percent going to the tier 1 institutions that include the Denver Art Museum, Denver Botanic Gardens, Denver Museum of Nature and Science, the Denver Zoo, and the Denver Center for the Performing Arts.[52] Receiving 75 percent approval, the SCFD is an example of regional cooperation (see Chapter 5) that Governor Hickenlooper said is "a bedrock foundation of collaboration in metro Denver that you don't see in other places."[53] Seeing the benefits of shared costs of arts and cultural amenity public goods across many municipalities, voters reaffirmed the SCFD in 1994, 2004, and 2016 with nearly 65 percent approval. The tax district generates approximately $40–$50 million annually and continues to be promoted and marketed along the themes that "culture [helps] make Colorado a great place to live, work and play." An economic impact study by the Colorado Business Committee for the Arts estimated that in 2013 the Denver regional arts, cultural, and scientific organizations generated $1.85 billion in total economic activity, including 10,205 jobs and an attendance of 14.2 million.[54] This voter-approved regional collaboration in culture-led development remains a "highly respected national model."[55]

Around the same time in the 1980s, Denver's Mayor Peña enacted the "1 Percent for Public Art" ordinance, which stipulates—"One percent of the design and construction budget of any single City capital improvement project over $1 million must be set aside for the inclusion of art in the new project."[56] For Denver this has resulted in a citywide collection of over three hundred public art pieces. For example, during the construction of the Denver International Airport, Luis Jiménez's sculpture *Mustang* (Figure 22a) was placed along the roadside entrance to the airport to welcome visitors to Denver and the West. But the seemingly sinister look of its piercing red eyes generates an ongoing debate about its presence as officially sanctioned city art. On the other hand, outside the Colorado Convention Center is Lawrence Argent's *I See What You Mean*, more commonly known as "the Blue Bear" (Figure 22b), which has become an iconic piece of beloved public art. Argent sought to produce something that represented the breadth of Colorado and decided to re-create the growing instances of wildlife interacting with people communities—especially as the city expands further into the foothills of the Rocky Mountains. With the blue bear peering into the Colorado Convention Center and looking at the people inside, it has quickly become a widely recognized symbol in downtown Denver—helping construct a newer image of the more sophisticated city engaged with its surrounding natural environments. More recently the $600 million hotel (opened in 2015) and transit complex at Denver International Airport included $6 million spent on six pieces of public art. In one piece titled *Shadow Array*, Denver artist Patrick Marold installed 235 beetle-kill spruce logs (from southern Colorado) along the landscaped bowl that surrounds the new DIA commuter rail station.[57] In these examples of public art, the sanctioned images of the city reflect Denver's long ties to its hinterland, in both the historic periods of resource extraction as well as recreationalism in the natural surroundings.

Perhaps most distinctive of the Denver art scene is the Clyfford Still Museum. It opened in 2011, and its origin is an interesting piece in the Denver-as-art-town story. As one journalist noted, Clyfford Still is the most influential abstract expressionist you've never heard of.[58] He laid the groundwork of the mid-twentieth-century abstract expressionism movement, more famously known by the works of Jackson Pollock, Willem de Kooning, and Mark Rothko. Still became reclusive in the 1950s and ended his relationship with commercial art galleries. Thus, virtually all his work (94 percent) remained in his possession, kept from public view and knowledge despite his influence on such an important movement.

Upon his death, Clyfford Still's personal will made an unusual stipulation. He bequeathed all his works *to an American city* that would create and maintain a museum devoted exclusively to his art. Such a city had to procure museum quarters for the Still collection, was to become the "caretaker" for

Figure 22. Public art in Denver. (a) Luis Jiménez's *Mustang* at Denver International Airport (*left*); and (b) Lawrence Argent's *I See What You Mean* outside the Colorado Convention Center, downtown Denver (*right*). (Image sources: E. Eric Boschmann.)

the collection, and had to raise sufficient funds to provide for a maintenance and operation endowment. Though no connection between Still and the city of Denver existed, Mayor Hickenlooper, highly supportive of cultural-led economic development, ambitiously sought this opportunity to increase the city's appeal to arts and culture tourists. Denver eventually won the bid for the collection and built a museum according to the strict and mostly quirky guidelines of the will, including no museum restaurant or auditorium, specific ceiling heights, and Benjamin Moore color #14-4 for the wall paint.[59] And furthermore, the entire Still collection (over twenty-five hundred pieces) must remain together and cannot be separated or sold. Therefore, because so few Clyfford Still pieces are on display anywhere else in the world, the museum collection is all the more attractive. Denver took this unusual opportunity to house a collection of tremendous international importance in an effort to make itself more of a cultural destination. This agenda is certainly not masked in one of the museum's promotional pamphlets. One pop-out tagline says: "The Clyfford Still Museum. An Experience Unlike Any Other in ~~Denver.~~ the World."

Finally, while cultural plans are rather commonplace among the entrepreneurial cities movement, Denver's latest cultural plan,[60] Imagine 2020, does address some of the main critiques levied against most traditional plans.[61] The overarching goal of Imagine 2020 is to "enhance Denver's quality of life and economic vitality through premier public venues, arts, and entertainment opportunities."[62] But while many plans rely on an export base theory, this one places more emphasis on art by and for locals. Export base approaches rely on the patronage of outside visitors to come and spend their money, thus creating a great external budgetary dependency. In Imagine 2020, local residents are clearly placed at the center, with explicit outcomes related to local quality of life. It emphasizes the importance of culture as an economic base and identifies Colorado as a leader in creative industries, ranking fifth in concentration of this sector (186,000 jobs). The plan articulates that raising Denver's national and international profile in part begins with making the city a place where local artists can thrive. Imagine 2020 also considers minorities and equity in access as central components to the plan. While Denver residents widely participate in the arts, the plan identifies challenges to inclusivity and access to arts based on age, income, and ethnicity. Finally, while many cultural plans focus on building cultural districts as anchors of attraction for planning and promotional purposes, Imagine 2020 takes a cultural dispersion approach to better meet goals of quality of life, equity in access, and greater local economic impacts. The plan therefore aspires to improve the city's integration of arts in the daily life of all its residents, and "cultural deserts" are identified, denoting neighborhoods lacking access to artistic, cultural, and creative activities. This initiative demonstrates a unique shift in cultural planning practices, whereby Denver seeks a greater inward and localized approach to development, rather than an external visitor-dependent vision.

Chapter 5

Political Landscapes

As metropolitan areas have grown in both population and land area, they have encompassed an increasing number of municipalities and counties, thus confronting both state and local governments with concerns about regional cooperation and collaboration. As we have detailed in previous chapters, the Denver metropolitan area has grown dramatically, especially since the 1950s when it expanded well beyond the City and County of Denver to include an increasing number of suburban and exurban municipalities and counties. This post-1950 decentralized growth has created numerous governance challenges, the same sorts of which have affected every other large metropolitan area in the United States during this time. Denver has adopted many regional governance strategies that are similar to other U.S. metropolitan areas, but because of Denver's particular geographic, historical, and political circumstances, its experience with regionalism is a unique story that has resulted in a number of successful innovations in recent years.

The historical development of regionalism in the Denver area can be divided into four phases of urban expansion and efforts toward regional integration. In the first phase, the early development of Denver saw the expansion of the central city through annexation, the absorption of the surrounding streetcar suburbs into the city, and the creation of the City and County of Denver. This was a phase of metropolitan consolidation. The second phase of independent suburban growth occurred mostly in the period after World War II, when the Denver metropolitan area expanded rapidly and new development spread into neighboring counties. However, this was also a period of growing central city–suburban tensions that were addressed primarily through formal structures of metropolitan and regional planning, many of which were encouraged by the federal government. However, these early top-down efforts to foster and promote regional collaboration were not so successful, and regional discord prevailed. The period from 1960 to 1990 in particular featured tensions that strained the relationship between the City and County of Denver and surrounding suburban jurisdictions, which affected regional organizations involved in economic development, transportation, and environmental planning. The third phase, starting around 1990, is one of increasing regional collaboration, unified by a smart growth vision that has focused on regionally based economic development, improving air quality, creation of a new rail transit system, and development of higher-density urban centers. The fourth phase of extended regionalism includes efforts at coordinating growth within the emerging Front Range urban megaregion from Fort Collins, to the north, to Colorado Springs and Pueblo, to the south. The expanded megaregion also extends to the west via the Interstate 70 corridor and interaction with mountain towns and major ski resorts, including Arapahoe Basin, Aspen, Breckenridge, Copper Mountain, Keystone, Steamboat Springs, Vail, and Winter Park, as well as the gambling centers of Blackhawk and Central City.

Phase 1: Metropolitan Consolidation

In the early years of its existence from 1860 to 1900, Denver annexed newly developed areas as the city grew outward. From its central core near the confluence of the South Platte River and Cherry Creek, Denver annexed nearby settlements, such as Auraria and Highland, and adjusted its boundaries as it expanded outward. In 1902, the city of Denver, which initially was a part of Arapahoe County, incorporated a number of streetcar suburbs and outer territories to form a newly consolidated city and county. As with many other cities at this time, annexation and consolidation were regarded by local businesses and city governments to be crucial for securing the funding and provision of infrastructure, such as water, electricity, and sewerage, to new development in unincorporated areas.[1] Moreover, as cities grew both in terms of population and size of incorporated territory, it became easier for public agencies to raise capital and sell bonds for improved services. Likewise, local businesses, such as banks, retailers and service contractors, benefited from the expanded customer base that came with new development.[2]

By the turn of the twentieth century, annexation was regarded as one of the most important tools in the box of booster tactics deployed by central-city municipal governments throughout the country,[3] and Denver was no exception in this respect.[4]

While the City and County of Denver continued to annex nearby land, an increasing number of suburban communities resisted annexation and were incorporated separately from Denver. Similar to other metropolitan areas, town leaders and residents perceived the benefits of separate incorporation to be greater than the benefits of joining the central city. Service considerations aside, Denver, like other U.S. central cities, was perceived by outsiders as congested, dirty, unhealthy, and politically corrupt, with a tendency toward unscrupulous activity, such as drinking, gambling, and prostitution. Many cities, including Denver, were run by machine politics, which led to the emergence of suburban political jurisdictions that sought a more businesslike managerial approach to city government and separation from increasing ethnic and working-class populations in the city. Thus, even though there were significant economic, political, and service benefits in joining the central city, many suburban towns chose to remain separate. While these towns began to grow more steadily in the 1920–50 period owing in part to the popularity of automobile transportation but also the failure to extend mass transit systems, they initiated a pattern whereby the City and County of Denver found it more difficult to grow, either through increased density or land annexation. Property owners in suburban areas, in particular, were increasingly reluctant to incur extra taxes to fund improvements to area-wide services, and Denver was unable to convince its voters of the need to expand transit and other services to communities outside its boundaries.[5]

Phase 2: Fragmented Suburban Growth

In the post-1945 period, suburban growth exploded around Denver and just about every other major U.S. city. Driven by the growth in automobile ownership and use, new highways, and new homes made more affordable by mass production techniques and favorable loan programs, suburbs became the destination of choice for most middle-class white families in postwar America. In recognition of the rapid pace of suburban growth, all levels of government—federal, state, and local—began to pay more attention to issues of regional collaboration and metropolitan governance. The federal government in the postwar era became more involved in urban issues, including slum clearance, urban renewal, interstate highways, mass transportation, housing, environmental pollution, and metropolitan planning. In recognition that many of these issues transcended local governmental boundaries and required a collaborative approach to solving regional problems, the federal government encouraged and supported regional planning efforts. Section 701 of the Housing Act of 1954 provided federal grants in support of regional councils of government and metropolitan planning agencies to promote cooperation in helping to solve regional problems. In 1959, the Advisory Commission on Intergovernmental Relations (ACIR) was created "to explore new government structures and policies to address suburban growth problems and improve coordination of federally-aided programs and projects."[6] The Federal Aid Highway Act of 1962 required the "establishment of a continuing and comprehensive transportation planning process carried out cooperatively by states and local communities" as a condition for receiving federal funds in support of highway projects.[7] This "3-C" (continuing, comprehensive, and cooperative) process became a hallmark of metropolitan transportation planning that still exists today and underscored the need for a regional approach to planning.

To support transportation and other planning activities, most metropolitan areas began to establish regional planning agencies, councils of governments, or metropolitan special districts. In Colorado, charter members Adams, Arapahoe, and Jefferson Counties and the City and County of Denver formed the Inter-County Regional Planning Association (ICRPA) in 1955 "to plan for the development of the metropolitan area . . . and to meet the common problems that confront the four counties."[8] The first ICRPA resolution supported a major east-west highway route through the metro area later developed as Interstate 70. In 1958, the association's name was changed to the Inter-County Regional Planning Commission (ICRPC), and the first regional transportation plan was approved. The ICRPC signed the first memorandum of agreement with the Colorado Department of Highways (CDOH) in 1963 after the Federal Aid Highway Act established the 3-C planning process.[9] In 1968, its name was changed again to the Denver Regional Council of Governments (DRCOG) to "signify the responsibility of the core city to its neighbors."[10] Today, the DRCOG district includes all of nine counties—Adams, Arapahoe, Boulder, Broomfield, Clear Creek,

Denver, Douglas, Gilpin, and Jefferson—plus the southwestern portion of Weld County.

Postwar Highway Expansion and the 1960s "Freeway Revolt"

Similar to many other U.S. cities in the postwar period, Denver developed an incredibly ambitious plan to build highways throughout the metropolitan area. Besides the major north-south Interstate Highway 25 (the Valley Highway through Denver) and east-west Interstate 70, Denver had plans to build freeways that would have crisscrossed the entire city.

While some of these highways—such as I-25, I-70, I-225, U.S. 36 northwest to Boulder (the Denver-Boulder Turnpike), U.S. 6 west (Sixth Avenue) to Golden, U.S. 85 south (Santa Fe Drive) to Littleton, and U.S. 285 west (Hampden Avenue west of Santa Fe Drive) to Conifer—were built, many others were not. The proposed Skyline, Columbine, Mountain North, Mountain South, Quebec, and Outerbelt Perimeter Freeways would have changed the landscape of Denver in dramatic fashion. The Skyline Freeway, for example, would have connected I-70 with I-25 (and beyond toward the southwest) by cutting a path through Lower Downtown Denver paralleling Larimer Street. Near Larimer and Park Avenue West, it would have intersected with the Columbine Freeway, thus creating a major highway interchange in an area near where Coors Field is located today. The Skyline Freeway would have torn through the heart of Lower Downtown (LoDo) and would have eliminated many of the classic red-brick former warehouse buildings that constitute the architectural signature of contemporary gentrified LoDo. The freeway would also have likely caused the demolition of nearby Union Station, now the centerpiece of the rail transit renaissance in Denver (see Chapter 6). The Columbine Freeway was proposed to slice through the east-side neighborhoods of Capitol Hill and Washington Park, which are today some of the most densely populated, vibrant, and desirable residential neighborhoods in Denver.

By the mid-1960s and 1970s, the public fascination with freeways began to wane, and citizen groups in cities across the country formed to oppose the construction of freeways through the middle of active, thriving neighborhoods. After several unsuccessful attempts by citizen groups to oppose freeway building in several north Denver neighborhoods, POWUR (Preserve Our Way of Urban Residence) was formed in 1965, which led to the creation of a

Citizens Advisory Committee (CAC) within the Denver Metropolitan Area
Transportation Study (DMATS) that resulted in successful efforts to stop plans
for many of the proposed freeways.[11] These antihighway efforts also included
greater support for mass transit development, eventually culminating in the
creation of the Regional Transportation District in 1969 (see Chapter 6).

   Among the areas that were not successful in resisting the highway intru-
sion were the north Denver neighborhoods of Globeville, Elyria, and Swansea,
which became the site of Interstate 70 just to the east of its interchange with
I-25 (known as "the mousetrap"). These neighborhoods started as towns that
were sites of mining smelters, rail yards, and stockyards in the late 1800s, and
they each developed residential communities of mostly eastern European
immigrant workers in smelting, meatpacking, and other nearby industries. By
the mid-twentieth century, they remained as working-class neighborhoods for
many lower- and middle-income households, including increasing numbers
of Hispanic/Latino and African American groups. In 1947, Denver officials
suggested that a future east-west highway through Denver should follow the
Forty-Sixth Avenue route east of the Valley Highway (later to become I-25).[12]
In 1955, the Inter-County Regional Planning Association (later to become the
Denver Regional Council of Governments) agreed to route Interstate 70
directly through these neighborhoods on an elevated viaduct, splitting them
in half. Highway construction began in the late 1950s and was completed in
1964. In Globeville, thirty-one homes were demolished and replaced with a
formidable wall that directly abutted houses and even a church (Figure 23).[13]
The intrusive highway ripped through the social fabric of these neighborhoods, cutting off access between their northern and southern portions, and
contributed to an exodus of population and socioeconomic decline over the
ensuing fifty years.

   In 2014, the Colorado Department of Transportation (CDOT) produced
a plan to refurbish the highway by removing the overhead viaduct and
creating a partially covered highway trench through the Elyria-Swansea
neighborhood as part of its preferred alternative.[14] The partial cover lowered
alternative would: (a) widen the highway by two lanes in each direction for
ten miles, creating a ten-lane template, (b) remove the viaduct in the
Elyria-Swansea neighborhood, (c) rebuild the highway below grade, and
(d) place a four-acre cover to create a park over the highway between
Columbine Street and Clayton Street (a distance of three city blocks) next to
Swansea Elementary School.[15] Alternatives that considered relocating the
highway along the existing I-270 and I-76 routes were rejected because of the

Figure 23. Saint Joseph's Church with Interstate 70 wall along Forty-Sixth Avenue. (Image source: Andrew R. Goetz.)

additional mileage, cost, and travel time required. It is expected that the preferred alternative will improve the visual aesthetics of the neighborhoods and permit more accessibility via bridges over the highway trench. A Record of Decision (ROD) was released in January 2017 by the Federal Highway Administration (FHWA) approving the preferred alternative identified by CDOT.[16] While FHWA, CDOT, and the City and County of Denver are all in favor of the preferred alternative, local community groups such as Ditch-the-Ditch are vehemently opposed to the project and would prefer a different alternative to the one that has been selected.[17]

In 1969, DRCOG supported legislation that created the Regional Transportation District (RTD), and in 1971, it entered into a memorandum of agreement with CDOH and RTD to jointly plan the region's transportation facilities.[18] RTD was established as a metropolitan special district by the

Colorado legislature in 1969 "to develop, maintain, and operate a mass transportation system" in Denver and all or parts of five surrounding counties (Adams, Arapahoe, Boulder, Douglas, and Jefferson).[19] Today, RTD serves an eight-county region, including Boulder, Broomfield, Denver, and Jefferson Counties, as well as parts of Adams, Arapahoe, Douglas, and Weld Counties (Figure 24). Prior to RTD, the Metropolitan Sewage Disposal District had become the region's first metropolitan special district in 1960, created for the purpose of sewage treatment for approximately 75 percent of the metro area.[20]

But these and other efforts at regional collaboration faced serious opposition, as many suburban jurisdictions remained wary of the central city and jealously guarded their municipal powers. An effort by the Colorado state legislature in 1961 to create a metropolitan capital improvement district ended when the Colorado Supreme Court ruled that the district violated the Colorado Constitution's home rule provisions.[21] Subsequent plans in 1965, 1967, and 1968 to create an urban supercounty to consolidate services were rejected by the state legislature.[22] Many suburbs, including Aurora, Englewood, and Westminster, developed their own water systems so as not to be dependent on the Denver Water Department. During a period of frequent droughts and rapid suburbanization in the 1950s, the Denver Water Department established a "blue line" around the metropolitan area, beyond which it refused to supply water.[23] But a large number of special water districts and independent water systems were developed to provide water supply to areas outside the blue line. Thus, restricted access to the Denver water system, which could have been an important growth management tool, did not inhibit expanded growth. In contrast, a blue line established around Boulder in 1959 was more successful in limiting growth.

One of the sometimes hidden motivations behind the creation and growth of suburban jurisdictions in postwar America was the desire for white families to leave central cities, which were experiencing increased growth of minority, especially African American, populations. This "white flight" phenomenon occurred in virtually every U.S. city at this time and was a major factor in the popularity of suburbs. At the same time, the civil rights movement was beginning to realize hard-fought victories against racial segregation and oppression, such as the 1954 *Brown v. Board of Education* Supreme Court decision, which ruled that school systems segregated by race were inherently unequal, and the Civil Rights Act of 1964, which outlawed discrimination based on race, ethnicity, gender, and religion.

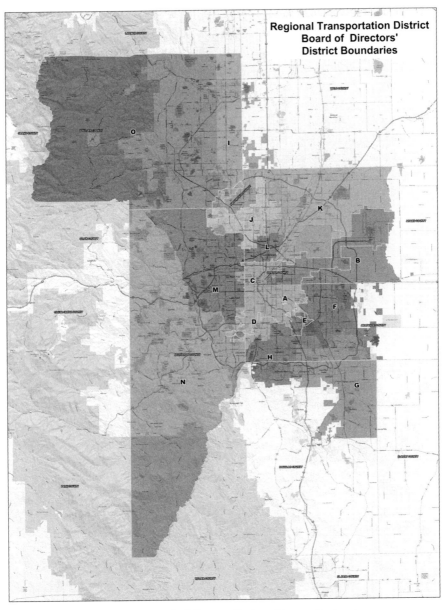

Figure 24. RTD region and board of director districts. (Source: Regional Transportation District. 2017. Regional Transportation District Board of Directors' District Boundaries Map. http://www.rtd-denver.com/documents/directors-district-map.pdf [accessed August 18, 2017].)

While the *Brown v. Board of Education* decision initially affected many southern school districts by forcing the abandonment of dual school systems based on race, the decision also had ramifications for many other school districts in the North and West that were de facto segregated. One such case was the Denver school district, which was the subject of the *Keyes v. School District No. 1* lawsuit filed in 1969. The *Keyes* case was initiated by parents of African American and Latino students in the Park Hill neighborhood who argued that Denver school district officials had intentionally acted to create racially segregated schools. As African American and Latino families began to move into some Denver neighborhoods that had been predominantly white, Denver school district officials allegedly took actions to keep minority students at predominantly minority schools, thus maintaining predominantly white schools in neighborhoods such as Park Hill. The case eventually was heard by the U.S. Supreme Court, which ruled in 1973 that: (1) Hispanic and black students should not be considered as desegregating each other because the inequities they suffered from were similar, (2) proof of de jure segregation in a substantial portion of the school district is enough to assume that the entire district was similarly affected, and (3) the burden of proof should be on the school board to show that other portions of the city were not affected by similar policies.[24] Accordingly, the Denver school board was instructed to desegregate the entire district "root and branch," which eventually resulted in a program of pairing schools and busing students to achieve a more balanced racial and ethnic mix.[25]

The court decisions and desegregation plans were met by anger and, in some cases, violent reactions. In 1970, forty-six school buses were dynamited at a Denver Public Schools parking facility. The home of the judge who presided over the initial lawsuit was bombed, as was the Keyes home in Park Hill. An antibusing member of the school board also received a letter bomb in the mail.[26] The fortunes of local politicians at this time rose and fell based on their views regarding busing.[27]

Within this tumultuous climate, political efforts were mounted to limit the annexation abilities of the City and County of Denver so as not to allow the Denver school district to expand its geographic service area, and thus bring more schools into its desegregation plan. Faced with the possibility that the City and County of Denver would annex part of the southeast office park of Greenwood Plaza, Greenwood Village mayor Harold Patton insisted, "we will fight Denver in all ways possible like Poland did when Hitler decided he needed more land. . . . We will fight until they are as bloody as a bull's hock."[28] The effort to limit Denver's ability to annex land was led by Freda Poundstone, a political lobbyist who was later elected mayor of Greenwood Village, a small, wealthy, and predominantly white suburban enclave located just southeast of Denver. In 1974, Poundstone proposed an amendment to the Colorado Constitution pertaining to annexation by a county (or a city and county, such as Denver) that would require voter approval from the entire county from which the area would be annexed, rather than just the specific area to be annexed. One of the strategies used to generate support for the amendment among voters on Colorado's western slope (areas west of the Continental Divide) was to invoke concerns about an expanded Denver and its need to siphon off even more water from the western slope. Western slope voters were fearful that Denver Water, which had already developed a system of mountain reservoirs and diversion tunnels west of the Continental Divide, would have stronger justifications for diverting even more western slope water if Denver continued to annex more territory.[29] With the strong support of the western slope and suburban Denver counties, Colorado voters approved the so-called Poundstone Amendment to the Colorado Constitution by a margin of 58 percent to 42 percent.[30]

This change in annexation policy effectively ended the City and County of Denver's ability to annex land outside of its borders because the suburban counties remained very hostile to annexations by Denver. In fact, there has been only one time that Denver annexed land since the installation of the Poundstone Amendment, and that was in 1988 when Adams County voted in favor of allowing Denver to annex land to build Denver International Airport (DIA). It should be noted that the Poundstone Amendment did not affect suburban municipality annexations. In fact, the suburb of Aurora continued to annex land in Adams and Arapahoe counties to rival the size of Denver, experiencing a 111 percent growth rate in the 1970s, the fastest of any U.S. city over one hundred thousand.[31] Aurora city councilman and future mayor Paul Tauer commented at the time, "I could see us having a twin-city relationship like Minneapolis–St. Paul, with Aurora in the role of Minneapolis and Denver playing St. Paul."[32]

While that comparison may have been an overstatement, the city of Aurora had nevertheless grown substantially from a population of 11,421 in 1950 to 222,103 by 1990, making it the second-largest city in the metropolitan area. A number of military facilities were built in Aurora before, during, and after World War II including Fitzsimons Army Hospital, Lowry Air Base, and Buckley Field, which led to its strong residential growth after the war. Nearby Stapleton Airport and the Rocky Mountain Arsenal (which manufactured chemical weapons) also provided employment opportunities for Aurora residents. A sprawling city of subdivisions without a recognizable core area, Aurora has had an aggressive annexation policy, which resulted in a 2015 population of 359,407 within a total land area of 154 square miles, stretching across parts of Adams, Arapahoe, and Douglas counties. While its population is just over half the size of Denver's, Aurora's land area is now slightly larger than Denver's. Fitzsimons Army Hospital was decommissioned in 1999, but it and the nearby area has been transformed into a major medical center, housing the Fitzsimons Life Science District, the Anschutz Medical Campus of the University of Colorado–Denver, the University of Colorado Hospital, and Children's Hospital. Interestingly, Aurora's recent population growth has resulted in a much more racially and ethnically diverse community, with 47.3 percent white alone not Hispanic or Latino, 28.7 percent Hispanic or Latino, 15.7 percent black or African American alone, 5.2 percent two or more races, 4.9 percent Asian alone, and 1.0 percent American Indian alone.[33] While not quite achieving "twin city" status with Denver, Aurora is by far the largest suburb in the Denver metropolitan area and a major player in regional planning and decision making.

Even though regional planning agencies such as DRCOG and RTD had been created, regional discord still plagued planning efforts in the 1970s and 1980s. Pressure was mounting for improving transportation facilities as highway traffic congestion grew worse with growing suburban populations. Even though RTD made numerous attempts to start a rail rapid-transit system in the years after it was created in 1969, these efforts proved fruitless through the end of the 1980s (see Chapter 6). In 1987, unhappy with RTD's lack of progress in developing a rapid-transit system, the Colorado state legislature authorized a private sector–led group, the Transit Construction Authority (TCA), to lead efforts to plan and build a light rail line in the southeast corridor between downtown Denver and the burgeoning Denver Technological Center edge city to help relieve traffic pressure on Interstate 25. The TCA effort was short-lived, however, after DRCOG selected RTD's southwest corridor instead of TCA's southeast corridor as the preferred alternative to be submitted for federal funding consideration.[34]

Also in the late 1980s, concerns were raised about DRCOG's ability to forge a regional approach to transportation and other issues. Former Colorado governor Richard Lamm said in 1989, "For all the money we've put into DRCOG, the returns are marginal. When you try to list the dynamic things

DRCOG has done, nobody can think of anything."[35] One regional leader once described DRCOG's impact as "beige."[36] Concerns such as these led governor Roy Romer and the Colorado state legislature in 1990 to create the Metropolitan Transportation Development Commission "to develop a comprehensive, regional solution to transportation problems plaguing the metropolitan area."[37] The commission produced a report that called for a new regional transportation plan, including both highways and rail transit that, according to public surveys, should be managed by a new regional authority. No new authority was created, but changes in the existing transportation agencies had begun to occur. In 1991, the Colorado Department of Highways (CDOH) was reorganized by the state legislature and changed its name to the Colorado Department of Transportation (CDOT) to reflect the increasingly intermodal character of statewide transportation planning.[38] Also in 1991, the U.S. Congress promulgated the Intermodal Surface Transportation Efficiency Act (ISTEA), which restructured planning processes by elevating metropolitan planning organizations (such as DRCOG) to the lead role in regional transportation planning in cooperation with state departments of transportation and regional transit agencies.[39] Still, many were skeptical of the ability of DRCOG, RTD, and CDOT to forge a regional consensus to improve multimodal transportation.[40]

Phase 3: Regional Collaboration

In their book *The Metropolitan Revolution*, Brookings Institution authors Bruce Katz and Jennifer Bradley include a chapter about the four referenda that showcased how metropolitan Denver progressed from a region bitterly divided by tensions over race, schools, growth, and transportation to one that began to forge a regional consensus around issues confronting the region.[41] The first referendum was the aforementioned Poundstone Amendment, which represents the nadir of efforts to develop a collaborative approach to regional problems. But in 1988, Adams County, which had been staunchly opposed to previous annexation efforts by Denver, voted in favor of allowing Denver to annex fifty-three square miles to build a new international airport, the only time Denver has been allowed to annex land since the adoption of the Poundstone Amendment (see Chapter 2). Also in 1988, voters throughout metropolitan Denver approved 75 percent to 25 percent a 0.1 percent sales and use tax to fund the Scientific and Cultural Facilities District in support of art, music, theater, dance, zoology, botany, natural history, and cultural history organizations (see Chapter 4).[42] And finally, in 2004, voters in the Regional Transportation District approved 58 percent to 42 percent a 0.4 percent sales tax increase to build a 122-mile regional rail transit system expansion called FasTracks (see Chapter 6). These four votes illustrate the trajectory of changing attitudes in the Denver area toward greater regional collaboration.

One of the factors prompting the increased collaboration was the collapse of the energy boom in the early 1980s, and the ensuing downturn in regional economic fortunes during the rest of the 1980s. As a result, local attention shifted to economic development strategies, and more examples of regional cooperation began to occur. As early as 1984, Aurora and Denver agreed to a revenue-sharing compromise over the Galleria Shopping Center, which would be built in Aurora but would be located close to the Denver city limits.[43] Aurora also agreed to support expansion of the Denver Fire Academy to train firefighters in both Denver and Aurora.[44] And then in 1988, Adams County and municipalities therein supported the ballot measure to allow Denver to annex land for the purpose of building DIA. The expected economic benefits for the jurisdictions close to the new airport were a powerful inducement for collaboration.[45]

Another factor in the increased level of regional collaboration was the role of business and civic organizations. The Greater Denver Chamber of Commerce, composed of over three thousand metropolitan area businesses, played a leading role in developing regional support for Denver International Airport and other economic development initiatives in the late 1980s, 1990s, and 2000s, as well as helping to forge a new regional identity. Chamber president Richard Fleming said in 1990, "The world sees Denver as you see it from an airplane—without artificial boundaries. We should treat it that way and deal together on common problems of air pollution, economic development, transportation, and water. We need to market Denver as a five-county metropolis and let prospects see all the alternatives. That's a lot better than having each county try to build itself up by running down the others."[46]

One of the key regional issues that concerned the chamber and the major political jurisdictions was air pollution. As a result of the postwar boom in suburban housing and automobile use, vehicle miles traveled increased dramatically, and so did air pollution. The problems were particularly severe in Denver owing to its geographic site in a river basin with the Front Range of the Rocky Mountains located just twenty miles to the west. This physical setting results in frequent temperature inversions during the winter months whereby colder air drains into the basin and can be trapped by warmer air above, resulting in a potential build-up of particulate matter, carbon monoxide, nitrogen oxides, and other pollutants over the city. Through much of the 1970s and 1980s, Denver was infamous for its "brown cloud" problem, and in some years it was exceeded only by Los Angeles for the worst air quality in the country. By the late 1980s, though, concerted efforts by the State of Colorado Air Pollution Control Division, the Regional Air Quality Council, and metropolitan jurisdictions contributed to substantial reductions in air pollution readings. Denver violated the federal carbon monoxide standard only seven times in 1989, while in 1975 it had exceeded that standard sixty-five times, despite a 57 percent increase in vehicle miles traveled during that time.[47]

In response to concerns about the ability of agencies such as DRCOG and RTD to conduct regional planning, groups such as the chamber and the Metro Mayors Caucus began to exert a greater voice on regional issues. The Metro Mayors Caucus (MMC) was formed in 1993 as a voluntary, consensus-based organization of thirty-two metropolitan area mayors[48] focused on addressing issues of regional importance.[49] The mayors felt there was a need for a more cooperative and collaborative forum to exchange ideas and viewpoints outside of the more traditional and confrontational arenas. The metro-area mayors were also members of the Colorado Municipal League (CML) and DRCOG, but CML had a more state-oriented focus, and because DRCOG allocated regional transportation funding, it had been characterized by more adversarial relationships among the jurisdictions. The MMC has nevertheless worked closely with both DRCOG and CML, and agreements made within the context of MMC have extended to agreements at these other organizations. A good example is the consensus that was forged in support of DRCOG's Metro Vision 2020 plan in 1997, which represented a strong statement in support of smart growth policies for the region.[50]

In the mid-1990s, DRCOG began its long-range Metro Vision 2020 planning process. Partly as a result of accords developed in the MMC and with support from the chamber, DRCOG embarked on a more focused regional planning exercise to address pressing growth-related issues that were impacting the Denver region. These included rapid urbanized land expansion that was on pace to exceed one thousand square miles by 2020, a notorious air pollution problem that resulted in nonattainment of federal air quality standards, rapidly increasing vehicle miles traveled and traffic congestion, and continuing battles over funding and approval for suburban beltways. Regional officials and DRCOG realized that a coherent vision of the region's future was necessary. The resulting Metro Vision 2020 plan focused on growth and development, the natural environment, and transportation and clearly embraced a smart growth approach to regional planning.[51] Features of Metro Vision included a voluntary urban growth boundary/area that was initially set not to exceed seven hundred square miles, a focus on higher-density development in specified urban centers, designation of four free-standing communities, improving air quality in the region, and most significantly, a rail transit system that would serve as the backbone of the regional transportation system (see Chapter 6).[52]

One of the criticisms of DRCOG has been that as a voluntary association, it has had limited enforcement mechanisms to implement its plans. In recognition of this shortcoming, DRCOG, along with the Metro Mayors Caucus, spearheaded an effort to create the Mile High Compact, which would legally obligate jurisdictions to abide by the elements of the Metro Vision plan. In 2000, thirty cities and counties signed the Mile High Compact thus agreeing to incorporate the principles and components of the regional Metro Vision 2020 plan into their legally binding local comprehensive/master plans. By 2010, forty-five cities and counties had signed the compact, representing 89 percent of the region's population.[53]

Relationships between the City and County of Denver and other metropolitan area jurisdictions have improved greatly over time. Former Denver mayor Wellington Webb was part of the initial group of mayors who started the Metro Mayors Caucus in 1993, and from 2003 to 2011, Denver mayor John Hickenlooper extended the spirit of collaboration throughout the region. Both Webb and Hickenlooper worked with other metro-area mayors on several regional initiatives including economic development, transportation, and sustainability. Other former or current mayors in the metro area, such as Margaret Carpenter of Thornton, Don Parsons of Northglenn, Susan Thornton of Littleton, Nancy Sharpe of Greenwood Village, Chuck Sisk of Louisville, and Linda Morton and Bob Murphy of Lakewood have been instrumental in helping to develop regional collaboration.[54]

Hickenlooper, who later became governor of Colorado, was mayor of Denver at the time of the FasTracks sales-tax vote, and he claimed that a crucial factor for the success of the FasTracks initiative was the leading role of many suburban mayors, even though in previous cases they had been bitterly opposed to regional initiatives involving Denver. Soon after becoming mayor,

Hickenlooper invited other mayors in the region to accompany him on economic development trips to market the Denver metropolitan area, rather than just the City and County of Denver. The California planner Bill Fulton has dubbed Hickenlooper's leadership style "brewpub regionalism," because of Hickenlooper's early activities as owner of the Wynkoop brewpub in Denver's Lower Downtown district before eventually running for mayor.[55] In the late 1980s, while still the owner of the Wynkoop, Hickenlooper joined other LoDo business owners in an effort to save the historic Union Station building that was slated for demolition. The resulting Save Our Station group was ultimately successful in preserving Union Station, which was eventually purchased by RTD, the City and County of Denver, DRCOG, and CDOT, and later became the intermodal centerpiece of the FasTracks plan. Hickenlooper's growing involvement with other LoDo businesses as part of the Downtown Denver Partnership led directly to his political career as mayor and later as governor. A regularly invited speaker on the national conference circuit of urban professionals, Hickenlooper called "collaboration the new competition" when describing the Denver approach to city regionalism and regional transport provision.[56]

While regional cooperation has improved greatly over time, the contemporary political landscape of the most populous counties of metropolitan Denver still exhibit a significant range across the ideological spectrum, and some fundamental disagreements remain. The City and County of Denver has continued to be more liberal than the rest of the metro area, and the First Congressional District, which is based in Denver proper, has been a solid Democratic Party stronghold since the early 1970s. In fact, during the past forty years this seat has been held by just two Democratic representatives, Patricia Schroeder (1973–97) and Diana DeGette (1997–present). Among active registered voters in Denver, 48 percent are Democrats, 35 percent are unaffiliated, and only 16 percent are Republicans.[57] Moving outward from the City and County of Denver, the political landscape becomes more conservative, although each suburban county has its own particular political profile. Adams County, to the northeast of Denver, has also been a Democratic stronghold but has featured more middle-class and working-class Democrats who tend to be more conservative than the Democratic base in Denver.[58] Tensions between Denver and Adams County were heightened by recent disagreements over Denver's proposed plan to develop an airport city at DIA (see Chapter 2). While Denver's relationship with the city of Aurora has improved greatly over time, Aurora recently tried to lure the National

Western Stock Show as part of a hotel and conference center proposed by Gaylord Entertainment.[59] In response, Denver has prepared a plan for a new National Western Center to ensure that the show remains in Denver.[60]

Both Arapahoe County, just southeast of Denver, and Jefferson County, just west of Denver, have historically been more Republican than Democratic but have become swing counties in recent years as a result of changing demographics. Today, they are split relatively evenly—Arapahoe County's registered party affiliations are 35 percent unaffiliated, 33 percent Democrat, and 32 percent Republican, while those for Jefferson County are 37 percent unaffiliated, 30 percent Democrat, and 32 percent Republican.[61] Douglas County, to the south of Denver, is the wealthiest and most conservative county in the Denver metro area, with nearly half of all voters registered as Republicans, and unaffiliated voters outpacing Democrats 33 percent to 20 percent. Despite these differing political orientations and some continued disagreements, many local officials in metropolitan Denver have been able to forge working relationships with one another so as to accomplish important initiatives for the good of the entire region.

Phase 4: Extended Regionalism

Much of the discussion on regionalism in the Denver area focuses on the more traditional delimitations of the Denver region, such as the metropolitan statistical area, or the DRCOG and RTD service areas. In many respects, however, the extended Denver region has expanded beyond the immediate metropolitan area to include other nearby metro areas such as Boulder, Fort Collins, Greeley, Colorado Springs, and Pueblo along the Front Range urban corridor, as well as numerous mountain communities, like Blackhawk and Central City, along the I-70 corridor west of Denver. The emerging Denver-Boulder megaregion, which Richard Florida ranked as the twenty-ninth-largest global megaregion based on a measure of light-based regional product, had a population of 3.7 million and was among the top ten global megaregions in innovation/patents and star scientists in 2008.[62] The increasing level of interaction between and among communities in the extended megaregion has contributed to increased highway traffic along Interstates 25 and 70, and the need for increased coordination to address future growth concerns.

To gain insight into the emergence of the megaregion, we provide a focus on some of the notable places that characterize this extended region.

Boulder

The city of Boulder (2015 population of 107,349) is located in Boulder County about thirty miles northwest of the Denver central business district. At an elevation of 5,430 feet above sea level, the city is located where the high plains meet the Flatirons, a particularly scenic section of the foothills of the Front Range of the Rocky Mountains. Boulder received its name from the many boulders strewn about from the steep creek (named Boulder Creek) that emptied onto the plains from the foothills. Boulder County (2015 population of 319,372) includes the cities of Boulder, Lafayette, Longmont, and Louisville. While it is included in the DRCOG and RTD service areas, Boulder County is designated as a separate metropolitan statistical area, although it is included in the Denver-Aurora Combined Statistical Area (CSA). The separate metropolitan designation suits many in Boulder just fine as Boulder has long resisted association with Denver. Boulder prefers to be a freestanding community that maintains a physical separation from the Denver metro area through an open space greenbelt that prevents sprawling development from filling in the U.S. 36 highway corridor between Denver and Boulder.

Indeed, Boulder has a long history of open space preservation and growth control. As early as the late 1800s, the U.S. Congress acted to preserve open space in the foothills near Boulder to preserve the watershed and scenic vistas of the Flatirons. In 1959, Boulder enacted a "blue line" that prevented water system expansion to areas above fifty-seven hundred feet in elevation. Boulder created a greenbelt around the city through the purchase of land starting in 1967 for the purpose of open space preservation. In 1972, Boulder enacted a height-restriction ordinance on new buildings, and in 1976 Boulder was one of the first U.S. communities to limit building permits for residential units by specifying that no more than four hundred units could be built per year. Despite these efforts, Boulder's population has continued to grow strongly from nearly twenty thousand in 1950 to over one hundred thousand today. All these actions have had the effect of limiting housing supply in Boulder, and with continued residential demand, housing prices have increased substantially in recent years. The median house or condominium value in Boulder in 2012 was $477,200, while in 2000, it was $272,200. The median house or condo value in Colorado for 2012 was $234,900.[63]

Boulder is the site of the University of Colorado (CU), which opened in 1877. As the flagship university in the state of Colorado, CU enrolled nearly thirty-two thousand students in 2013. It is one of thirty-four U.S. public institutions belonging to the Association of American Universities (AAU), and the only member in the Rocky Mountain region.[64] Because of the strong influence of the university, Boulder's population is more highly educated and younger than that of most other cities in Colorado. Several national research laboratories, such as the National Center for Atmospheric Research (NCAR) and the National Institute of Standards and Technology (NIST) are located in Boulder.

Because of the university and its location at the edge of the Flatirons, Boulder is known for its active, outdoors-oriented lifestyle. Boulder typically ranks highly for its overall quality of life, and for being a very health-conscious place. Biking, running, skiing, hiking, climbing, rafting, and camping are major pastimes for Boulder residents. Boulder has an extensive network of cycling paths throughout the city and ranks among the most bike-friendly communities in the United States. The League of American Bicyclists designated Boulder as at the highest level (platinum) of bicycle-friendly communities, one of only four in the entire United States (Fort Collins, Colorado; Davis, California; and Portland, Oregon, are the other three). Boulder is home to many professional bicyclists, including the Garmin-Sharp professional cycling race team that competes in major international cycling events such as the Tour de France. Boulder has hosted the annual "Bolder Boulder" ten-kilometer running race on Memorial Day every year since 1979, which now draws over fifty thousand participants, the largest timed race in the United States. The Eldora ski resort is located close to Boulder, just southwest of the mountain town of Nederland, and numerous other ski resorts are within a two-hour drive from Boulder.

Because of the university, the national research labs, and its high quality of life, Boulder is home to a concentration of high-tech, information technology, aerospace, biotech, cleantech, and natural and organic product companies. Boulder was ranked first among all U.S. metropolitan areas in Richard Florida's creativity index in 2012, based on the percentage of the labor force engaged in creative-class occupations.[65] As a result, Boulder has a wealthier population on average, with a 2011 median household income of over $57,000, and a median family income of over $113,000.

In political and cultural terms, Boulder is very liberal and is known as a somewhat quirky place. During the 1960s and 1970s, Boulder became a popular destination for hippies, some of whom have remained ever since. It is fair to say that the number of shops and organizations promoting New Age ideas, organic and natural products, herbal teas, and eastern mysticism would likely exceed the national average. Boulder also has a relatively large number of retail marijuana stores, although Denver has by far the largest number in the state. Politically, Boulder is one of the most liberal cities in Colorado, and even the entire county has more than twice as many registered Democrats than Republicans. Boulder's brand of political persuasion is so liberal, sometimes radical, that it is jokingly referred to as the People's Republic of Boulder by both residents and outsiders alike.[66] Its racial and ethnic profile is not too diverse, with 83 percent white alone, not Hispanic or Latino, 8.7 percent Hispanic or Latino, 4.7 percent Asian alone, 2.6 percent two or more races, 0.9 percent black or African American alone, and 0.4 percent American Indian alone.[67]

Fort Collins

The city of Fort Collins (2015 population of 161,175) is the fourth-largest city in Colorado and is the county seat of Larimer County, located about sixty-five miles north of Denver where the Cache La Poudre River exits the nearby foothills of the Rocky Mountains. It was founded in 1864 as a military fort named for Lieutenant Colonel William Collins who was the commander of Ohio Cavalry troops headquartered at Fort Laramie, Wyoming. The city of Loveland (2015 population of 75,182) is located just south of Fort Collins, and together they are the principal cities of the Fort Collins–Loveland Metropolitan Statistical Area (MSA), which is composed of Larimer County (2015 population of 333,577). The most populous parts of the Fort Collins–Loveland MSA and the Greeley MSA together constitute the North Front Range metropolitan planning organization.

Fort Collins has a relatively strong local economy, being home to Colorado State University (CSU), which was founded in 1870 as the Colorado Agricultural College. As a major land-grant institution with an enrollment of approximately thirty thousand, Colorado State University is the largest employer in Fort Collins and has an impact on the city similar to the impact of CU on Boulder. CSU has strong research programs in fields such as infectious diseases, atmospheric science, clean energy technologies, environmental science, and biomedical technology, and its professional programs in veterinary medicine, occupational therapy, journalism, agriculture, and construction management are ranked among the nation's best.[68] These emphases have had a positive spillover effect on the employment profile of Fort Collins, which features Hewlett-Packard, Agilent Technologies, Eastman Kodak, Avago Technologies, and other high-tech and information technology companies. Fort Collins is also home to several very successful craft brewers including New Belgium and Odell brewing companies. Because of the university and technology focus, Fort Collins is a relatively wealthy community with a median household income of $64,459, and a median family income of $89,332.

Fort Collins has experienced significant population growth in recent decades. In 1950, Fort Collins was a relatively small town of 14,937 people, and it has grown over tenfold since then. In response to the strong rate of growth, Fort Collins and Larimer County have engaged in growth management planning by establishing a sixty-five-square-mile growth management area (GMA) through an intergovernmental agreement first adopted in 1980 and revised in 2000. The GMA identifies those areas that are suitable for urban development within the boundary, while areas outside the GMA boundary and not part of another municipality will not be provided public services and facilities at urban levels.[69] Unlike Boulder, however, Fort Collins has not placed a limit on the number of housing units that can be built. In addition to open space preservation, the city of Fort Collins has a strong program of historic preservation. The Old Town district in downtown Fort Collins contains a number of protected properties that preserve the historic character of this district. Its racial and ethnic profile is very similar to Boulder's, with 83.1 percent white alone not Hispanic or Latino, 10.1 percent Hispanic or Latino, 3.1 percent two or more races, 2.9 percent Asian alone, 1.2 percent black or African American alone, and 0.6 percent American Indian alone.[70]

Similar to Boulder, Fort Collins is known for its high quality of life. It regularly ranks high on lists of best places to live, including that of *Money* magazine, which designated the city the best place to live in 2006, and *Time* magazine, which named Fort Collins America's Most Satisfied City in 2014. Part of the high quality of life ranking is due to the emphasis on physical activities and healthy lifestyles of residents. Bicycling, hiking, rafting, skiing, and other outdoor activities are very popular in Fort Collins. The League of American Bicyclists has designated Fort Collins as a platinum-level bicycle city, its highest level shared with only three other cities (Boulder; Davis, California; and Portland, Oregon). The National League of Cities in conjunction with Let's Move named Fort Collins the top city in the country for Healthy Efforts in September 2014.

Greeley

The city of Greeley (2015 population 100,883) is the county seat of Weld County, located about fifty miles northeast of Denver where the Cache La Poudre River joins the South Platte River. Greeley is the main urbanized area of the Greeley Metropolitan Statistical Area (2015 population 285,174) which is composed of Weld County, including the cities of Dacono, Evans, Fort Lupton, and parts of Brighton, Northglenn, and Thornton. Greeley has grown at a pace similar to Boulder, from a 1950 population of just over twenty thousand to today's population just over one hundred thousand. But while Boulder has enacted relatively stringent growth control measures, Greeley has not. Greeley differs from both Boulder and Fort Collins in many ways, especially its more conservative political orientation. It also has a somewhat more diverse population, with 59.3 percent white alone not Hispanic or Latino, 36.0 percent Hispanic or Latino, 3.4 percent two or more races, 1.7 percent black or African American alone, 1.3 percent Asian alone, and 1.2 percent American Indian alone.[71]

Greeley started as a utopian agricultural community (the Union Colony) founded in 1869 by Nathan Meeker, a former agricultural reporter of the *New York Tribune* newspaper. The *Tribune*'s editor, Horace Greeley, encouraged Meeker to establish the colony that today bears Greeley's name. The Union Colony was based on strict moral values, including temperance, and an emphasis on hard work, education, and religious principles. Owing to its initial start as an agricultural colony, and the fertility of the nearby river valleys, Greeley and much of Weld County thrived as major agricultural communities, producing cattle, pigs, grain, and sugar beets. Some of the largest cattle and pig feedlots in the world are located near Greeley, and the Swift meatpacking plant in Greeley is one of the largest employers in the city. Weld County is the fourth most productive agricultural county in the United States, based on the value of its agricultural products.

Greeley is the home of the University of Northern Colorado, which was founded in 1889 as the Colorado State Normal School. With an enrollment today of over twelve thousand students, it has continued its emphasis on ed-ucating teachers, in addition to developing programs in business, music, and the arts and sciences. One of its most famous alumni is the author James A. Michener, who received his master's degree and taught there in the 1930s. Michener's classic novel *Centennial*, the story about several generations of a western family, was based on his experiences living and studying in Greeley. The library at the university is named for Michener and is the repository for his papers and archives.

Other factors have also fueled growth in Greeley. From 2000 to 2010, the Greeley MSA was one of the fastest growing MSAs in the country, with a 39.7 percent growth rate due to continued strength in its core economic ac-tivities and proximity to the rapidly growing metro areas of Denver, Boul-der, and Fort Collins. Because of strong employment growth and rising housing prices in the nearby MSAs, Greeley and Weld County became popu-lar sites for reasonably priced residential development. Parts of southwest-ern Weld County are included in the DRCOG and RTD areas, while many commuters working in Larimer and Boulder Counties live in Weld County. In recent years, Greeley and Weld County have been the sites of intensive oil and gas development, including widespread use of hydraulic fracturing, or "fracking" technologies. The fracking boom is tapping into significant de-posits in the Denver-Julesberg basin, and while other municipalities and counties have tried to limit this activity, the governments of Greeley and Weld County have wholeheartedly embraced oil and gas development.

Politically, Greeley and Weld County are much more conservative than Denver, Fort Collins, and especially Boulder. Among registered voters in Weld County, 38 percent are unaffiliated, 37 percent are Republicans, and 23 percent are Democrats.[72] In 2013, faced with Democratic Party control of the governor's office and both the state senate and house, several Weld County commissioners proposed the secession of Weld County and several other northeastern Colorado counties to form the new state of North Colo-rado.[73] These commissioners said that a "collective mass" of statewide issues, including increasing renewable energy standards, new regulations on oil and gas production, and new background checks on gun sales, had accumulated over recent years, which isolated rural Colorado from the rest of the state, putting rural counties at a disadvantage.[74] Indeed, similar to other parts of the United States, the state of Colorado had become increasingly polarized in political terms, characterized broadly by an urban/rural split in ideolo-gies and party affiliations. The Front Range urban corridor has continued to grow significantly in population, including an increasing number of immigrants from other states representing more liberal and moderate voters. At the same time, populations in the more conservative rural portions of the state, such as the eastern plains and the western slope, have declined or increased more slowly, resulting in a more evenly divided electorate.

Historically, Colorado has been a more conservative and Republican-oriented state. Of the thirty-six presidential elections since 1876, when Colorado achieved statehood, the state's electoral college supported twenty-two Republican candidates, but only thirteen Democrats and one Populist (James Weaver in 1892). Since 1952, Coloradans have voted in favor of twelve Republican candidates for president, and only five Democrats. But in recent years, the Colorado electorate has swung toward Democrats, supporting: (1) Barack Obama for president in both 2008 and 2012,[75] and Hillary Clinton in 2016; (2) for governor, Bill Ritter in 2006 and John Hickenlooper in 2010 and 2014; and (3) for the U.S. Senate, Ken Salazar in 2004, Mark Udall in 2008, and Michael Bennett in 2010 and 2016 (Republican Cory Gardner interrupted this Democratic streak by defeating Udall in 2014). Confronted by these political dynamics, the commissioners from Weld and ten other counties were successful in placing the secession measure on the ballot in November 2013, but the proposed secession effort failed in six of the eleven counties, including Weld.[76] Nevertheless, a message of dissatisfaction from Weld County and rural Colorado had been sent. Another message was sent in 2016, as Weld and most rural Colorado counties voted strongly in favor of Donald Trump for president.

Colorado Springs

Colorado Springs (2015 population 456,568) is the second-largest city in Colorado after Denver, and is located sixty miles south of Denver in El Paso County. Its site at the edge of the southern Front Range of the Rocky Mountains is dominated to the west by Pikes Peak, the 14,115-foot mountain famous for inspiring the words to "America the Beautiful." Similar to other Front Range cities, Colorado Springs has experienced very rapid population growth, expanding nearly tenfold from just over forty-five thousand in 1950. Colorado Springs is the principal city for the Colorado Springs Metropolitan Statistical Area (2015 population 697,856), which includes cities and towns such as Security-Widefield, Fountain, Fort Carson, Black Forest, Manitou

Springs, Woodland Park, Monument, and others in El Paso County (2015 population 674,471) and Teller County (2015 population 23,385) directly to the west. The Colorado Springs metropolitan area is represented by the Pikes Peak Area Council of Governments as its designated metropolitan planning organization.

Colorado Springs was founded in 1871 by railroad promoter William Jackson Palmer, who started the Denver and Rio Grande Railroad and purchased land to create the city of Colorado Springs along the railroad's route south of Denver. During his first visit to the area in 1869, Palmer envisioned Colorado Springs as a great resort city thanks to the region's numerous natural springs, pleasant climate, and outstanding scenic beauty.[77] From Palmer's vision, Colorado Springs developed into an elite resort enclave featuring high-end hotels, tourist attractions, spas, and health sanitariums. Visitors and migrants from eastern cities, such as Boston, New York, and Philadelphia, as well as from London, England, lent a sophisticated air to the city and helped to establish numerous cultural, educational, and religious institutions.[78] Palmer himself donated land to help establish the private Colorado College in 1874, and as a result of wealth generated from the Cripple Creek gold rush of the 1890s, millionaire Spencer Penrose built the world-famous Broadmoor Hotel and Resort in 1916 and established the Cheyenne Mountain Zoo in 1926.

During World War II and the postwar era, Colorado Springs became a major military-oriented city. In the 1940s, Colorado Springs was chosen as the site for Camp Carson, a U.S. Army base, later renamed Fort Carson, and Peterson Field, a U.S. Army Air base, which later became Peterson Air Force base. In 1954, the U.S. Air Force Academy was established in Colorado Springs to be followed by the establishment of the U.S. Space Command, North American Aerospace Defense Command (NORAD) and Cheyenne Mountain Air Station, and Schriever Air Force base. A large number of defense-related aerospace companies established facilities in Colorado Springs, including Boeing, General Dynamics, Lockheed Martin, and Northrop Grumman. Today, the military and defense industries remain the largest employers in Colorado Springs and help to explain much of the population growth since 1950.

Another factor accounting for the remarkable growth of Colorado Springs has been its attraction as a tourist center, which has also spawned permanent relocations of visitors to the area. Similar to Denver, people who stayed in Colorado Springs either because of military deployment or while on vacation developed an attachment to the area that many times translated into a permanent relocation. Colorado Springs, like Denver, has served as a gateway to the Rocky Mountains for skiing, camping, hiking, rafting, fishing, and other outdoor activities, which has contributed to the economic profile of the city. Beyond these activities, Colorado Springs is the headquarters of the U.S. Olympic Committee and home to the U.S. Olympic Training Center, which brings many athletes regularly to the city. Colorado Springs has also become the home of many religious organizations, especially Evangelical Christian and other Christian groups. Focus on the Family and Family Talk, both founded by James Dobson, and the New Life Church, founded by Ted Haggard, are some of the most notable organizations, but there are many others as well. Several of these religious organizations moved to Colorado Springs from southern California in the early 1990s and have contributed to the area's strong population growth.

Politically, Colorado Springs is very conservative, owing to its strong military presence and the preponderance of conservative Christian religious organizations. Among registered voters in El Paso County, 41 percent are Republicans, 36 percent are unaffiliated and 21 percent are Democrats, which is similar to Douglas County just to the north in the Denver metropolitan area.[79] The Fifth Congressional District of Colorado is centered in Colorado Springs and has elected a Republican representative in every election since it was created in the early 1970s.

Pueblo

The southernmost metropolitan area along the Colorado Front Range urban corridor is anchored by the city of Pueblo (2015 population 109,412), located 112 miles south of Denver along the Arkansas River. The Pueblo Metropolitan Statistical Area is composed of Pueblo County (2015 population 163,591) and is represented by the Pueblo Area Council of Governments as its metropolitan planning organization.

Pueblo started as a series of trading forts established between 1821 and 1846 along the Arkansas River, which was at that time the boundary between the United States and Mexico. Pueblo was incorporated as a city in 1870, and in its early years it was considered to be the saddle-making capital of the world. William Jackson Palmer's Denver and Rio Grande (D&RG) Railroad reached Pueblo in 1872, leading to the development of South Pueblo as the main depot and site of railroad-oriented development. The D&RG built rail lines from Pueblo to coalfields near Trinidad and Walsenburg by 1876, to the agricultural San Luis Valley by 1878, and to silver mines in Leadville by 1881. Other rail companies, such as the Atchison, Topeka, and Santa Fe (ATSF); Missouri Pacific; Rock Island; and Denver, Texas, and Fort Worth Railroads all came to Pueblo by the early 1890s, turning Pueblo into a major railroad center rivalling Denver.[80]

As a result of its central location in proximity to mineral resources and its railroad connections, Pueblo developed as the most important early industrial center in the western United States. Its location near coalfields and iron deposits in southern Colorado led Palmer to start the Colorado Coal and Iron Company in 1879, which was renamed the Colorado Fuel and Iron (CF&I) Company in 1892.[81] Initially focused on smelting, CF&I eventually expanded into steel manufacturing and quickly grew into the largest steel works in the western United States by the early twentieth century. Pueblo became known as the "Pittsburgh of the West," and steel manufacturing continued to be its major industry through much of the twentieth century. Pueblo's success as a steel center attracted thousands of industrial workers representing a wide diversity of racial and ethnic groups, including Irish, Italian, German, Slovenian, Greek, Lithuanian, Russian, Hungarian, Japanese, and African Americans. Pueblo became a cultural melting pot and displayed more cultural diversity than most other cities in Colorado and the western United States.[82] By the 1980s, the steel industry across the United States had declined, and steel production in Pueblo had dwindled accordingly. CF&I filed for bankruptcy protection on several occasions in the 1980s and experienced changes in ownership in the 1990s and 2000s. Today the steel facilities in Pueblo are owned by the Evraz Group, one of Russia's major steel companies, which still is engaged in manufacturing steel rails for railroads, rods and bars for construction, and seamless pipes.[83]

Pueblo has not experienced the same degree of population growth as Colorado Springs, Greeley, Fort Collins, Boulder, or Denver. Its population grew rapidly in the late 1800s and early 1900s, reaching 41,797 in 1910, making it the second-largest city in Colorado (after Denver) at that time. Pueblo also had a major growth spurt in the late 1940s and 1950s, growing from 52,162 in 1940 to 91,181 in 1960. Since then, Pueblo's growth has been slow, even losing population during the 1980s. Similar to other cities dependent on heavy manufacturing, Pueblo's economy has suffered and has not diversified enough to offset the decline of the steel industry. Of the largest cities in Colorado, Pueblo has the least expensive residential real estate, with a median home value in 2013 of \$108,900, compared to the state median home value of \$254,000.[84]

Blackhawk and Central City

The two mountain towns of Blackhawk (2010 population 118) and Central City (2010 population 663) are historic mining settlements located in Gilpin County, about thirty-four miles west of Denver. Even though Gilpin County is part of the Denver-Aurora-Lakewood Metropolitan Statistical Area and the DRCOG area, its mountainous terrain has historically isolated its communities, making travel to and interaction with Denver more difficult.

Central City and Blackhawk were the sites of major gold discoveries in 1859, thus precipitating the gold rush that led to their growth and the growth of Denver in the early 1860s. The construction of successful ore smelters, and the completion of the Colorado Central rail line from Golden to Blackhawk, ensured the continuation of hard-rock mining through the late 1800s. But by the early 1900s, the mining boom had tapped out, and both Blackhawk and Central City declined sharply in population and economic relevance.

While several attempts to revive mining in these communities during the twentieth century were short-lived, economic development strategies turned to tourism. The area was designated the Central City/Blackhawk Historic District in 1961, which protected the original historic buildings, and the communities were marketed as authentic western gold-mining towns. The fortunes of both towns changed dramatically when a statewide referendum in 1990 made limited-stakes gambling legal in both Central City and Blackhawk, as well as the gold-mining town of Cripple Creek near Colorado Springs.[85] Very quickly, casinos were built in both towns, and while local small businesses had hoped to cash in on the introduction of gambling, major casino companies have taken over much of the gaming business.

Interestingly, gambling establishments in Blackhawk have been more numerous and successful than those in adjacent Central City. Blackhawk was the first town that visitors would reach driving up from Denver along U.S. Route 6 and Colorado Highway 119, thus geographical proximity to Denver favored Blackhawk over Central City. Also, Central City had a building height restriction of fifty-three feet so that historic properties would not be obscured. In contrast, Blackhawk built larger and swankier casinos with large parking garages that made it easier for travelers from Denver to access the casinos. In response, Central City town leaders pushed efforts to build the Central City Parkway, an 8.4-mile four-lane highway linking Interstate 70 directly with Central City, and in 2009, they removed the building height restriction.[86] While Central City backers hoped the new parkway and re- moved restrictions would favor Central City over Blackhawk, the number of casinos and revenues generated in Blackhawk have continued to be much larger than in Central City.

While gambling activities in Blackhawk and Central City have generated significant revenues, with some of the proceeds used for tourism, historic preservation, and community college funding, concerns have been raised about the social and environmental impacts of gambling in Colorado.[87] The relatively inaccessible mountain locations of Blackhawk and Central City are not necessarily the best places to host casino activities, which are mar- keted toward residents of metropolitan Denver and other Front Range com- munities located over thirty-five miles away. After the start of gambling in 1991, traffic accidents in Gilpin County increased, fuelled in part by a rise in gamblers, sometimes intoxicated after a night in the casinos, driving on dangerous mountain roads. While some of the revenues are targeted for his- toric preservation, some commentators have argued that the historical char- acter of the mountain towns has actually been destroyed by the casinos.[88] Despite repeated efforts, Colorado voters have rejected all other proposals to expand gambling in other communities throughout the state.

Efforts at Megaregion Connectivity

Owing to the growth of the Denver, Boulder, Fort Collins, Greeley, and Col- orado Springs metropolitan areas, and the increasing overlap in commuting and spatial interaction along the Front Range urban corridor and the nearby mountain communities, efforts to coordinate planning for transportation and other issues facing this emerging megaregion have increased. In partic- ular, traffic along Interstate 25, which links together the urban corridor, has grown significantly, creating major congestion problems within and between these metropolitan areas. Traffic on Interstate 70 west of Denver has also in- creased, especially on weekends as travelers seek to access ski resorts during the winter and other outdoor activities at other times of the year. Eastbound I-70 traffic is particularly bad on Sundays, when travelers are returning to

Denver after a weekend in the mountains. Efforts to widen Interstates 25 and 70 have been conducted in piecemeal fashion by the Colorado Department of Transportation (CDOT) in coordination with the relevant metropolitan planning organizations. Along many sections of both I-25 and I-70, it is difficult and extremely costly to widen the highways, thus leading to other ideas of how to link the extended region.

One such idea was the proposed Prairie Falcon Parkway Express (PFPE), formerly known as the Front Range Toll Road, and nicknamed "Super Slab" by opponents. The project was proposed in 2006 by a private firm that hoped to construct a four-lane median-divided toll road together with rail and utility lines between north of Fort Collins and south of Pueblo about twenty to thirty miles east of I-25. It was controversial because numerous landowners in the proposed corridor area were vehemently opposed to the project, and organized to stop it.[89] Adding to the concerns was the authority that the private company had acquired by interpretation of an obscure mining law to obtain land for the toll road through eminent domain, without public approval. This legal loophole has since been closed, now requiring the entire planning process for this or any privately sponsored transportation project to go through a public approval process as part of CDOT planning requirements. Because of landowner concerns and lack of political and financial support for such a massive highway project, plans for the Super Slab have been shelved.

In addition to expanding highway capacity, efforts have also been mounted to develop passenger rail service along the Front Range urban corridor and along the I-70 mountain corridor. Partly as a result of successful rail transit development in Denver, and national efforts to develop high-speed rail, communities along the I-25 and I-70 corridors have increasingly been asking whether passenger rail service could provide a viable alternative to congested highway travel. In response, CDOT created the Division of Transit and Rail in 2009, produced a state rail plan in 2012, and is preparing a statewide transit plan. In 2016, a new interregional express bus service (called the Bustang) from Denver to Fort Collins, Colorado Springs, and Glenwood Springs was initiated by CDOT to provide a transit alternative to driving and to gauge demand for possible intercity rail passenger service. The CDOT state rail plan includes development of commuter rail service from the Denver metropolitan area to Fort Collins in its short-range investment program and several initiatives in its long-range program, including: (1) extension of intercity commuter rail from Denver to Colorado Springs and Pueblo;

(2) projects to extend intercity rail service throughout Colorado and to Cheyenne, Wyoming, and El Paso, Texas; and (3) high-speed rail projects with highest priority being the line from the Denver metropolitan area to the Eagle County Airport, just west of Vail, along the I-70 mountain corridor.[90] While these projects have been identified in the plan, it is not at all clear how the funding and financing would be generated to build the lines and operate the services. To help address these questions, the Colorado legislature in May 2017 created the Southwest Chief and Front Range Passenger Rail Commission, charged with preserving and expanding Amtrak's Southwest Chief service through southeastern Colorado as well as drafting legislation to facilitate the development of a Front Range passenger rail service in and along the Interstate 25 corridor.[91] The momentum for developing rail passenger service along the I-25 corridor is building, and as the region continues to grow and traffic congestion worsens, the pressure to develop rail alternatives will increase.

*   *   *

Similar to other metropolitan areas in the United States, the Denver metropolitan area has experienced significant suburban and exurban growth since at least the 1950s, which has created challenges for regional governance and collaboration. While the City and County of Denver accounted for nearly 75 percent of the region's population in 1950, it accounted for only 25 percent by 1990. Growth in outlying Adams, Arapahoe, Boulder, Broomfield, Douglas, and Jefferson Counties, including the suburban municipalities of Aurora, Lakewood, Thornton, Westminster, Arvada, and Centennial, and the freestanding community of Boulder, has outstripped that of the central city during this time. This shift in regional population has created a need for interjurisdictional collaboration across a variety of issues including transportation, land use, air quality, economic development, water supply and treatment, and waste disposal. Despite efforts to address regional problems through regional associations, such as the Denver Regional Council of Governments (DRCOG) and the Regional Transportation District (RTD), the Denver area historically had been characterized by fragmentation and discord, with only limited successes in establishing regional collaboration.

Since 1990, however, efforts at regional collaboration have been much more successful. The creation of the Metro Mayors Caucus in 1993, and the expanded role of the Denver Metro Chamber of Commerce, together with a more effective DRCOG and RTD, led directly to progress on regional issues of transportation, land use, economic development, and air quality. The 1988 vote in Adams County to allow Denver to annex land to build Denver International Airport was an important breakthrough in developing a stronger regional consciousness. DRCOG's Metro Vision 2020 smart growth plan was another major initiative that led to the Mile High Compact, in which forty-five cities and counties have agreed to incorporate regional growth boundary/area limits into their master/comprehensive plans, and to support the development of an intermodal transportation system. Agreement on Metro Vision was an important precursor to the regional support developed for the RTD FasTracks program in 2004. At the same time, the growth of the Front Range urban corridor, extending from Fort Collins to the north to Pueblo to the south, and the I-70 mountain corridor west of Denver, has created a need for interjurisdictional planning within this extended megaregion.

Chapter 6

Sustainable Futures

Contemporary urban development in the United States and, to some extent, the rest of the world, is torn between two paradigms. On the one hand, post-1950 style suburbanization and exurbanization, facilitated by increasing automobile use and expanded highway systems, continues to be a dominant paradigm, as measured by increasing urban land cover, vehicle miles traveled, and new edge-city developments on the urban fringe. But at the same time, there has been a surge of interest in sustainable urban growth, featuring concepts such as smart growth, new urbanism, growth management, affordable housing, in-fill and transit-oriented development, and urban growth boundaries. Many cities and metropolitan areas have adopted plans and policies that promote one or more of these aspirational visions for the city of the future.[1]

A particularly good example of this changing paradigm is found in Denver, which exhibits a historical legacy as a sprawling cow town at the same time that it espouses an eco-friendly vision of new urbanist developments and a growing commitment to rail transit and transit-oriented development. In 2004, metro-area voters approved a 122-mile expansion of the rail transit system as part of the Regional Transportation District's FasTracks program, which laid the foundation for an aggressive transit-oriented development initiative in the City and County of Denver and other metro-area jurisdictions. But despite these efforts, the continued popularity of very low density one- to forty-acre "ranchettes" on the urban fringe creates a mixed and contradictory image of the Denver region. The case of Denver is important because it represents a significant effort by a relatively large U.S. metropolitan region to change its urban growth trajectory from continuing low-density sprawl to higher-density, mixed-use, and transit-oriented urban centers. In recognition that the status quo is neither desirable nor sustainable, Denver has been able to forge a consensus for action that can serve as a reference for other metropolitan regions facing similar issues.

This chapter is organized as follows. After a theoretical section discusses some of the relevant themes and concepts that relate directly to sustainable futures, Denver's experience with growth control and smart growth is presented. A focus on post-1950s suburban growth in Denver serves to provide the context for the 1970s growth control movement, which found fertile ground in the Denver area. This period proved to be an important precursor to the post-1990s smart growth phase, which has featured a new Metro Vision, new redevelopment projects, and a new commitment to rail transit and transit-oriented development.

Competing Urban Growth Paradigms

The dominant urban growth paradigm since at least 1945 in the United States has been decentralized suburban growth, characterized by low-density development in newly urbanizing areas on the metropolitan fringe facilitated by automobiles and highway transportation.[2] Terms, models, and concepts such as multiple-nuclei cities, Fordist suburbs, urban realms, the outer city, the galactic metropolis, suburban downtowns, edge cities, the peripheral city, splintering urbanism, and edgeless cities have all been used to describe various aspects of the suburbanization process.[3] The economic, political, social, cultural, and technological forces that have combined to support suburban development have been powerful and successful in terms of profitability and popular appeal. Numerous industries have benefited tremendously from suburban growth, and the suburban population has enjoyed a substantial improvement in the quality of life as compared to the pre-1945 period.

But the individual quality-of-life improvements associated with suburbanization have come with increasing economic, social, and environmental costs due to the sprawling nature of this development.[4] According to a report from Smart Growth America, urban sprawl is defined as a process whereby the spread of development across the landscape far outpaces population growth. Urban sprawl is characterized by: (1) widely dispersed population in low-density development, (2) rigidly separated residential, commercial, and employment land uses, (3) a network of roads that creates huge blocks and subdivisions that limit accessibility, and (4) a lack of town centers or major activity nodes.[5] Studies have shown that there are considerable costs associated with urban sprawl including higher energy costs, especially gasoline consumption, higher levels of traffic congestion, increased water consumption, and the need to provide additional infrastructure (transportation, electrical, water, sewer systems) and public facilities (schools, fire, police, libraries) to newly developed areas.[6] There are also considerable environmental costs associated with sprawling development including increased greenhouse gas emissions, air pollution, water pollution, flooding, noise, erosion, loss of prime agricultural land, loss of open space and wetlands, loss of scenic amenities, and habitat encroachment. Urban sprawl has been implicated in declining public health in the United States as people who live in counties with sprawl-style development have higher rates of obesity and higher blood pressure.[7]

In response to the realization of the costs of urban sprawl and limited alternatives to suburban-style development, many city planners, developers, architects, and advocacy groups have been espousing a "smart growth" approach to urbanization. Relying on concepts such as new urbanism, in-fill development, affordable housing, historic preservation, transit-oriented development, and urban growth boundaries, the main thrust of the smart growth movement is to encourage more high-density development in already urbanized areas that contain a mix of land uses close enough together to encourage more walking, biking, and public transit use. New urbanism, a leitmotiv of smart growth,[8] features higher-density, mixed-use neotraditional neighborhoods with sidewalks and narrower streets and is viewed as a viable alternative to suburban sprawl, providing residents and workers a greater choice of lifestyle options that do not depend exclusively on automobile use and long-distance travel to access needed activities. It has been estimated that the savings from a controlled-growth scenario as opposed to uncontrolled growth in the United States for the period 2000–2025 include four million acres saved from conversion to urban land, $12.6 billion saved in water and sewer infrastructure costs, $109.7 billion saved in road infrastructure costs, and 49.6 million daily vehicle miles not traveled, which would result in substantially improved air quality and significantly lower greenhouse gas emissions.[9]

In a seminal paper, Burchell, Listokin, and Galley analyze the smart growth movement in contrast to previous urban policies and find that while it echoes previous efforts such as urban renewal, inner-area revitalization, growth control, and growth management, it also emphasizes newer approaches such as new urbanist design innovations and a much stronger commitment to multimodal transportation.[10] The proponents of smart growth have also been able to learn from previous mistakes in urban policy, while a much broader coalition, including large segments of governments at all levels, the public-at-large, and the development community have come together in support of smart growth.

A distinguishing characteristic of smart growth has been its acceptance and embrace of neoliberal approaches to urban redevelopment, featuring public-private partnerships, and in many cases private sector–led development. Krueger and Gibbs maintain that smart growth represents a "third wave" of sustainability initiatives in the United States after the growth control efforts of the 1970s, and growth management in the 1980s.[11] While some growth control and growth management measures were criticized for being "antibusiness," many smart growth initiatives have explicitly included the business community. Smart growth builds on but is different from the previous waves, especially in its emphasis on a market-based approach to limit sprawl and encourage in-fill development. Furthermore, the transition from growth control to smart growth can be seen as part of a broader shift in American political economy away from government intervention and regulatory control toward market solutions, deregulation, and public-private partnerships.

Support for the smart growth movement can also be explained by the rise of "new regionalist" approaches in urban development.[12] Eschewing the top-down approach of U.S. federal policies in support of regional governments and regional planning, the new regionalism has emphasized a bottom-up approach, featuring informal networks of local government, business, and citizen advocacy groups to forge coalitions in support of regional policies (see Chapter 5). Support for many smart growth policies has been a product of nontraditional new regionalist networks.[13]

U.S. cities are notorious for their automobile dependency, high energy consumption, and high carbon emissions per capita,[14] but many of the largest U.S. cities are trying to change these patterns by starting new or expanding existing rail transit systems and encouraging transit-oriented development (TOD). Reconnecting America has identified a total of 643 potential new fixed-guideway projects in 106 metropolitan regions.[15] Of these projects, 138 are in the construction and engineering phase that will yield 1,464 miles of new transit. Most of the cities with these projects have witnessed an upsurge in interest for residential, office, and retail development in areas directly served by their rail transit systems. Demographic changes, frustration with motor vehicle traffic congestion, high gasoline prices, and other factors are creating strong demand for housing, retail, and offices in walkable, mixed-use neighborhoods close to transit.[16]

But while some communities have embraced transit-oriented development and other smart growth principles, other metropolitan areas have been less enamored by these initiatives and have preferred to continue growing in a more low-density, auto-dependent fashion. The Denver metropolitan area represents an interesting case study that has embraced smart growth planning but still exemplifies both paradigms of urban growth.

Post-1950 Suburbanization and the 1970s Growth Control Movement

As already detailed in Chapter 3, population growth in the Denver metropolitan area increased significantly after 1950, as the region experienced a typical U.S. postwar suburbanization process. Colorado having been home to a number of military bases during World War II, many veterans who were stationed in Denver or Colorado moved to Denver after the war, thus contributing to substantial population in-migration. Denver also benefited from its location and orientation as a Sunbelt city, with its dynamic economy and quality of life attracting population especially from the U.S. Midwest and Northeast. The availability of Federal Housing Administration and Veterans Administration long-term low-interest mortgages helped to fuel the suburban housing boom, along with increased automobile ownership and construction of interstate highways. In 1950, Denver's urbanized population was just under 500,000, of which 416,000 (83 percent) lived in the city of Denver. By 1990, the urbanized population had expanded more than threefold to over 1.5 million, of which only 467,000 (31 percent) lived in the City and County of Denver. The total urbanized land grew more than fourfold from 105 to 459 square miles during that same time period, thus resulting in a more sprawling urban landscape.[17]

While the Denver metropolitan area was sprawling outward during the 1950–90 period, there were some countermovements that began to sow the seeds of development alternatives to the low-density suburban and exurban model. The first rumblings of dissent occurred in the late 1960s and 1970s as part of the nationwide growth control and environmental movement that produced groundbreaking legislation such as the National Environmental Policy Act of 1969, which created the Environmental Impact Statement process, and the cabinet-level Environmental Protection Agency, which was created through an executive order by President Nixon in 1970. That was followed by federal legislation regulating air quality, water quality, the use of coastal zones, the disposal of hazardous and toxic wastes, and other aspects of the natural environment. In land use planning, states began to impose growth controls on local development to protect critical areas as part of the so-called Quiet Revolution.[18] A number of rapidly growing and higher-income municipalities and counties began to enact different measures to curb residential growth, such as limiting residential permits or requiring that developers bear more of the costs of growth. By the 1970s, Colorado was developing a reputation as a more eco-friendly, slow growth area. For example, the city of Boulder enacted growth control measures starting in 1976 that sought to limit residential growth to no more than 2 percent per year.[19]

In Denver, a movement led by a Colorado state representative Richard Lamm opposed the hosting of the 1976 Winter Olympics based on environmental and financial concerns, and a general uneasiness about the pace and character of growth in Denver and the nearby mountain areas. In a 1972 referendum, Colorado voters rejected hosting the Winter Olympics, the only time in history that a city has turned down an invitation from the International Olympic Committee to host the Olympic games. On the heels of this movement, Lamm was elected governor of Colorado in 1974. In 1977, he stopped plans for a circumferential interstate beltway to be built around Denver, citing concerns about sprawl and automobile dependency during a period in which an energy crisis had driven gasoline prices to record high levels. Lamm vowed to "drive a silver spike" into the heart of the I-470 beltway project to kill the proposal, though many other constituencies in the metropolitan area were strongly in favor of the project.[20] Eventually pieces of the beltway did spring back to life in the 1980s in the form of the C-470 state highway and in the 1990s and 2000s as public-private toll roads E-470 and the Northwest Parkway.

While the growth control movement had some impact in Colorado and some other states in the 1970s, a neoliberal anticontrol backlash typified federal, state, and local policies in the 1980s. The regional economy in Denver and Colorado during the 1970s benefited from the activities of energy exploration companies that sought to expand their operations in the oil and gas fields of Colorado, Wyoming, and other western states as a result of high energy prices at that time. But just as quickly as the boom occurred, by the early 1980s, the price of oil and gas began to plummet owing to new sources being developed throughout the world. In 1982, Exxon announced that it was pulling out of its western Colorado oil shale project and closed its Denver office, thus initiating a series of energy company closures in Colorado. By the mid-1980s, Denver proper was actually losing population, and attention turned away from growth control to prodevelopment strategies. Efforts to reinvigorate the state and city economies included the construction of large public projects such as Denver International Airport, the Colorado Convention Center in downtown Denver, and Coors Field in the Lower Downtown (LoDo) area. Coors Field was built for the Colorado Rockies baseball team, which started playing in 1993, supporting Denver's major league sports credentials, twenty years after rejecting the Winter Olympics. Plans for building a circumferential beltway around the metropolitan area were resurrected and paved the way for new suburban residential and commercial ventures, such as the massive Highlands Ranch development in Douglas County, which eventually grew to a population of nearly one hundred thousand by 2010 (see Chapter 3). Other areas in the nearby foothills and mountain communities were similarly impacted from highway construction, thus expanding the urban footprint.

1990–2010: Smart Growth, New Urbanism, and Regional Planning

The economic downturn lasted only a short while, and by the early 1990s, Denver was growing again. There was a large spike in population migration from California in the early 1990s in the wake of several major earthquakes in California, the Rodney King incident in Los Angeles, and subsequent fallout from these events. Depressed real estate prices in Denver proved to be an inviting catalyst that prompted many Californians and others to discover the natural amenities and relatively high quality of life in the Denver area. The 1990s population boom was also a result of a more diversified economic base that benefited from the development projects started in the late 1980s. The Denver metro area grew by 30.7 percent during the 1990s, thus leading to a reconsideration of how growth should be best accommodated in the future.

As a result of a growing regional consensus in the early 1990s to address numerous growth-related factors that were impacting the Denver region (see Chapter 5), the Denver Regional Council of Governments (DRCOG) embarked on its Metro Vision planning process. First, analyses indicated that if development were to expand to the limits allowed within the land-use plans of every county and municipality in the region, the composite build-out would exceed one thousand square miles for an area that at that time covered only five hundred square miles. Second, as a result of the tightening of air quality restrictions as identified in the Clean Air Act Amendments of 1990, the Denver region faced significant problems for noncompliance of air quality standards. Denver had a notorious "brown-cloud" air pollution problem in the 1970s and 1980s that was a result of increased particulates and temperature inversion smog especially during the winter months (see Chapter 1). Third, compounding the air quality problem, both vehicle miles traveled and traffic congestion were increasing much faster than population growth. And finally, the Denver area was still battling over funding and approval for additional suburban beltways. Even though Colorado's Governor Lamm had initially stopped the I-470 beltway from being constructed in the 1970s, pieces of the beltway eventually were built. In the 1980s, the state of Colorado built C-470 in the southwestern quadrant of the metropolitan area, and a private tolling authority was moving forward to build E-470 in the eastern half of the metropolitan area. DRCOG realized that a coherent vision of the region's future was necessary.

The resulting Metro Vision 2020 plan focused on growth and development, the natural environment, and transportation.[21] The counties and municipalities of the DRCOG region agreed to the concept of a voluntary urban growth boundary/area (UGB/A) that was initially set not to exceed seven hundred square miles.[22] In order to accommodate the expected future growth, there would be a focus on higher-density development in designated urban centers throughout the region. Four outlying communities (Boulder, Longmont, Brighton, and Castle Rock) would remain freestanding communities set apart from the contiguous development of the Denver urbanized area. Special attention was focused on improving air quality in the region by instituting regional clean air programs, including the introduction of ethanol and other oxygenated fuels in area gasoline stations, bans on wood burning, and more frequent street sweeping of sand after winter snowstorms. And most significantly, DRCOG agreed that a regional rail transit system should be built as the backbone of an intermodal transportation system to help focus development in designated urban corridors and centers, to provide transport alternatives to roadway traffic congestion, and to improve air quality.

Regional support for the smart growth–oriented Metro Vision plan was much more broadly based than support for the growth control measures of the 1970s. The most important difference was the support of business and civic organizations for the smart growth plan. The Denver Metro Chamber of Commerce, composed of over three thousand metropolitan area businesses, and other regional business associations have been supportive of many elements in Metro Vision, especially measures to improve air quality and traffic congestion. The mayors and county commissioners have also been unified in support and have forged new regional alliances through organizations such as the Metro Mayors Caucus (MMC). The MMC was formed in 1993 as a voluntary, consensus-based organization focused on addressing issues of regional importance. The mayors felt that there was a need for a more cooperative and collaborative forum to exchange ideas and viewpoints outside of the more traditional and confrontational arenas.[23] The MMC and the Chamber of Commerce promoted a more cohesive vision for the region than had previous planning efforts, which had been typified by discord and parochialism (see Chapter 5).

While a regional consensus about economic development and growth was starting to emerge, the City and County of Denver had already begun to implement several of the ideas contained in the Metro Vision 2020 plan, including the redevelopment of downtown Denver. In 1982, Denver closed off its Sixteenth Street downtown retail district to automobile traffic and created a pedestrian mall with natural gas–fueled buses providing frequent service. The Sixteenth Street Mall has been successful in maintaining a retail base in downtown Denver and has continued as a central corridor for commercial, office, convention, and tourist activity.

The commercial core of Upper Downtown Denver (closer to the Colorado state capitol building and Civic Center Park) went through a period of urban renewal in the 1960s and 1970s when many new high-rise office buildings were built with the support of the Denver Urban Renewal Authority Skyline District. Lower Downtown Denver (LoDo) (closer to Denver Union Station and the South Platte River) had been the main warehouse and rail station area that boomed during the period of railroad dominance from the 1870s to the 1930s, but it had declined substantially during the era of interstate highways, trucking, and air transportation. By the 1950s, LoDo was already a classic "zone-in-transition" area of the city, containing many flop-houses and skid-row activities.[24] But LoDo was initially excluded from the Denver urban renewal district, thus many of its old red-brick warehouse buildings were not demolished to build new high-rises. Instead, by the 1980s, historic preservation groups, led by Dana Crawford, realized and publicized the unique character of the buildings in LoDo, and they played a critical role in the 1986 Downtown Area Plan, which identified LoDo as a "sensitive" and "vulnerable" section of downtown, and which sought to "protect its historic character by preserving the existing buildings."[25] In the late 1980s, the success of a few pioneering businesses, including the Wynkoop brewpub started by John Hickenlooper (who later became mayor of Denver and governor of Colorado), sparked a revival of this moribund area and initiated one of the most impressive transformations of a downtown district of any city in the United States. In 1990, because of the historic preservation movement and the early pioneering businesses, the owners of the Colorado Rockies expansion baseball team decided to build the Coors Field baseball park in LoDo, thus catalyzing tremendous real estate development in the form of restaurants, nightclubs, and residential lofts throughout LoDo during the 1990s and 2000s. The district has become a major destination for residents and visitors alike, and one of the busiest and most popular areas of the city.

As detailed in Chapter 2, the City and County of Denver decided in the mid-1980s to build the new Denver International Airport and to close Stapleton Airport to all aviation activity. In 1995, Stapleton Airport was closed, and Denver proposed to redevelop the forty-seven-hundred-acre former airport site into a mixed-use development based on Peter Calthorpe's new urbanist principles as reflected in the Stapleton Development Plan (a.k.a. the "Green Book"). Planners and builders supported a wide range of housing styles from apartments, townhomes, and rowhouses to larger single-family dwellings that would result in Stapleton becoming a mixed-income neighborhood with substantial affordable housing. These same groups also pressed for more schools to be built to encourage more families to move there. In 1998, Denver hired Forest City Enterprises to lead the massive redevelopment effort, which was expected to occur over a long time horizon. As of 2010, Stapleton had nearly ten thousand residents, six schools, and more than two hundred shops, restaurants, and services.[26] The full build-out calls for twelve thousand residential units, ten million square feet of office space, three million square feet of retail space, and eleven hundred acres of parks and open space.[27] Stapleton is already one of the largest urban in-fill projects in the United States, and it has received several national and international awards for sustainable urban development.

In Lakewood, a major suburb just west of Denver, the Villa Italia retail mall, which had opened in 1966, had entered a period of decline by the mid-1990s. The city of Lakewood contracted with developers Continuum Partners in the late 1990s to redevelop the old mall into a shopping, dining, entertainment, and residential district called Belmar that was expected to become the "new downtown" for Lakewood. Construction started in 2002, and as of 2010, there were over seventy shops and services, fifteen dining options, a 1.1-acre central plaza, a 2.1-acre urban square park, and fifteen hundred residents living in apartments, condominiums, and townhomes.[28] The design is based on a traditional downtown area with three- to four-story buildings, wide sidewalks, narrow grid streets, and both onstreet and offstreet parking (Figure 25).

An effort to expand growth management planning throughout Colorado, however, was not as successful. In 2000, the Colorado Voter Approval

Figure 25. The Belmar "new urbanist" redevelopment of a former shopping mall in the suburb of Lakewood, featuring pedestrian-oriented commercial, office, and residential activity. (Image source: Andrew R. Goetz.)

of Growth Act (Amendment 24) sought to change the State of Colorado Constitution by requiring voter approval of growth area maps that identified areas for future development in counties greater than ten thousand population and cities and towns greater than one thousand population. These jurisdictions would also have been required to identify "committed areas" where growth would be allowed to occur without voter approval, and to provide information to voters about the impacts of proposed growth. Despite strong support from the Colorado Public Interest Research Group (COPIRG), the Sierra Club, and other environmental organizations, Amendment 24 was defeated in November 2000 by a 70–30 margin. Key to the measure's defeat was vigorous opposition from the development industry within and outside Colorado, exemplified by a $6 million advertising campaign to influence voters to reject the amendment.[29] Since then, smart growth efforts have largely been confined to the local or regional scale, and mostly in Denver, other Front Range cities, and fast-growing mountain communities.

The most ambitious smart growth project in the metropolitan area has been the Regional Transportation District (RTD) FasTracks program, which will add 122 miles of light and commuter rail transit and 18 miles of bus rapid transit in six corridors radiating outward from a redeveloped Union Station. Before discussing the FasTracks plan, an overview of how rail transit declined and was reintroduced in Denver is provided.

The Decline and Reintroduction of Rail Transit in Denver

In its early years, Denver entrepreneurs started horse railway services within the city, which eventually were converted to electric streetcars in the 1880s. A number of private companies, such as the Denver City Railway Company; the Denver Electric and Cable Company; the Denver, Lakewood, and Golden Railway; and the Denver and Northwestern Railway started intra- and interurban services during the 1885–1901 period.[30] By 1914, all these railway companies had been merged to form the Denver Tramway Company, which operated streetcar service until 1950.[31]

From the 1880s through the 1920s, electric streetcars were the dominant form of intraurban transportation in nearly all large U.S. cities, but from the 1920s onward, private automobiles began to take over a larger percentage of urban travel and effectively spelled the end for most streetcar systems. Only the very largest cities, which had built subway, elevated rail, or metro systems (e.g., New York, Boston, Philadelphia, Chicago) and a few other cities were able to maintain some form of rail transit during the period of automobile dominance. From the 1920s to the 1950s many cities, including Denver, shut down their streetcar systems, replacing them with motor bus services. By the 1960s, most transit companies were facing financial difficulties, and many of these services were transferred to cities or regional public agencies. In 1971, the bus operations of the Denver Tramway Company were sold to the City and County of Denver. Two years before that, the Colorado General Assembly had created the Regional Transportation District (RTD) to "develop, maintain, and operate a mass transportation system," and it provided RTD with the ability to levy a sales tax for its funding support.[32] In 1973, a 0.5 percent sales tax measure to develop a regional transit system was approved by voters. In 1974, RTD acquired all the ongoing bus services from the City and County of Denver.

Once RTD became the principal transit operator in the region, several plans were formulated in the 1970s and 1980s to develop a rail transit system. In 1972, RTD proposed to build a ninety-eight-mile personal rapid-transit system that would have entailed the use of twelve-person vehicles to run on an aerial track providing nonstop, demand-responsive service based on passengers' input regarding choice of destination. A funding application for $1.06 billion (1973 dollars) was submitted to the Urban Mass Transportation Administration (UMTA), which subsequently rejected the proposal in 1975. In 1976, RTD redrafted a plan based on a slightly different automated rapid-transit system technology that would feature eighty miles of fixed guideways, not aerial tracks, on which twelve- to twenty-passenger vehicles would operate. RTD again applied to UMTA for federal funding, but the $1.77 billion plan was rejected. According to UMTA, Denver was seen as "an automobile-dominated city with congestion not yet severe enough to warrant federal investment."[33]

Still, RTD continued to press the case for rail transit. In 1980, RTD put together another regional transit plan that focused on building a light rail line in the Southeast Corridor paralleling Interstate 25 from the Denver central business district (CBD) south to Arapahoe Road, as part of a seventy-three-mile system. Instead of submitting an application for federal funding, this time the RTD board decided to place a referendum on the November 1980 ballot to increase the regional sales tax by 0.75 percent for fourteen years in order to build the Southeast Corridor and five other regional corridors. Despite early polls that suggested the measure would be approved, voters ultimately denied the referendum 54 percent to 46 percent. At the same time, voters also approved an initiative that required elections for RTD board members, rather than board appointments by mayors and county commissioners.[34]

After this stinging defeat, RTD did not initiate any transit referenda during the rest of the 1980s. Instead, several scaled-back plans were drafted that at least kept alive the possibility of rail transit development in the future. But as some political leaders and area businesses expressed their concerns about worsening traffic congestion and air quality, the Colorado General Assembly grew impatient with the lack of action by RTD and, in 1987, promulgated House Bill 1249, which created a private-oriented entity, the Transit Construction Authority (TCA), to design and build a rail transit line between downtown Denver and the Denver Technological Center edge-city development along the southeast I-25 corridor. As a part of this bill, the General Assembly directed RTD to develop plans for rapid transit in seven additional corridors. The resulting sixty-mile regional system proposed by RTD was called the Fastrack Program but did not include the TCA's Southeast Corridor.[35] Instead, RTD proposed the Southwest Corridor along Santa Fe Drive as the preferred initial corridor to be developed. Both RTD and TCA applied for federal funding to conduct feasibility analyses of their preferred alternatives, but because federal regulations allowed only one feasibility analysis per metropolitan area at a time, the area's metropolitan planning organization, the Denver Regional Council of Governments (DRCOG), was asked to compare the two corridors to determine which one was better suited for transit.[36] The resulting *Southeast/Southwest Transit Threshold Analysis* identified the Southwest Corridor as more cost-effective.[37] TCA folded shortly thereafter, while RTD requested funding from UMTA for an alternatives analysis in the Southwest Corridor, which was granted in 1991. Still concerned about the state of transportation in the region and skeptical of the ability of both DRCOG and RTD to forge a regional consensus, Colorado governor Roy Romer and the General Assembly created yet another entity, the Metropolitan Transportation Development Commission, "to develop a comprehensive, regional solution to transportation problems plaguing the metropolitan area."[38] The report concluded that "they [the public] don't trust government and they don't have a lot of faith that they will get their money's worth. That seems to be why they favor a new governing authority, and why they want some form of continuing public monitoring process."[39]

In addition to suggested roadway improvements, there was a rail transit plan contained in this report that was essentially the same as the RTD plan from 1987.

By the end of the 1980s, there was increasing interest in developing a rail transit system, but infighting between rival agencies and authorities clouded the picture. Members of the political and business communities had become skeptical of the ability of RTD to develop an effective regional transportation system. Frequent concerns were raised about the elected board members of RTD, with claims that "RTD managed to attract a string of candidates known for personal problems and political gaffes," including several convicted felons and outright opponents of public transit.[40] The RTD board developed a negative reputation that cast a shadow over everything that RTD tried to do. In 1990, the Colorado General Assembly passed Senate Bill 208 (SB 208), which required approval by the relevant metropolitan planning organization of the financing and technology for all proposed fixed-guideway projects in the state.[41] This was yet another sign of the skepticism the state legislature had toward RTD's ability to plan and deliver a rail transit system.

As the 1990s began, the Denver region began to experience another population growth surge, with many new residents arriving especially from California. Traffic congestion and air quality continued to worsen, and demands for regional transportation solutions grew louder. While the decision to build a new airport (Denver International Airport) was ratified in the late 1980s, some observers suggested that a regional rail transit system was actually a more pressing transportation need.[42]

In light of these pressures, RTD continued to explore rail transit alternatives. At the same time that RTD requested federal funding for an alternatives analysis for the Southwest Corridor, they conducted the *Northeast Corridor Alternative Alignment Study*, which recommended a 7.5-mile light rail line from downtown Denver to Stapleton Airport. As a result of public input and opposition from neighborhoods in northeast Denver, the proposed line was scaled back to a terminus at Thirtieth and Downing Streets in the Five Points neighborhood just outside of the Denver CBD, instead of Stapleton Airport. The renamed Metro Area Connection (MAC) line was also proposed to extend south of downtown to Broadway and I-25 to cover a total distance of 5.3 miles. In 1989, the RTD board had directed that "a separate account be established to receive all funds due RTD from the imposition of the Use Tax, and that all revenues in this fund be set aside for construction of rapid transit,"[43] which was then dedicated to building the MAC line as a demonstration project.[44] In

1991, the board also earmarked $40 million from unrestricted funds of its investment portfolio to the MAC line to allow construction to begin in 1992 subsequent to approval from DRCOG, as part of the SB 208 process.[45] Soon after construction began, the name of the project was changed to the Central Corridor light rail line to "represent the project's role in a larger, regional system."[46] On October 7, 1994, the Central Corridor became the first light rail transit line to open in Denver since the era of the electric streetcars.

Meanwhile, planning continued for the Southwest Corridor with the completion of the federally funded Alternatives Analysis/Major Investment Study in 1994 in which light rail was selected as the preferred alternative. In 1995, the Preliminary Engineering/Environmental Impact Statement (EIS) was completed, and $3.9 million in federal funds were allocated for final design work, pending approval of the EIS by the Federal Transit Administration (FTA). After the EIS was approved, in 1997 the FTA authorized $120 million in a federal full funding grant agreement to begin constructing a light rail line in this corridor with a target completion date in the year 2000.

While RTD finally achieved some success with the completion of the Central Corridor and the beginning of the Southwest Corridor light rail lines, planning continued on other corridors previously identified in its regional plan. In 1995, Clarence (Cal) Marsella was hired as general manager of RTD, and he aggressively sought to expand rapid transit in the Denver region. In 1997, Marsella and RTD proposed a long-term comprehensive plan called "Guide the Ride," which sought to expand rapid-transit service by one hundred miles using a combination of light rail, commuter rail, and bus/carpool lanes in the major corridors. The proposed $6 billion plan would be funded by a 0.4 percent hike in the regional sales tax in a referendum that was presented to voters in November 1997. While Marsella and the RTD staff received support for the Guide the Ride plan from many political and business leaders in the region, including the Transit '97 coalition that formed to support the campaign, the RTD board was sharply divided on the issue. One board member, Jon Caldara, actually led the campaign against Guide the Ride, while board chairman Ben Klein and board member Jack McCroskey actively feuded with other board members, RTD staff, Transit '97, and each other over a litany of issues.[47] The voting public was once again left with the impression that the RTD board was split and dysfunctional, and that RTD could not be trusted with $6 billion of public money to build a rapid-transit system. Concerns were also expressed that too many ambiguities remained regarding the specific technologies to be employed in each of the corridors. Despite early polls showing public support, the Guide the Ride referendum was defeated 58 percent to 42 percent.

After the defeat of Guide the Ride in 1997, RTD continued to work on rail transit development in an incremental fashion. After the full funding grant agreement from the FTA was received in 1997, construction began on the 8.7-mile Southwest Corridor extending along an existing freight railroad right-of-way from the I-25 and Broadway terminus of the Central Corridor south through the suburb of Englewood to its eventual terminus at Mineral Avenue in the suburb of Littleton. This was the first light rail line to extend to some of Denver's suburbs and was seen as being a real test case of light rail's viability in Denver. The Southwest Corridor was completed in summer 2000 on time and within its $177 million budget. Projected to carry eight thousand four hundred passengers per weekday in 2002, it averaged nearly eighteen thousand passengers per weekday that year.[48]

In 1999, RTD approved a plan to add to the Central Corridor by creating a short spur through the Central Platte Valley (CPV) from the Auraria station (campus for the University of Colorado at Denver, Metropolitan State University, and Community College of Denver) to Union Station in Lower Downtown (LoDo) Denver. The CPV line would connect major sports and entertainment venues such as Sports Authority Field at Mile High (Denver Broncos football and outdoor concerts), the Pepsi Center (Denver Nuggets basketball, Colorado Avalanche hockey, and indoor concerts), Six Flags Elitch Gardens Amusement Park, and Coors Field (Colorado Rockies baseball). Public and private funds totaling $47 million were combined to build the 1.8-mile spur. Construction began in 2001, and the spur was completed in 2002.

As RTD focused its efforts on the Central and Southwest Corridors, and while the ill-fated TCA effort collapsed in 1990, little attention was given by RTD to the Southeast Corridor along I-25. But in 1995, a major investment study for the Southeast Corridor was begun by the Colorado Department of Transportation (CDOT), and in 1996, the study recommended that a light-rail line was the most appropriate solution. Governor Roy Romer supported the light rail recommendation and, with the help of the legislature, appropriated state funds for preliminary engineering and environmental impact assessment. He also supported the dedication of $340 million of state funds to help build the line, if $510 million of federal funds could also be obtained.[49] But in November 1998, Bill Owens was elected governor of Colorado, and he withdrew the commitment for state light rail funding, instead supporting a highway-widening option for I-25. After considerable discussion and negotiation among the governor's office, CDOT, RTD, DRCOG, and local municipalities, a new plan was formulated that included both light rail and highway-widening in the Southeast Corridor. The highway widening portion of the project was proposed as one of twenty-eight statewide transportation projects that would be funded through the issuance of Transportation Revenue Anticipation Notes (TRANS bonds) based on future federal transportation dollars. The light rail portion of the project would be funded through bonding from sales tax revenues, federal funds from the FTA, and local matching funds.[50] Both bond initiatives were placed before state voters in November 1999, and, with broad-based political and business support, they were both approved. In 2000, the FTA provided a $525 million full funding grant agreement for the nineteen-mile Southeast Corridor light rail line, which would extend from the Broadway and I-25 terminus of the Central Corridor southeast along the I-25 corridor to the I-225 interchange at the Denver Tech Center, terminating at Lincoln Avenue in suburban Douglas County. The line would also extend along the I-225 corridor northeast to the Nine Mile station at Parker Road. In 2001, a consortium of private-sector engineering and construction firms (Southeast Corridor Constructors) was awarded a design-build contract for the project, which was renamed the Transportation Expansion (T-REX) project, and construction began shortly thereafter. T-REX became one of the largest transportation projects in the United States at that time and was distinctive because of its design-build feature, which allowed the private contractors the flexibility to make small design changes as the project unfolded, thus making the construction process more efficient and saving both time and money. Upon completion in 2006, the $1.67 billion project was 3 percent under budget and was finished twenty-two months ahead of the projected completion date. While initial passenger estimates called for 38,100 riders per day by 2020, actual daily ridership in 2015 was over 43,000.[51]

In spite of voter disapproval of the Guide the Ride plan in 1997, RTD was nevertheless able to build thirty-five miles of light rail transit in an incremental fashion from 1994 to 2006 in the form of the Central, Southwest, and Southeast Corridor rail lines. Each of these lines was built on time and within budget, with actual ridership exceeding projections. Historically skeptical of RTD's ability to build and operate a rail transit system, political and business leaders, as well as the general public, began to change their impression of RTD and also began to believe in the viability of rail transit in Denver. In the face

of continued population and employment growth in Denver, traffic congestion continued to be a major problem. The annual Urban Mobility Report
produced by the Texas Transportation Institute found that in the early 2000s
Denver was experiencing some of the worst traffic congestion in the country.
Increasingly, metro-area residents perceived that rail transit could be a useful
strategy to provide alternative mobility options to congested highways.

_____

The FasTracks Plan

Sensing that the Denver metropolitan area was ready to support a major
build-out of the rail transit system, Cal Marsella and the newly elected pro-
rail transit RTD board developed a plan in the early 2000s that would dramatically expand the system. The so-called FasTracks plan proposed a major
expansion of transit facilities throughout the region over a ten-year period,
including:

1) Construction of 122 miles of light and commuter rail transit along six
   new travel corridors and extension of the three existing corridors together with an eighteen-mile bus rapid-transit line along U.S. 36 from
   Denver to Boulder (see Figure 26). The six new rail transit corridors
   included:
   a. the 12.1-mile light rail West Line to Lakewood and Golden
   b. the 11.2-mile electric commuter rail Gold Line to Arvada and
      Wheat Ridge
   c. the 41-mile diesel commuter rail Northwest Line to Boulder and
      Longmont
   d. the 18.4-mile electric commuter rail North Metro Line to Commerce
      City, Northglenn, and Thornton
   e. the 22.8-mile electric commuter rail East Line to Denver Inter-
      national Airport, and
   f. the 10.5-mile I-225 light rail line through Aurora connecting the
      Southeast Corridor with the East Corridor
2) Addition of twenty-one thousand new parking spaces. Besides building thirty-one new park-n-rides, spaces would be added to the existing park-n-rides.

3) Improvement in the overall bus network by adding more feeder buses to the rapid-transit stations/stops and by development of FastConnects—transit hubs where the transfer time will be reduced by arrival of the buses and trains at the same time.

4) Remodeling the Denver Union Station into an intermodal hub that would not only connect people to all the rapid-transit lines but also to regional, express, and local buses, the Sixteenth Street Mall shuttle, a new downtown bus circulator, Amtrak intercity rail passenger service, the Ski Train from Denver to Winter Park Ski area, Greyhound Bus services, and a bicycle service center.

5) Improvement of the facilities and amenities provided to passengers at the stations/stops and park-n-rides.

The plan was initially estimated to cost $4.4 billion and would require a 0.4 percent increase in the regional sales tax. When the plan was first announced, Republican governor Bill Owens and state transportation officials were not in favor of the proposed tax hike because of its high cost and the potential negative effects on highway funding.[52] Nevertheless, transit advocates had learned from the mistakes of the Guide the Ride vote in 1997 and were determined to create a stronger coalition in support of FasTracks:

Following all of that political mess in 1997, the actual founding fathers and mothers sat around the table in November and what they decided was we really needed a coalition of key stakeholders who needed to be what I like to call the three pillars of strength to be on the public-private partnership. You needed a public sector that we got through the participation of various cities and counties around the region. But we needed the private sector and they primarily went after the chambers and the economic development groups. The last pieces we needed were those advocates; the environmental community was really not on board for Guide the Ride, nor were they at the table to start to conceptualize how this would change the landscape of metropolitan Denver and what the contribution would be in how we would rebuild all those objectives as organizations. So we were getting all of that diverse group of interests around the table to start to build a more collaborative plan, a more visionary plan, and some of the other key pieces that you needed to go back to [the public], which we did in seven years time.[53]

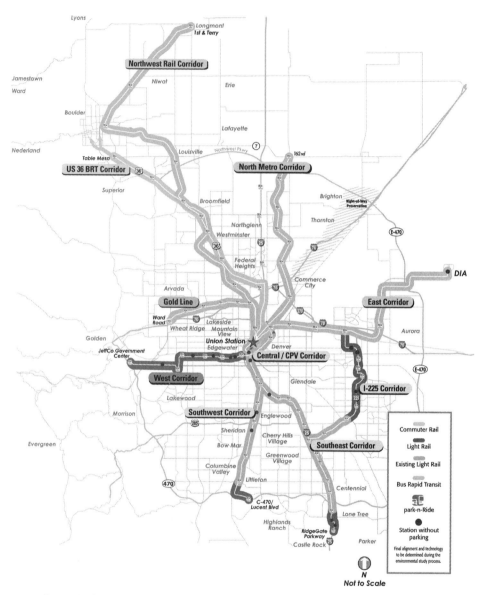

Figure 26. The RTD FasTracks plan. (Source: Regional Transportation District. 2010. FasTracks home page. http://www.rtd-fastracks.com/main_1 [accessed July 19, 2010].)

In November 2004, voters in the RTD area approved by a 57 percent to 43 percent margin a 0.4 percent sales tax increase to fund the $4.7 billion FasTracks expansion.[54] In a metropolitan area that had previously voted down efforts to build a regional rail system in the 1970s, 1980s, and 1990s, the 2004 vote in favor of a vastly expanded rail transit system was a significant departure from the automobile/highway orientation of the postwar period. Residents had become disenchanted with the ever-worsening traffic congestion on the major interstates and arterial roads, and after having seen RTD deliver the Central and Southwest Corridor rail lines on time and under budget, and with actual ridership exceeding projections, they felt that rail transit could provide a more efficient and environmentally friendly mode of urban transportation. The local business community as represented by area chambers of commerce was very supportive of the rail transit expansion, and all thirty-one mayors in the Denver Metro Mayors Caucus also supported the initiative. In addition, the Alliance for Regional Stewardship (cofounded by John Parr, a regional leader from Denver), an affiliate of the American Chambers of Commerce Executives committed to working across regional boundaries, played a strong role in support of FasTracks.

In the years since the 2004 vote, sharp increases in the cost of construction materials plus declining revenues due in part to the 2008–9 economic recession have resulted in a $2.4 billion funding gap to complete the entire program by 2017.[55] In 2011, the Burlington Northern Santa Fe (BNSF) Railroad announced that the cost for RTD to acquire access to the Northwest Corridor rail line would be $535 million, instead of the $66 million that was initially budgeted in 2004.[56] The total cost for the Northwest rail line alone jumped from $461 million in 2004 to $1.7 billion by 2012, and the cost of the entire FasTracks project increased to $7.4 billion by 2012.[57] In response, RTD considered several ways to cut costs, including shortening some of the lines, using single instead of double tracks at the ends of some lines, and lengthening the amount of time to build the system. The RTD board of directors also considered plans to ask voters again to increase the regional sales tax by another 0.4 percent to complete the entire system by 2017 but decided not to place the referendum on the ballot for November 2010, 2011, or 2012 in light of continuing economic concerns.

Instead of seeking another increase in the sales tax, RTD has aggressively pursued public-private partnerships to jump-start most of the FasTracks lines. RTD submitted a proposal in 2007 as part of a U.S. Department

of Transportation pilot program designed to encourage public-private partnerships in transportation projects.[58] The proposed Eagle P-3 project identified three of the FasTracks lines—the 22.8-mile East Line to Denver
International Airport, the 11.2-mile Gold Line northwest to Arvada and
Wheat Ridge, and an initial 6.2-mile segment of the Northwest line to
Westminster—as well as a commuter rail maintenance facility to be built
as part of a Design-Build-Finance-Operate-Maintain contract with a private partner. In 2009, RTD issued a request for proposals and in 2010 selected
Denver Transit Partners—a consortium including Fluor Enterprises, Uber-
ior Investments, Laing Investments, and other companies—for the project.
In 2011, the Eagle P-3 project received a $1.03 billion full funding grant
agreement from the Federal Transit Administration to begin work on the $2.2
billion project. Denver Transit Partners also arranged for $486 million in pri-
vate financing. Construction on the lines began in 2010 and was expected to be
completed by 2016.[59] While the University of Colorado A line[60] to the airport
opened in April 2016, and the B line to Westminster opened in July 2016, the
G line opening to Arvada and Wheat Ridge was delayed to 2018. There have
been software problems with the crossing gates that caused the Federal Railroad Administration not to allow testing to continue on the G line until the
issue is corrected on both the University of Colorado A line and the B line.[61]
The service on the Airport line was also disrupted by several lightning strikes
during summer 2016 that shut down the line for up to seven hours at a time. An
alternative design (a static wire above the overhead catenary system) that could
have been a useful safeguard in this area that is prone to frequent lightning
strikes was not implemented by Denver Transit Partners.[62]

In 2012, RTD received an unsolicited proposal to complete the 10.5-mile
I-225 line as part of a public-private partnership and, after a competitive
bidding process, selected Kiewit Infrastructure Company to complete the line.
Construction began in 2013 with expected completion by 2016.[63] The opening
of the newly named R line was delayed to 2017 owing to a faulty computer
circuit board on the electronic system.[64] In 2013, RTD signed a $343 million
contract with Regional Rail Partners (RRP) to design and build the first thirteen miles of the North Metro rail N line to 124th Avenue to be completed by
2018.[65] In May 2017, RTD and RRP announced that "current construction
challenges" will delay the projected opening of the N line indefinitely.[66]

As of 2017, most of the FasTracks plan has either been completed or is
under construction. In April 2013, the 12.1-mile West (W) line to Lakewood
and Golden was completed. In May 2014, a new regional twenty-two-bay bus

facility behind Union Station was opened, and in July 2014, the newly renovated Union Station was reopened, featuring locally owned restaurants and
the new 112-room Crawford Hotel in the historic building. In 2016, the East
(University of Colorado A) line, the initial segment of the Northwest (B) line,
and the Flatiron Flyer Bus rapid-transit line between Denver and Boulder
opened. In 2017, the I-225 (R) line opened, while the Gold (G) line is expected
to open in 2018. By the early 2020s, 13 miles of the 18.4-mile North Metro
(N) line should be open. The final 5.4 miles of the North Metro line, three
small extensions to the Central, Southwest, and Southeast lines, and 35 miles
of the Northwest (B) Line to Boulder and Longmont remain to be completed
as part of the original FasTracks plan.

Transit-Oriented Development

As espoused in DRCOG's Metro Vision statement, it was expected that a rail
transit system would help shape future growth in the region by encouraging
more high-density transit-oriented development (TOD) in transit corridors
and station areas. To help implement this vision, the City and County of
Denver produced a new land use and transportation plan in 2002 called
"Blueprint Denver," which created a new TOD zoning code allowing higher-
density, mixed-use development to occur in station areas and along transit
corridors. Denver also produced TOD strategic plans in 2006 and 2014,
wherein they developed a TOD Station Typology for the station areas, recognizing that "one size does not fit all."[67] Other metro-area jurisdictions
through which rail transit lines are or will be running have also developed
plans for their station areas.

These planning efforts and increased private-sector real estate interest
has led to a TOD boom in Denver. Development already built or under construction within half a mile of existing or planned station areas include
31,819 residential dwelling units, 7,586 hotel rooms, 8.1 million square feet
of office space, 5.7 million square feet of retail space, and 7.5 million
square of medical space.[68] Most of the development has been built within
the downtown area along the Central Corridor and the Central Platte Valley
lines. This includes a considerable amount of development activity in proximity to Union Station, especially the area between Union Station and the
South Platte River, which is in the midst of a major transformation from
abandoned rail yards into a residential, office, commercial, and recreational

district. Union Station itself has been redeveloped as part of the FasTracks program into an intermodal hub that serves as the focal point for light rail, commuter rail, Amtrak, regional express bus, and intercity bus service, as well as office, retail, hotel, and restaurant development. Outside of the city of Denver, the inner-ring suburb of Englewood redeveloped an old mall into a new transit-oriented development (along the Southwest Corridor) called CityCenter Englewood that now houses the Englewood Civic Center with city offices, courtrooms, and library, along with onsite retail and residential development. And in Aurora (along the I-225 R line corridor), the Anschutz/ Fitzsimons Medical Campus, which is the new home of the University of Colorado Health Sciences Center, has been expanding rapidly with ambitious plans for additional growth in the future. Much of the transit-oriented development in Denver was built in the 2006–9 period, followed by a slowdown from 2010–12 due to the Great Recession. The number of TOD residential units completed in 2014 (2,885) and 2013 (2,781) are the second- and third-highest totals since data collection started in 1997. Projections indicate strong growth is expected in residential, retail, and especially office transit-oriented development.[69]

Impacts of TOD and Smart Growth Planning in Denver

When comparing TOD to overall development in the Denver region, TOD is becoming a larger piece of the big picture. In its Metro Vision plan, DRCOG designated 104 higher-density urban centers throughout the Denver region, many of which are located along rail transit lines. One of the goals identified in the Metro Vision 2035 plan is to accommodate 50 percent of the region's new housing and 75 percent of the region's new employment in these urban centers by 2035. While these may be very ambitious goals, recent evidence suggests some progress in attaining them. From 2005 to 2010, 21 percent of the region's housing growth occurred in the urban centers (accounting for only 1 percent of the total land area of the region). The percentage of new housing units built in urban centers has increased from 5 percent in 2004 to nearly 50 percent in 2010. In 2009, as measured by square footage, 66 percent of new residential development, 60 percent of new office development, and 19 percent of new retail development throughout the region was located in TOD areas.[70] From 2005 to 2013, 55 percent of new employment in the region was located in urban centers.[71]

The development in transit-served locations and smart growth planning efforts are having an effect on the land use and urban form of the Denver metropolitan area, although the designated urban growth area continues to expand. One of the goals of the DRCOG Metro Vision 2035 plan is to increase overall urban density by 10 percent between 2000 and 2035. While an ambitious goal, average density in the region has been increasing. From 1990 to 2000, urbanized area density increased from 3,309 to 3,979 persons per square mile.[72] Between 2000 and 2010, residential density within the designated urban growth boundary/area increased by 5.3 percent.[73] Very dense housing is now found in and near the downtown transit zone, and mixed-use transit areas have higher residential densities than the overall Denver region.[74] At the same time, however, urban land consumption continues to grow. In the year 2000, the urban land area for the Denver region was 635 square miles, which grew to 717 square miles by 2006, representing a 12.9 percent increase. At this rate of urban land expansion, the entire urbanized area would cover 1,106 square miles by 2035, thus exceeding the urban growth boundary/area of 980 square miles that was established in the Metro Vision 2035 plan. Large lot development in outlying jurisdictions continues to contribute to the expansion of urbanized land area. The Metro Vision plan now includes a goal of limiting the total households in semiurban development by 2035 to 3 percent of the region's total households, which is the estimated level as of 2006. Semiurban development is defined as residential subdivisions or groupings of ten or more residential parcels with an average residential lot size greater than or equal to one acre and less than ten acres.[75]

The investment in rail transit and transit-oriented development in Denver is also having an effect on travel behavior. Recent data show that transit ridership has been increasing, from 78.9 million boardings in 2003 to 103.4 million boardings in 2015.[76] The mode share of single-occupant vehicle (SOV) use is slowly declining throughout the region, going from 77.1 percent in 2005 to 74.9 percent in 2012, and vehicle miles traveled (VMT) per capita is also slowly declining, going from 24.7 in 2005 to 23.9 in 2012.[77] The Metro Vision plan includes a goal to reduce SOV mode share to 65 percent by 2035, and to decrease VMT per capita by 10 percent to 22.3 by 2035. Denver is now among the top ten U.S. cities where the percentage of commuters riding a bike to work has increased the most, growing from 1 percent in 2000 to 2.3 percent during the 2008–12 period.[78] And growing car-sharing options, such as ZipCar and car2go, as well as transportation network companies like Uber and Lyft, are providing more flexibility in travel choices.

Table 7. Transportation Mode Share Comparisons: Downtown Denver, Denver City, Denver-Aurora-Lakewood Metropolitan Statistical Area, and the U.S. Average

	Denver Downtown	Denver City	Denver MSA	U.S. Average
Drive alone	34.7%	68.6%	75.6%	76.3%
Transit	47.2%	7.2%	4.4%	5.0%
Carpool	4.6%	8.7%	9.1%	9.7%
Bicycle	7.3%	2.9%	1.1%	0.6%
Walk	4.5%	5.0%	2.4%	2.8%

Sources: 2014 Downtown Denver Commuter Survey, 2012 U.S. Census Bureau, and American Community Survey (ACS) yearly estimates.

Within the Denver region, commuting by transit is highest in the downtown area, where nearly half of all commuters use transit and only 35 percent drive alone. Bicycling is also higher for commuters in the downtown area. Moving away from downtown, mode share statistics for the City and County of Denver and the Denver MSA are closer to the U.S. averages, although bicycling mode shares in both the city and MSA remain higher than the U.S. average (Table 7).

While Denver still remains a relatively low-density city that relies heavily on the automobile and highway transportation, there has nevertheless been a clear change in regional policy that is encouraging more transit, bicycling, and pedestrian mobility, as well as higher-density transit-oriented development. The change in policy is having a recognizable impact on Denver's land use, urban form, and travel behavior. There is certainly no better example than downtown Denver, where the majority of commuting access is now by transit, bicycles, and walking, instead of cars. Conventioneers, tourists, and others from the region enjoy the area for its accessibility, cultural amenities, and ambiance. Redevelopment of Union Station into a regional transportation hub and the mixed-use pedestrian-oriented development nearby should continue this change in urban form into the future. It is too early to determine how much of a regional change in land use patterns and urban form will occur from the completion of the FasTracks program. However, it certainly appears that tying transit development to land use development is causing Denver to think and plan for the future in a different way than it has in the past concerning what will best utilize the transit system as an integral part of the existing and future land use pattern.

*   *   *

The Denver metropolitan region is an interesting example of the two major paradigms of urban growth in the post-1950 era. From 1950 to 1990, Denver followed the classic U.S. postwar suburban and exurban low-density development model with increasing dependence on automobiles and highways. Edge-city developments, retail malls, and large-lot developments on the urban fringe contributed to a massive expansion of urbanized land and the accompanying economic and environmental costs associated with urban sprawl. But in response to concerns over rapid population growth, urban land expansion, air quality, and increasing traffic congestion, Denver reached a watershed moment in the early 1990s with the development of its Metro Vision regional planning process, which supported higher-density, mixed-use, in-fill development and a regional rail transit system to link urban activity centers. Since 1990, the Denver area has been increasing its population and employment density, especially in its transit- and pedestrian-oriented urban centers. The overall population density of the region has increased in spite of continued increases in urbanized land area.

The Denver metropolitan region also represents an interesting case study of how the smart growth movement of the 1990s and 2000s has been more successful than previous efforts at growth management. While a number of growth control measures were initiated in the 1970s, such as the rejection of the Winter Olympics and the cancellation of the I-470 interstate beltway project, the support for these actions was relatively short-lived and faded away during the economic decline and subsequent economic development efforts of the 1980s. Principally associated with the firebrand governor Richard Lamm, who was known for his incendiary expressions such as "driving a silver stake" through the beltway project, the 1970s growth control movement in Colorado antagonized the development community and other powerful growth machine interests. By contrast, the smart growth movement of the 1990s and 2000s has largely sought to include the development community, as well as a broader coalition of government and business interests in supporting specific smart growth programs and projects. The redevelopment of Lower Downtown Denver, especially the Union Station area, as well as Stapleton, Belmar, and other new urbanist–influenced projects were the result of public-private partnerships and a wider recognition of the benefits of infill development. The approval of the 122-mile addition to the rail transit system known as FasTracks was a result of unprecedented collaboration among mayors, county commissioners, and chambers of commerce in the Denver metropolitan region, who largely supported the rail transit expansion. The rise of nontraditional "new regionalist" organizations such as the Metro Mayors Caucus and the Alliance for Regional Stewardship was critical to the support for FasTracks. And the FasTracks build-out would not have been possible without the public-private partnerships that have jump-started most of the rail lines. Simply put, the smart growth initiatives of the 1990s and 2000s have been more widely supported, longer lasting, and ultimately more successful than the growth control efforts of the 1970s.

Nevertheless, not all initiatives have been successful. The failure of Amendment 24 in 2000 has limited smart growth planning to major urban areas rather than the entire state. And the continued popularity of ultra-low-density (one- to forty-acre "ranchettes") residential developments on the exurban fringe undermines the purpose and effectiveness of the region's voluntary urban growth boundary/area. Even though density within the region has been increasing since 1990, the urbanized land area has also been increasing at a rate that would exceed the maximum growth area defined in the Metro Vision 2035 plan.

It is not clear whether smart growth planning in Denver will engender a full paradigm shift away from lower-density, auto-oriented suburban development toward higher-density, mixed-use, transit- and pedestrian-oriented urban centers. But it is clear that the smart growth movement has been more successful at implementing the new paradigm than previous efforts. Given the substantial economic, social, and environmental costs of sprawling suburban development, it is likely that more sustainable urban design approaches will continue to be implemented and slowly replace the previous low-density suburban development paradigm.

The Next Frontier

In its more than 150 years of existence, Denver has come a long way toward becoming one of the leading urban centers in the United States. From its origins as a mining boom town, through its phases as a sleepy cow town, followed by its postwar population explosion, Denver has evolved and matured into a cosmopolitan metropolis. Today it boasts continued growth, a robust economy, a diverse and highly educated population, and a strong commitment to the arts and outdoor recreation. After the postwar period of rapid suburbanization, automobile orientation, and divisive policies and planning, the Denver region has committed itself to a more sustainable future with an emphasis on regional economic development, smart growth, rail transit development, and enhanced regional collaboration.

Looking back, there was nothing inevitable about Denver's rise as a major metropolitan center. Denver's geographic location did not presage its urban development. It is not located near a natural coastal harbor, as are New York and San Francisco, or where a river empties into an ocean, sea, or lake. The confluence of the South Platte River and Cherry Creek at Denver pales in comparison to Pittsburgh's Three Rivers confluence or St. Louis's Mississippi-Missouri confluence.

While gold discoveries were the initial impetus behind Denver's founding and early growth, the boom-and-bust nature of mining did not lend itself to sustained growth. Other cities in the region could have become a major metropolis instead of Denver. In its very early years, Denver vied with the fledgling town of Auraria on the southeast bank of Cherry Creek to determine which place would become the leading city of the confluence area. Once Denver town leaders were able to lure the Leavenworth and Pikes Peak Express stagecoach line to locate its terminus in Denver, Auraria relinquished its claim to be the leading city. Denver competed with Golden to determine which city would become the principal gateway to the gold mining area at Blackhawk and Central City. When the Union Pacific Railroad announced it would be routing its transcontinental rail line through Cheyenne, Wyoming, both Golden and Denver developed plans to build a spur rail line to connect to the Union Pacific line. While the Colorado Central Railroad from Golden was able to build only four miles north of Denver by 1870, the Denver Pacific Railroad from Denver completed the 106-mile line to Cheyenne, thus establishing Denver, not Golden, as the railroad hub for the region.[1]

When the Union Pacific had announced that Cheyenne, not Denver, would be on the main transcontinental line, expectations were that Cheyenne would become the major city along the eastern edge of the Rocky Mountains. But the Denver Pacific spur line and subsequent rail connections via the Kansas Pacific Railroad, the Denver South Park and Pacific Railway, and the Denver and Rio Grande Railway solidified Denver's position as a railroad hub and regional economic center, thus allowing Denver to eclipse Cheyenne. Later in the early twentieth century, it appeared that the city of Pueblo, with its advantageous location along the Arkansas River, its proximity to coal and iron ore resources, and its position as a hub for an emerging rail network, might overtake Denver as the major city along Colorado's Front Range. Instead, Denver leaders opened the Moffat Tunnel in 1927, providing Denver with a more direct railroad route to the West, and invested in building Denver Municipal Airport (later named Stapleton Airport) in 1929 in anticipation of the expected growth in air transport. Thus, Denver solidified its position as the leading metropolitan center in Colorado and the Rocky Mountain region.[2]

In more recent years, metropolitan area voters have faced decisions that have influenced the future growth and character of the Denver area. In the late 1980s, voters in Adams County and Denver faced momentous decisions about whether to go forward with plans to build a new airport for the metropolitan area. The decision to build Denver International Airport was crucial to ensure that Denver remained a major aviation center with frequent and reliable air service important for long-term economic development. Also in the late 1980s, metropolitan area voters decided to fund the Scientific and Cultural Facilities District (SCFD) in support of arts and cultural programs. And, then in the early 2000s, metropolitan area voters approved the Regional Transportation District (RTD) FasTracks rail transit program, which,

together with other smart growth initiatives in the region, is directly influ-
encing Denver's future growth patterns.

The establishment of Denver as one of the leading urban centers in the
country owes as much, if not more, to leadership initiatives and community
support, as to natural advantages that it possessed. Certainly, its proximity
to natural resources such as minerals, fertile agricultural land, and oil and
gas, as well as its natural amenities of sun, snow, mountains, and crisp air
played a significant role in its economic and population growth. But Denver's
story is very much about how its leaders have taken initiatives to capitalize
on these resources and how its citizens have supported these initiatives to
put Denver in a position to emerge as a leading metropolitan area.

Contemporary Denver: The "Next Frontier"

In 2010, the Brookings Institution Metropolitan Policy Program released its
State of Metropolitan America report, in which it categorized the one hundred largest U.S. metropolitan areas into seven typologies based on different
levels of population growth, population diversity, and educational attainment. Denver was placed in the "Next Frontier" group, characterized by levels of population growth, diversity, and education that exceed national
averages. Joining Denver in this group were Albuquerque, New Mexico; Austin, Dallas–Fort Worth, and Houston, Texas; Sacramento, California; Seattle,
Washington; Tucson, Arizona; and Washington, D.C. According to Brookings, the Next Frontier cities "attracted immigrants, families, and educated
workers during the 2000s thanks to their diversified economies (including
government employment in several) and relatively mild climates. In some
ways the demographic success stories of the 2000s, Next Frontier areas are
generally younger, are growing more rapidly, and are more economically
dynamic than other metro areas. One price of their success is their higher
levels of both educational and wage inequality."[3]

What does it mean to be a Next Frontier city? With population growth,
diversity, and educational attainment exceeding national averages, it would
appear that this group of cities is in an advantageous position. Certainly, the
Next Frontier cities are much better positioned than the "Industrial Core"
cities, such as Buffalo, Cleveland, and Detroit, that are typified by low growth,
low diversity, and low educational attainment.[4] Most of the Next Frontier
cities are among those that are representative of Richard Florida's creative

cities. They tend to be places that have strong diversified economies specializing in sectors such as information technology, telecommunications, tourism, aerospace, defense, and government activities. They possess cultural amenities, such as vibrant arts communities and "hip" urban neighborhoods that younger age groups, especially the millennial generation, find attractive. Certainly metropolitan Denver fits this characterization quite well.

At the same time, however, there are concerns as suggested by the Brookings characterization. Strong population and economic growth has led to patterns of educational and wage inequality. In Denver, similarly to other rapidly growing metropolitan areas, income polarization is growing and is being displayed in spatial form through an increasing number of both extremely affluent and extremely poor neighborhoods. The number of high- and extreme-affluence census tracts increased from 19 to 40, while the number of high- and extreme-poverty tracts jumped from 49 to 140, between 2000 and 2010 in the Denver metropolitan area.[5] The spatial polarization of wealth and poverty has ramifications for educational disparities because local school districts are funded through local property taxes, which can and do result in wide variations in school funding levels depending on the district. So, while Denver boasts a highly educated population, the local school districts across the metropolitan area vary greatly in the educational resources available to them.

As a Next Frontier city, Denver has a greater-than-average level of diversity among the top one hundred U.S. metropolitan areas. With 78 percent white alone not Hispanic or Latino, 22.5 percent Hispanic or Latino, 5.6 percent black or African American alone, 3.7 percent Asian alone, 3.6 percent two or more races, and 1 percent American Indian alone, the Denver metropolitan area has a relatively diverse profile.[6] Yet levels of racial and ethnic segregation for African Americans and Latinos in Denver are higher than national averages for the top one hundred metropolitan areas, and while they have declined for African Americans since the 1970s, they have been on the increase for Latinos since then. Public school segregation for both African Americans and Latinos in Denver is also higher than the national average. The overall diversity profile masks some disturbing trends regarding racial and ethnic segregation. Furthermore, in light of recent events in Ferguson, Missouri; New York; Cleveland; Chicago; and other places involving police homicides of unarmed African American males, and the ensuing protests across the country, it is clear that issues of racial and ethnic inequality are as relevant today as they were fifty years ago.

The Future of Denver

In 1983, Federico Peña was elected mayor of Denver, running on the slogan "Imagine a Great City." To a considerable degree, that imagination and sustained efforts from city leaders and citizens have brought tangible and positive results. Today, Denver is well positioned among U.S. metropolitan areas and is generally a desirable place to live.

Looking forward, the major issues facing Denver are those of growth and inequality. Natural resources and amenities have been an important part of Denver's growth in the past, and they will continue to be important in the future. Water is a critical resource throughout the arid western United States, and Denver's continued growth depends on access to it. While water conservation will reduce per capita demand, continued population growth will necessitate the acquisition of additional water resources. Denver has taken significant strides toward the accommodation of future population growth through its smart growth planning approaches. Recent regional collaboration initiatives also bode well for the future of the metropolitan area. Still, important challenges remain around integrating an increasingly diverse population and providing opportunities for all members of society regardless of socioeconomic strata or racial or ethnic background. These are challenges not only for Denver but for all U.S. metropolitan areas. Metropolitan Denver will not be alone as it seeks to reconcile its future growth with access to opportunities for all its residents.

Notes

Preface

1. Whitman, Walt. 1887. *Specimen Days in America*. London: Walter Scott, 227; cited in Leonard, Stephen J., and Thomas J. Noel. 1990. *Denver: Mining Camp to Metropolis*. Boulder: University of Colorado Press, 123.

Introduction

1. Olinger, David. "Denver Is Flourishing." *Denver Post*, September 18, 2015, 1A, 9A.

2. Leonard, S., and T. Noel. 1990. *Denver: Mining Camp to Metropolis*. Boulder: University of Colorado Press, 169.

3. Of particular note: Leonard, S., and T. Noel. 2016. *A Short History of Denver*. Reno: University of Nevada Press; Leonard, S., and T. Noel. 1990. *Denver: Mining Camp to Metropolis*. Boulder: University of Colorado Press; and Dorsett, L., and M. McCarthy, 1986. *The Queen City: A History of Denver*. Boulder: Purett, 2nd ed. For the wider Colorado region, see Abbott, C., et al. 2005. *Colorado: A History of the Centennial State*. 4th ed. Boulder: University Press of Colorado; Philpott, W. 2013. *Vacationland: Tourism and Environment in the Colorado High Country*. Seattle: University of Washington Press. Finally, Leonard and Noel 2016 contains an extensive bibliography of Denver history books and articles.

4. Quoted in Leonard and Noel 2016, 12–13.

5. Barth, Gunther. 1975. *Instant Cities: Urbanization and the Rise of San Francisco and Denver*. New York: Oxford University Press.

6. Brosnan, Kathleen A. 2002. *Uniting Mountain and Plain: Cities, Law, and Environmental Change Along the Front Range*. Albuquerque: University of New Mexico Press.

7. Julie Speer (director and writer), Mariel Rodriguez-McGill (writer). 2013. "Colorado Philanthropy." In History Colorado and Rocky Mountain PBS (producers), *Colorado Experience*. Denver: Rocky Mountain Public Broadcasting Network.

8. Leonard and Noel 1990, 235.

9. Grove, Noel, Ted Spiegel, and William H. Bond. "Air: An Atmosphere of Uncertainty." *National Geographic Magazine*, April 1987, [502]+.

10. Brooke, James. "Denver Seeing the Light Past Its 'Brown Cloud.'" *New York Times*, April 21, 1998, A10.

11. A quote from Dana Crawford: "I had a friend who used to call Denver the 'locker room' of the Rockies." In Stephen Edwards, "Full Steam Ahead for Downtown Denver." *National Geographic Traveler*, August–September 2014, 14.

12. McPhee, Mike. 2015. *Dana Crawford: 50 Years Saving the Soul of a City*. Denver: Upper Gulch, 221.

13. Philpott, William. 2013. *Vacationland: Tourism and Environment in the Colorado High Country*. Seattle: University of Washington Press, 239.

14. Adapted with permission from the biographical profile of former 9News (NBC, Denver) personality Brooke Thacker. As she stated, this summarized her actual experience of vacationing in Colorado one spring and moving permanently the following year (personal e-mail correspondence September 9, 2010).

15. Population projection figures are from U.S. Census Press Release CB 15-215, December 22, 2015; the Colorado State Demography Office; and http://www.america2050 .org/front_range.html.

16. Kemp, Rob. 2015. *Colorado Migration in 2013*. State Demography Office, Colorado Department of Local Affairs.

17. Campoy, Ana, and Dan Frosch. 2015. "Denver Job Market Lures Millennials." *Wall Street Journal*, July 23, A3.

18. Limerick, Patricia Nelson, with Jason L. Hanson. 2012. *A Ditch in Time: The City, the West, and Water*. Golden, Colo.: Fulcrum, 4.

19. Based on U.S. Census and Bureau of Labor Statistics.

Chapter 1. Physical Landscape and Natural Surroundings

1. Wyckoff, William. 1999. *Creating Colorado: The Making of a Western American Landscape, 1860–1940*. New Haven, Conn.: Yale University Press.

2. With the exception that the South Platte River basin through Denver and northeast Colorado is slightly lower in elevation than other portions of the eastern plains.

3. The Front Range is the first range of the Rocky Mountains encountered in central Colorado traveling from the east astride the fortieth parallel. The urban areas just to the east of the Front Range (i.e., Denver, Boulder, Fort Collins, Colorado Springs, and Pueblo) are collectively referred to as the Front Range urban corridor.

4. Quoted in Abbott, C., et al. 2005. *Colorado: A History of the Centennial State*. 4th ed. Boulder: University Press of Colorado, 2.

5. Abbott et al. 2005.

6. Rodriguez-McGill, Mariel (writer), and Speer, Julie (writer and director). 2013. "The Original Coloradans." In History Colorado and Rocky Mountain PBS (producers), *Colorado Experience*. Denver: Rocky Mountain Public Broadcasting Network.

7. Nelson, Sarah, et al. 2008. *Denver: An Archaeological History*. Boulder: University Press of Colorado.

8. Both of these are cited as aesthetic influences on the unique architectural design of the Jeppesen Terminal at Denver International Airport (Nelson et al. 2008).

9. Blake, Kevin. 2002. "Colorado Fourteeners and the Nature of Place Identity." *Geographical Review* 92 (2): 155–79.

10. Matthews, Vincent, ed. 2009. *Messages in Stone: Colorado's Colorful Geology.* 2nd ed. Denver: Colorado Geological Survey.

11. Colorado Climate Center. 2003 Climate of Colorado. http:// ccc.atmos.colostate .edu/climateofcolorado.php.

12. See Philpott, William. 2013. *Vacationland: Tourism and Environment in the Colorado High Country.* Seattle: University of Washington Press, 64 and n. 98 for other sources.

13. Nelson, Mike, and the 9News Weather Team. 1999. *The Colorado Weather Book.* Englewood, Colo.: Westcliffe.

14. Ferril, Thomas Hornsby. 1944. *Trial by Time.* New York: Harper and Brothers.

15. U.S. Department of the Interior, Bureau of Reclamation. *The Law of the River.* http://www.usbr.gov/lc/region/g1000/lawofrvr.html (accessed July 2015).

16. Wolfe, Dick, and Joseph Grantham. 2001. "Synopsis of Colorado Water Law." Colorado Division of Water Resources, Department of Natural Resources.

17. Bunch, Joey. 2016. Colorado Household Rain Barrel Law Takes Effect Wednesday. *Denver Post*, August 5, 2016. http://www.denverpost.com/2016/08/05/colorado-house hold-rain-barrel-law-takes-effect-tuesday/ (accessed December 2016).

18. See *The Great Divide* (2015), a Havey Productions film, for an excellent documentary on the historic complexity of water laws in Colorado, and future long-term implications.

19. Limerick, Patricia Nelson, with Jason L. Hanson. 2012. *A Ditch in Time: The City, the West, and Water.* Golden, Colo.: Fulcrum.

20. McKee, Thomas, Nolan Doesken, John Kleist, and Catherine Shrier. 2000. "A History of Drought in Colorado: Lessons Learned and What Lies Ahead." 2nd ed. Colorado Climate Center. http://climate.atmos.colostate.edu/pdfs/ahisto-ryofdrought.pdf.

21. Ryan, Wendy, and Nolan Doesken. 2013. "Drought of 2012 in Colorado." Colorado Climate Center. http://ccc.atmos.colostate.edu/pdfs/climo_rpt_13_1.pdf.

22. The Hayman fire was started by a U.S. Forest Service employee who, during severe drought conditions and a total burn ban, was burning letters from her estranged husband in a fire ring before the fire got out of control.

23. Brooke, James. "Denver Seeing the Light Past Its 'Brown Cloud.'" *New York Times*, April 21, 1998, A10.

24. Hobbs, Gregory J. Jr. 2004. "To See the Mountains: Restoring Colorado's Clean and Healthy Air." *University of Colorado Law Review* 75: 433–96.

25. Finley, Bruce. "Denver Aims to Cut Carbon Emissions 80 Percent by 2050." *Denver Post*, December 3, 2015.

26. Philpott 2013.

27. Salcido, Rachel. 2014. "The Rocky Mountain Arsenal National Wildlife Refuge: On a Rocky Road to Creating a Community Asset." *John Marshall Law Review* 47 (4): 1401–32; Leonard, S., and T. Noel. 1990. *Denver: Mining Camp to Metropolis.* Boulder: University of Colorado Press, 351–53.

28. Rachel Carson. 1962. *Silent Spring.* Paperback ed. Greenwich, Conn.: Fawcett, 47–48.

29. This quote is attributed to the *Denver Post*, November 27, 1988, as referenced in Leonard and Noel, 1990, 351 (see n. 17 of chapter 25).

30. Leonard and Noel, 1990, 354.

31. Speer, Julie (director). 2014. "Colorado's Cold War." In History Colorado and Rocky Mountain PBS (producers), *Colorado Experience.* Denver: Rocky Mountain Public Broadcasting Network; Leonard and Noel, 319–21.

32. Salcido 2014.

33. U.S. Fish and Wildlife Service. "Rocky Flats National Wildlife Refuge." http://www.fws.gov/refuge/rocky_flats/ (accessed November 2015).

34. Salt Lake City, Utah; Kansas City, Missouri; and Albuquerque, New Mexico, are closer cities but contain much smaller population clusters.

Chapter 2. Historical Development

1. Kelman, Ari. 2013. *A Misplaced Massacre: Struggling over the Memory of Sand Creek.* Cambridge, Mass.: Harvard University Press.

2. University of Denver. 2014. Report of the John Evans Study Committee, November 2014.

3. Limerick, Patricia Nelson. 1987. *The Legacy of Conquest: The Unbroken Past of the American West.* New York: Norton.

4. Leonard, S., and T. Noel. 1990. *Denver: Mining Camp to Metropolis.* Boulder: University of Colorado Press, 8.

5. Leonard and Noel 1990.

6. Dorsett, Lyle. 1977. *The Queen City: A History of Denver.* Boulder: Purett; Leonard and Noel 1990.

7. Quillen, Ed. 1994. "DIA Follows Colorado Tradition." *Denver Post*, April 5.

8. Dempsey, Paul Stephen, Andrew R. Goetz, and Joseph S. Szyliowicz. 1997. *Denver International Airport: Lessons Learned.* New York: McGraw Hill, 150.

9. Dorset 1977.

10. Noel, Tom. 1994. "By-Pass Phobia Leads Denver to Spin Giant Webs of Steel and Concrete." *Denver Post*, May 14.

11. Dempsey, Goetz, and Szyliowicz 1997, 151.

12. Greenwald, Gerald. 1995. "Future Bright for DIA and Denver." *Denver Post*, February 28.

13. Dorsett 1977; Leonard and Noel 1990.

14. Dorsett 1977, 24.

15. Leonard and Noel 1990, 39.

16. Wyckoff, William. 1988. "Revising the Meyer Model: Denver and the National Urban System, 1859–1879." *Urban Geography* 9 (1): 1–18.

17. Leonard and Noel 1990.

18. Limerick, Patricia Nelson. 2012. *A Ditch in Time: The City, the West, and Water.* Golden, Colo.: Fulcrum.

19. Turner, Frederick Jackson. 1894. *The Significance of the Frontier in American History.* Madison: State Historical Society of Wisconsin, 1.

20. Turner 1894.

21. Meyer, David R. 1980. "A Dynamic Model of the Integration of Frontier Urban Places into the United States System of Cities." *Economic Geography* 56 (2): 120–40; Wyckoff 1988; Kaplan, David H., James O. Wheeler, and Steven R. Holloway. 2004. *Urban Geography.* Hoboken, N.J.: Wiley.

22. Wyckoff 1988.

23. Leonard and Noel 1990.

24. Abbott, C., S. J. Leonard, and T. J. Noel. 2005. *Colorado: A History of the Centennial State.* 4th ed. Boulder: University Press of Colorado, 227.

25. Abrams, J. 2011. "In Search of Wealth and Health: Denver's Early Jewish Community." In *Colorado History 16: Denver Inside and Out*, ed. L. Borowsky, 71–82 (74–75). Denver, Colo: History Colorado, the Colorado Historical Society. The report referenced in the quote is from Health Committee of the City Club of Denver, *Tuberculosis in Denver*, Health Committee of the City Club of Denver. Pamphlet 6. Denver: City Club of Denver. 1925, page 5. 1925, 5.

26. Whitman, Walt. 1887. *Specimen Days in America.* London: Walter Scott, 227; cited in Leonard and Noel 1990, 123.

27. It is unlikely that a train from San Francisco to Denver would have been attacked by Sioux warriors because the Sioux nation was based in the Dakotas and the northern Great Plains, a long distance from the rail line between San Francisco and Denver.

28. Dempsey, Goetz, and Szyliowicz 1997.

29. Leonard and Noel 1990.

30. Leonard and Noel 1990.

31. Markusen, Ann, Peter Hall, Scott Campbell, and Sabina Deitrick. 1991. *The Rise of the Gunbelt: The Military Remapping of Industrial America.* New York: Oxford University Press.

32. Dorsett 1977, 261.

33. Markusen et al. 1991, 5.

34. Dorsett 1977; Leonard and Noel 1990.

35. Dorsett 1977.

36. Dorsett 1977; Leonard and Noel 1990.

37. Leonard and Noel 1990.

38. Phillips, Dave. 2009. "Stimulus Plan, Circa 1939: The Colorado Ski Industry." *Colorado Springs Gazette*, December 23, 2009. http://gazette.com/article/91267.

39. Donald, Robert Bruce. 2007. "The 10th Mountain Division and the Boom in Post-War Skiing in America." http://voices.yahoo.com/the-10th-mountain-division-boom-post-war-384375.html.

40. Coleman, Anne Gilbert. 2004. *Ski Style: Sport and Culture in the Rockies.* Lawrence: University Press of Kansas.

41. Coleman 2004.

42. Coleman 2004.

43. Philpott, William. 2013. *Vacationland: Tourism and Environment in the Colorado High Country.* Seattle: University of Washington Press.

44. Dorsett 1977.

45. Philpott 2013, 168.

46. Leonard and Noel 1990.

47. Dorsett 1977.

48. It is notable that Denver's first two professional sports franchises were in the American Football League (AFL) and the American Basketball Association (ABA), two upstart leagues that both began in the 1960s. They challenged the dominance and exclusiveness of the established National Football League (NFL) and National Basketball Association (NBA), by providing an opportunity for newer rapidly growing cities like Denver to have professional sports teams, which the older leagues were reluctant to do. See Pluto, Terry. 2007. *Loose Balls: The Short, Wild Life of the American Basketball Association.* New York: Simon and Schuster.

49. Goetz, Andrew R. 2013. "Suburban Sprawl or Urban Centres: Tensions and Contradictions of Smart Growth Approaches in Denver, Colorado." *Urban Studies* 50 (11): 2178–2195.

50. Outside of places like Denver and Houston, the energy "boom" was actually an energy "crisis," with high oil prices crippling the U.S. national economy.

51. Weiler, Stephan. 2000. "Pioneers and Settlers in Lo-Do Denver: Private Risk and Public Benefits in Urban Redevelopment." *Urban Studies* 37 (1): 167–79.

52. Goetz 2013.

53. Dempsey, Goetz, and Szyliowicz 1997; Goetz, Andrew R. 2015. "The Expansion of Large International Hub Airports." In: In Hickman, R., Givoni, M., Bonilla, D. & Banister, D. (eds.) *Handbook on Transport and Development.* Cheltenham: Edward Elgar.

54. Dempsey, Goetz, and Szyliowicz 1997.

55. While automated baggage systems are now a common feature in new airports, the scale and complexity of the proposed Denver system was well beyond technological capacity at that time. According to Richard de Neufville, "the enormous increase in complexity, that distinguishes the fully automated baggage system attempted at Denver from all others, represents much more than a simple evolution of technology. It is not just a change from a third to a fourth generation of technology, say; it is more like an attempted leap from the third to the fifth or sixth generation of baggage systems."

De Neufville, Richard. 1994. "The Baggage System at Denver: Prospects and Lessons." *Journal of Air Transport Management* 1(4) 1994, 231–32,

56. Dempsey, Goetz, and Szyliowicz 1997; Goetz 2015.

57. According to Douglas K. Fleming, and Yehuda Hayuth, centrality refers to the degree to which a city possesses higher-order central place characteristics, while intermediacy refers to strategic locations between important origins and destinations. Fleming, Douglas K. and Yehuda Hayuth. 1994. "Spatial Characteristics of Transportation Hubs: Centrality and Intermediacy." *Journal of Transport Geography* 2(1): 3-18,

58. Newmark, Knight, Frank Capital Group. 2012. DIA Porteos. http://www.denveraerotropolis.com/docs/Current_Economic_Impact-n-Airport_Efficiencies_DIA_Porteos.pdf (accessed August 16, 2012).

59. The Denver-Tokyo flight is operated by United Airlines using the Boeing 787 aircraft, which during its initial flights experienced several fires on board due to overheating of its lithium ion batteries, resulting in the FAA's decision to ground the plane until the problems could be fixed. After several delays, the 787 service for Denver-Tokyo was initiated in May 2013.

60. Denver International Airport. 2012. "The Wait Is Over; Denver to Tokyo Nonstop Begins March 2013." *WingTips Newsletter* (from DIA) 4 (6) (June 2012); Goetz 2015.

61. Wilbur Smith and Associates. 2008. "The Economic Impact of Airports in Colorado 2008." Prepared for Colorado Department of Transportation, Division of Aeronautics. May 2008. http://www.coloradodot.info/programs/aeronautics/PDF_Files/2008TechReport.pdf.

62. The airport rail link was completed in April 2016 as part of Denver's FasTracks rail transit program, which will result in a total of 157 miles of light and commuter rail throughout the Denver area; see. Goetz, Andrew R., Andrew E.G. Jonas, and Sutapa Bhattacharjee. 2011. "Regional Collaboration in Transport Infrastructure Provision: The Case of Denver's FasTracks Rail Transit Program." Final Report. National Center for Intermodal Transportation, University of Denver; Goetz 2015.

63. Davidson, Kelly. 2006. "Prairie Potential: DIA Corridor Will Create an 'Aeropolitan' of New Growth and Industry over Next 30 Years." *Colorado Construction* 9 (8): 18–23. http://colorado.construction.com/features/archive/0604_cover.asp (accessed August 17, 2012); Goetz 2015.

64. Harden, Mark. 2012. "Denver Unveils 'Airport City' Plan to Guide DIA Commercial Development." *Denver Business Journal*, April 26, 2012. http://www.bizjournals.com/denver/news/2012/04/26/denver-unveils-airport-city-plan-to.html (accessed August 17, 2012).

65. Robles, Yesenia. 2012. "Adams County: Denver Aerotropolis Bigfoots Prior Agreement." *Denver Post*, August 1, 2012. http://www.denverpost.com/breaking-news/ci_21211923/adams-county-denver-aerotropolis-big-foots-prior-agreement (accessed August 18, 2012).

66. Goetz 2015.

67. Clark, Tom. 2015. "DIA Agreement Opens Door for New Opportunities in Northeast Corridor." Metro Denver Economic Development Corporation, June 30, 2015. http://www.metrodenver.org/blog/posts/2015/06/dia-agreement-opens-door-for-new-opportunities-in-northeast-corridor/ (accessed December 8, 2016).

68. Goetz 2013. Goetz 2015.

69. Broomfield had been a city within the Denver metropolitan area but changed its status to a city and county in 2001.

70. Knox, Paul, and Sallie Marston. 2004. *Human Geography: Places and Regions in Global Context*. Upper Saddle River, N.J.: Prentice Hall.

71. Metro Denver Economic Development Corporation. 2016. "Metro Denver and Northern Colorado Key Industry Clusters." http://www.metrodenver.org/research-reports/industry-cluster-study/ (accessed December 9, 2016).

72. The Metro Denver Economic Development Corporation collects industry cluster data for the nine-county metro Denver and northern Colorado region, which includes Adams, Arapahoe, Boulder, Broomfield, Denver, Douglas, Jefferson, Larimer, and Weld Counties.

73. Metro Denver Economic Development Corporation 2016.

74. Metro Denver Economic Development Corporation 2016.

75. Metro Denver Economic Development Corporation 2016.

76. Metro Denver Economic Development Corporation 2016.

Chapter 3. Demographics and Culture

1. Metropolitan Policy Program. 2010. *State of Metropolitan America: On the Front Lines of Demographic Transformation*. Washington, D.C.: Brookings.

2. Barth, Gunther. 1975. *Instant Cities: Urbanization and the Rise of San Francisco and Denver*. New York: Oxford University Press.

3. Leonard, S., and T. Noel. 1990. *Denver: Mining Camp to Metropolis*. Boulder: University of Colorado Press; Leonard, S., and T. Noel. 2016. *A Short History of Denver*. Reno: University of Nevada Press.

4. Stephens, R., et al. 2008. *African Americans in Denver*. Charleston, S.C.: Arcadia.

5. Robertson, D., et al. *Denver's Street Railways*, vol. 1, *1871–1900—Not an Automobile in Sight, 1999*; vol. 2, *1901–1950—Reign of the Denver Tramway, 2004*; vol. 3, *The Interurbans*. Denver: Sundance.

6. Leonard and Noel 1990; Leonard and Noel 2016.

7. Leonard and Noel 1990; Leonard and Noel 2016. The city of Aurora started as the town of Fletcher in Adams County in 1891 but has since expanded into Arapahoe County. Today most of the city of Aurora is located in Arapahoe County.

8. Jackson, K. T. 1985. *Crabgrass Frontier: The Suburbanization of the United States*. New York: Oxford University Press.

9. Dorsett, L., and M. McCarthy. 1986. *The Queen City: A History of Denver*. Boulder: Purett. 2nd ed.

10. Gutfreund, O. 2004. *Twentieth Century Sprawl: Highways and the Reshaping of the American Landscape.* New York: Oxford University Press.

11. Denver Federal Executive Board. 2007. *The Impact of the Federal Government Facilities on the Denver Metropolitan Region and the State of Colorado.* http://www .colorado.feb.gov/useruploads/files/2007_federal_impact_report.pdf (accessed December 2010).

12. Based on author's calculations of 2010 U.S. Census data.

13. Regional agencies such as the Denver Regional Council of Governments (DRCOG) and the Regional Transportation District (RTD) still included Boulder County in their jurisdictions for planning purposes.

14. Sutton, P., T. Cova, and C. Elvidge. 2006. "Mapping 'Exurbia' in the Conterminous United States Using Nighttime Satellite Imagery." *Geocarto International* 21 (2): 39–45.

15. DRCOG (Denver Regional Council of Governments). 2009. "Regional Data and Maps: People and Households." http://www.drcog.org/index.cfm?page=Peopleand Households (accessed April 3, 2009).

16. Garreau, J. 1992. *Edge City: Life on the New Frontier.* New York: Doubleday.

17. *Denver Post,* March 17, 1983; quoted in Leonard and Noel 1990, 291.

18. Gutfreund 2004.

19. Source: http://www.publicpurpose.com/ut-cprof-den.htm. Based on 2000 U.S. Census data.

20. Mitchell, D. 2000. *Cultural Geography: A Critical Introduction.* Oxford: Blackwell, 130–35.

21. Highlands Ranch Metro District. 2010. www.highlandsranch.org (accessed April, 2, 2010).

22. Simon, S. 2006. "Cookie-Cutter Homes Suit Some Critics' Taste After All." *Los Angeles Times,* July 24.

23. Rusk, D. 2003. *Denver Divided: Sprawl, Race, and Poverty in Greater Denver.* Denver: University of Denver Morgridge College of Education.

24. Newman, P., and Kenworthy, J. 1989. "Gasoline Consumption and Cities: A Comparison of U.S. Cities with a Global Survey." *Journal of the American Planning Association* 55 (1): 24–37.

25. Rusk 2003.

26. Rusk 2003.

27. Fishman, R. 2005. "The Fifth Migration." *Journal of the American Planning Association* 71 (4): 357–66; see also Ehrenhalt, Alan. 2012. *The Great Inversion and the Future of the American City.* New York: Vintage Books; Gallagher, Leigh. 2013. *The End of the Suburbs: Where the American Dream Is Moving.* New York: Portfolio/Penguin.

28. Brooke, J. 1998. "Denver Stands Out in Mini-Trend Toward Downtown Living." *New York Times,* December 28, A10.

29. Borowsky, Larry. 2006. "Denver's Immigrant Legacy: Yesterday's Immigrants Shaped the Denver of Today." *University of Denver Magazine.* http://blogs.du.edu/today/magazine/denvers-immigrant-legacy.

30. Hosokawa, Bill. 2005. *Colorado's Japanese Americans from 1886 to the Present.* Boulder: University Press of Colorado. In the 1970s, the Japanese community was spread across nine blocks, but under a Denver Urban Renewal Authority redevelopment plan for the area, they decided to consolidate on the current one-block area, rather than divide and relocate.

31. Flores, Antonio. 2017. "Facts on U.S. Latinos, 2015: Statistical portrait of Hispanics in the United States." http://www.pewhispanic.org/2017/09/18/facts-on-u-s-latinos/ (accessed December 2, 2017).

32. Leonard and Noel 1990.

33. Jackson, Kenneth T. 1967. *The Ku Klux Klan in the City, 1915–1930.* New York: Oxford University Press.

34. Leonard and Noel 1990; Romero, Thomas I., II. 2013. "How I Rode the Bus to Become a Professor at the University of Denver Sturm College of Law: Reflections on Keyes's Legacy for the Metropolitan, Post-Racial, and Multiracial Twenty-First Century." *Denver University Law Review* 90 (5): 1023–1058.

35. Gould, Richard. 2007. *The Life and Times of Richard Castro: Bridging a Cultural Divide.* Denver: Colorado Historical Society, no. 14.

36. Romero 2013, 1046, 1054.

37. Leonard and Noel 1990, 377–80.

38. Leonard and Noel 1990, 385.

39. Singer, Audrey. 2004. *The Rise of New Immigrant Gateways.* Washington, D.C.: Brookings Institution.

40. 2013 American Community Survey, 2009–13 estimates.

41. 2011 American Community Survey, five-year estimates.

42. Mauck, Laura. 2001. *Five Points Neighborhood of Denver.* Chicago: Arcadia.

43. http://www.blackamericanwestmuseum.com/.

44. McDonald, John F. 2008. *Urban America: Growth, Crisis, and Rebirth.* Armonk, N.Y.: M. E. Sharpe.

45. Dwyer, C., and C. Sutton. 1994. "*Brown* Plus Forty: The Denver Experience." *Urban Geography* 15 (5): 421–34.

46. Source: based on 2000 census data compiled by the Piton Foundation, www.piton.org.

47. From 8,775 to 12,710 based on the U.S. Census, as compiled by the Piton Foundation www.piton.org.

48. Highland grew from 10,353 to 12,234; Union Station grew from 2,225 to 3,475; based on U.S. Census (2000) and American Community Survey (2008) data, as compiled by the Piton Foundation www.piton.org.

49. From 1,253 to 677 based on Denver Public Schools data, as compiled by the Piton Foundation www.piton.org.

50. Or the 2000 white, black, and nonwhite Latino population was 27.4 percent, 26.3 percent, and 42.9 percent, respectively, and in 2010, 57 percent white, 15.8 percent black, and 22.5 percent Latino. All compiled by the Piton Foundation. www.piton .org. Based on decennial U.S. Census data.

51. West, W. A. 1980. *Curtis Park: A Denver Neighborhood.* Boulder: Colorado Associated University Press, 14.

52. Turkewitz, Julie. 2017. "Denver Cafe 'Happily Gentrifying'? Neighbors Aren't So Happy." *New York Times,* November 27, A16.

Chapter 4. Image and Place Making

1. Philpott, William. 2013. *Vacationland: Tourism and Environment in the Colorado High Country.* Seattle: University of Washington Press.

2. Riebsame, William (general editor) and James Robb (director of cartography). 1997. *Atlas of the New West: Portrait of a Changing Region.* New York: W. W. Norton.

3. See Philpott 2013; and Park, L., and D. N. Pellow. 2011. *The Slums of Aspen: Immigrants vs. the Environment in America's Eden.* New York: New York University Press.

4. Philpott 2013.

5. Philpott 2013, 240.

6. Philpott 2013, 20–21; 302.

7. Philpott 2013, 7.

8. A place-specific promotional tagline to the local Coors beer company.

9. Peruzzi, Marc. 2006. "The Gore-Tex Vortex: Think Life in America's Favorite Outdoor Mecca Is Dreamy? Careful What You Wish For." *Outside Magazine,* August. http://www.outsideonline.com/adventure-travel/north-america/united-states/colorado/boulder/The-Gore-Tex-Vortex.html.

10. Pew Research Center. 2009. *Denver Tops List of Favorite Cities: For Nearly Half of America, Grass Is Greener Somewhere Else.* http://pewresearch.org/pubs/1096/community-satisfaction-top-cities.

11. Brooks, David. 2009. "I Dream of Denver." *New York Times,* February 9, A29.

12. "Colorado Travel Year, 2014 Final Report." Longwoods International, 2015; "Colorado Travel Impacts 1996–2014." Dean Runyan Associates, 2015; both reports available at www.colorado.com/research.

13. As in Samuel Bowles's 1869 *The Switzerland of America: A Summer Vacation in the Parks and Mountains of Colorado.* Springfield, Mass.: Samuel Bowles and Co.

14. Wyckoff, William. 1999. *Creating Colorado: The Making of a Western American Landscape 1860–1940.* New Haven, Conn.: Yale University Press.

15. Dorsett, L., and M. McCarthy. 1986. *The Queen City: A History of Denver.* 2nd ed. Boulder: Pruett.

16. Leonard, S., and T. Noel. 1990. *Denver: Mining Camp to Metropolis.* Boulder: University Press of Colorado.

17. Gorte, Ross W., Carol Hardy Vincent, Laura A. Hanson, and Marc R. Rosenblum. 2012. *Federal Land Ownership: Overview and Data*. Washington, D.C.: Library of Congress, Congressional Research Service.

18. Leonard and Noel 1990, 261.

19. Leonard and Noel 1990.

20. Nickname for mountains over fourteen thousand feet in elevation.

21. Donnie Betts (director and writer). 2013. "Lincoln Hills." In History Colorado and Rocky Mountain PBS (producers), *Colorado Experience*. Denver. Rocky Mountain Public Broadcasting Network.

22. Philpott 2013.

23. Abbott, C., S. J. Leonard, and T. J. Noel. 2005. *Colorado: A History of the Centennial State*. 4th ed. Boulder: University Press of Colorado.

24. Colorado and Denver Tourism Study. 2008. Report by Longwoods International; "Colorado Travel Year, 2012 Final Report." Longwoods International, 2013; available at www.colorado.com/research.

25. Colorado and Denver Tourism Study 2008.

26. Park and Pellow 2011, 38.

27. Park and Pellow 2011.

28. The ideas here are derived from Philpott 2013; quotes in this paragraph are from pp. 5, 204, and 162.

29. Because of widespread opposition of the environmental consequences and economic burden in hosting such an event, the people of Colorado later voted to decline the successful bid. The games were subsequently held in Innsbruck, Austria.

30. Jack Kerouac. 2007 (1957). *On the Road* (50th anniversary ed.). New York: Viking Penguin, chapter 5.

31. McPhee, Mike. 2015. *Dana Crawford: 50 Years Saving the Soul of a City*. Denver: Upper Gulch, 82.

32. McPhee 2015, 93.

33. Geologist, turned brew master and pub owner, turned politician, first as mayor of Denver from 2003 to 2011, and then as governor of Colorado from 2011 to 2019.

34. McPhee 2015, 178.

35. Morley, Judy Mattivi. 2006. "'The Most Famous Street in the West': Denver's Larimer Square." Chapter 2 in *Historic Preservation and the Imagined West: Albuquerque, Denver, and Seattle*. Lawrence: University of Kansas Press.

36. Rossi, Frances. Letter to the *Denver Post*, Perspective section, p. 2, July 20, 2014.

37. McPhee 2015.

38. Emilie Rusch. "King Soopers' Opening Signals Evolution of Downtown Denver." *Denver Post*, August 9, 2015.

39. Noel, Thomas J., and Amy B. Zimmer. 2008. *Showtime: Denver's Performing Arts, Convention Centers, and Theater District*. Denver: Denver's Division of Theater's and Arenas.

40. Murray, Michael. 2002. "City Profile: Denver." *Cities* 19 (4): 283–94.

41. Cities with at least one team from the NFL, MLB, NBA, NHL, and MLS sports leagues are New York City, Los Angeles, San Francisco, Chicago, Dallas, Philadelphia, Washington, D.C., Boston, and Denver. Cities with at least one team from these sports leagues except MLS are Miami, Phoenix, Detroit, and Minneapolis.

42. With the 2016 bankruptcy of Sports Authority, the future name remains uncertain.

43. Denver Municipal Code, ord. no. 255-12, § 1, 5-14-12.

44. Robinson, Tony. 2013. *The Denver Camping Ban: A Report from the Street*. A report by Denver Homeless Out Loud (DHOL). Available at: http://denverhomelessoutloud. org/homeless-survey/.

45. Calhoun, Patricia. "Snooze No Longer Supports City's Urban Camping Ban." *Westword*, April 9, 2013.

46. Sloan, Gene. 2007. "Denver's Art Scene Soars with New Galleries, Events." *USA Today*, October 25.

47. Commission on Cultural Affairs. 1989. *Cultural Denver: An Action Plan for the Development of the Cultural Environment of the City and County of Denver*.

48. Apple, R. W. 1998. "On the Road: A Cow Town That Acquired High Culture." *New York Times*, March 27; Sloan 2007.

49. Many of the ideas for what is unique about Denver's art scene come from personal interviews (conducted by author Eric Boschmann) with Adam Lerner, director of the Museum of Contemporary Art; Clark Richert, Denver artist; and the late Robin Rule, founder and owner of Rule Gallery in Denver.

50. Denver Arts and Venues. 2014. *Imagine 2020: Denver's Cultural Plan*, City and County of Denver.

51. Sloan 2007. Denver exhibits strong support for both the arts and sports. Attendance at Denver Broncos football games is legendary; the last home game that was not a sellout was in 1969.

52. http://scfd.org/.

53. Katz, Bruce, and Jennifer Bradley. 2013. "Denver: The Four Votes." Chapter 4 in *The Metropolitan Revolution: How Cities and Metros Are Fixing Our Broken Politics and Fragile Economy*. Washington, D.C.: Brookings Institution, 52.

54. Colorado Business Committee for the Arts. 2014. *Economic Activity Study of Metro Denver Culture: Like No Place Else*.

55. Ritchie, Daniel L. "Guest Commentary: SCFD Is Still Paying Off." *Denver Post*, May 9, 2015.

56. Denver Public Art, http://www.artsandvenuesdenver.com/public-art?

57. Marold, Patrick. 2013. "Shadow Array." http://patrickmarold.com/blog/shadow-array.

58. Brooks, Mary Jo. 2011. "Denver Opens a New Home to Clyfford Still." *PBS News Hour*, November 17.

59. City of Denver. 2004. "The Clyfford Still Art Collection Is Bequeathed to the City of Denver." Mayor's office press release, August 9.

60. The first plan, "Cultural Denver," came out in 1989 under Mayor Peña. In that short document is an interesting admission that Denver lacks a self-image, that the arts are not well linked to tourism, and that art has been rather elitist—with a need for more connection to small, emerging, experimental, ethnic organizations in the city, and the expressed goal to create Denver as the cultural capital of the Rocky Mountain region. Much has changed in the intervening years.

61. For a summary of cultural plan critiques, see Markusen, Ann, and Anne Gadwa. 2010. "Arts and Culture in Urban and Regional Planning: A Review and Research Agenda." *Journal of Planning Education and Research* 29 (3): 379–91.

62. Denver Arts and Venues 2014.

Chapter 5. Political Landscapes

1. Jackson, Kenneth T. 1985. *Crabgrass Frontier: The Suburbanization of the United States*. Oxford: Oxford University Press; Jonas, Andrew, E. G. 1991. "Urban Growth Coalitions and Urban Development Policy: Postwar Growth and the Politics of Annexation in Metropolitan Columbus." *Urban Geography* 12 (3): 197–225.

2. Cox, Kevin R., and Mair, Andrew J. 1988. "Locality and Community in the Politics of Local Economic Development." *Annals of the Association of American Geographers* 78 (2): 307–25.

3. Jackson 1985, 144–46.

4. Goetz, Andrew R., Andrew E. G. Jonas, and Sutapa Bhattacharjee. 2011. "Regional Collaboration in Transport Infrastructure Provision: The Case of Denver's FasTracks Rail Transit Program." Final report, National Center for Intermodal Transportation.

5. Goetz, Jonas, and Bhattacharjee 2011.

6. NJTPA (North Jersey Transportation Planning Authority). 2010. "History of MPOs—Parts I–IV." http://www.njtpa.org/Pub/Report/hist_mpo/default.aspx.

7. NJTPA 2010.

8. DRCOG (Denver Regional Council of Governments). 2010. "What Is DRCOG?" http://www.drcog.org/index.cfm?page=WhatisDRCOG? (accessed August 9, 2010).

9. DRCOG. 2005. "DRCOG 50th Anniversary History." http://www.drcog.org/documents/50th%20DRCOG%20history%20.pdf (accessed August 9, 2010).

10. DRCOG 2005; Jonas, Andrew E. G., Andrew R. Goetz, and Sutapa Bhattacharjee. 2014. "City-Regionalism as a Politics of Collective Provision: Regional Transport Infrastructure in Denver, USA." *Urban Studies, 51*(11), 2444–56.

11. See Litvak, Diana. 2007. "Freeway Fighters in Denver." MA thesis, University of Colorado at Denver; Denver Metropolitan Area Transportation Study Citizens Advisory Committee. 1967. "Analysis of Interim Report to the Executive Committee."

12. Colorado Department of Transportation. 2017. I-70 East Environmental Impact Statement. http://www.i-70east.com/project-overview.html (accessed November 22, 2017).

13. Doeppers, Daniel. 1967. "The Globeville Neighborhood in Denver." *Geographical Review* 57 (4): 506–22.

14. Colorado Department of Transportation. 2017. I-70 East Environmental Impact Statement. http://www.i-70east.com/project-overview.html (accessed November 22, 2017).

15. Colorado Department of Transportation. 2017. I-70 East Environmental Impact Statement. http://www.i-70east.com/alternatives.html#PIPA (accessed November 22, 2017).

16. Federal Highway Administration. 2017. "I-70 East ROD 1: Phase 1 (Central 70 Project)." http://www.i-70east.com/ROD/I-70EastEIS_ROD_Record-of-Decision.pdf (accessed August 14, 2017).

17. Tracey, Caroline. 2017. "Redlining Returns to Denver, but with a Neoliberal Twist." *Nation*, July 31, 2017. https://www.thenation.com/article/redlining-returns-to-denver-but-with-a-neoliberal-twist/ (accessed August 14, 2017).

18. DRCOG 2005.

19. Denver Metropolitan Study Panel. 1976. "Metropolitan Change in Denver: Past Approaches." Denver Metropolitan Study and National Academy of Public Administration; Jonas, Goetz, and Bhattacharjee 2014.

20. Denver Metropolitan Study Panel 1976.

21. Denver Metropolitan Study Panel 1976.

22. Leonard, S., and T. Noel. 1990. *Denver: Mining Camp to Metropolis*. Boulder: University of Colorado Press.

23. Leonard and Noel 1990; Jonas, Goetz, and Bhattacharjee 2014.

24. Horn, C. L., and Kurlaender, M. 2006. *The End of Keyes: Resegregation Trends and Achievement in Denver Public School*s. Cambridge, Mass.: Civil Rights Project at Harvard University.

25. Dwyer, Catherine F., and Christopher J. Sutton. 1994. "*Brown* Plus Forty: The Denver Experience." *Urban Geography* 15 (5): 421–34.

26. Dwyer and Sutton 1994.

27. Leonard and Noel 1990.

28. *Denver Post*, October 25, 1975; quoted in Leonard and Noel 1990, 293; Goetz, Andrew R. 2013. "Suburban Sprawl or Urban Centres: Tensions and Contradictions of Smart Growth Approaches in Denver, Colorado." *Urban Studies* 50 (11): 2178–95; Jonas, Goetz, and Bhattacharjee 2014.

29. Romero, Tom I., II. 2012. "The Color of Water: Observations of a Brown Buffalo on Water Law and Policy in Ten Stanzas." University of Denver Sturm College of Law Legal Research Paper Series, working paper no. 13-05. http://papers.ssrn.com/sol3/papers.cfm?abstract_id=2209270## (accessed January 10, 2015).

30. James, Franklin J., and Christopher B. Gerboth. 2001. "A Camp Divided: Annexation Battles, the Poundstone Amendment, and Their Impact on Metropolitan Denver, 1941–1988." *Colorado History* 5: 129–74.

31. Leonard and Noel 1990.

32. *Rocky Mountain News*, July 1, 1984; quoted in Leonard and Noel 1990, 358.

33. U.S. Census 2010.

34. Jonas, Goetz, and Bhattacharjee 2014.

35. O'Keefe, Mike. 1989. "Doctor No: Is the Denver Regional Council of Governments a Prescription for Metro Mediocrity?" *Westword*, November 8–14, 1989; quoted in Leonard and Noel 1990, 475; Jonas, Goetz, and Bhattacharjee 2014.

36. Goetz, Andrew R., Paul Stephen Dempsey, and Carl Larson. 2002. "Metropolitan Planning Organizations: Findings and Recommendations for Improving Transportation Planning." *Publius: The Journal of Federalism* 32 (1): 87–105. See also Dempsey, Paul Stephen, Andrew R. Goetz, and Carl Larson. 2000. *Metropolitan Planning Organizations: An Assessment of the Transportation Planning Process, a Report to Congress, Volumes I, II, and III*. Denver: University of Denver Intermodal Transportation Institute and National Center for Intermodal Transportation.

37. Metropolitan Transportation Development Commission. 1990. "A Regional Solution to Metropolitan Transportation, Final Recommendations to the Colorado General Assembly."

38. Goetz, Andrew R. 2007. "State Departments of Transportation: From Highway Departments to Transportation Agencies." In *Handbook of Transportation Policy and Administration*, ed. Jeremy Plant, 121–44. New York: Taylor and Francis.

39. Goetz, Dempsey, and Larson 2002.

40. Jonas, Goetz, and Bhattacharjee 2014.

41. Katz, Bruce, and Jennifer Bradley. 2013. *The Metropolitan Revolution: How Cities and Metros Are Fixing Our Broken Politics and Fragile Economy*. Washington, D.C.: Brookings Institution.

42. The Scientific and Cultural Facilities District includes Adams, Arapahoe, Broomfield, Boulder, Denver, Douglas, and Jefferson Counties.

43. Jonas, Goetz, and Bhattacharjee 2014.

44. Goetz, Jonas, and Bhattacharjee 2011.

45. Jonas, Goetz, and Bhattacharjee 2014.

46. Leonard and Noel 1990, 473; Jonas, Goetz, and Bhattacharjee 2014.

47. Denver Regional Council of Governments (DRCOG). 1992. *Mobility Management in the Denver Region: An Element of the Regional Transportation Plan*. Denver: Denver Regional Council of Governments.

48. The Metro Mayors Caucus now includes thirty-nine mayors.

49. It is interesting to note that the Metro Mayors Caucus holds its meetings at the Metro Denver Chamber of Commerce offices.

50. Jonas, Goetz, and Bhattacharjee 2014.

51. Denver Regional Council of Governments (DRCOG). 1997. *Metro Vision 2020 Plan*.

52. In the Metro Vision 2035 plan, the urban growth boundary/area was expanded to 980 square miles (Denver Regional Council of Governments. 2007. *Metro Vision 2035 Plan*. Denver, Colo.); Goetz 2013; Jonas, Goetz, and Bhattacharjee 2014.

53. Denver Regional Council of Governments. 2017. Mile High Compact. https://drcog.org/planning-great-region/metro-vision/mile-high-compact (accessed November 22, 2017).

54. Goetz, Jonas, and Bhattacharjee 2011.

55. See Fulton, Bill. 2007. "Brewpub Regionalism Could Cure City Ailments." *California Planning and Development Report*, June 25, 2007. http://www.cp-dr.com/node/1702 (accessed November 22, 2017). Fulton said the historical relationship between Denver and its suburban cities "could best be described as Iraq minus the militias and most of the checkpoints." Cited in Jonas, Goetz, and Bhattacharjee 2014.

56. See Jonas, Goetz, and Bhattacharjee 2014. Originally cited in Urban Omnibus. 2011. http://urbanomnibus.net/2011/07/ford-foundation-the-just-city/ (accessed March 20, 2012).

57. Murray, Jon. 2014. "New App Allows Denver Voters to Register, See Info on Smart Phones." *Denver Post*, September 8, 2014. http://www.denverpost.com/news/ci_26493082/new-app-allows-denver-voters-register-see-info (accessed January 10, 2015).

58. Bartels, Lynn. 2014. "Adams County: Changes Include Stunning Republican Victories," *Denver Post*, December 6, 2014. http://www.denverpost.com/election2014/ci_27083906/adams-county-changes-include-stunning-republican-victories (accessed December 15, 2014).

59. Raabe, Steve. 2011. "National Western Stock Show Picks Aurora for Proposed Relocation." *Denver Post*, June 28, 2011. http://www.denverpost.com/ci_18369490 (accessed January 2, 2015).

60. City and County of Denver. 2017. North Denver Cornerstone Collaborative, National Western Center. https://www.denvergov.org/content/denvergov/en/north-denver-cornerstone-collaborative/national-western-center.html (accessed November 22, 2017).

61. Arapahoe County Elections Division 2014. http://www.arapahoevotes.com/ and Coloradoan. 2014. Map: Colorado Voter Party Affiliation by County, October 16, 2014. http://www.coloradoan.com/story/news/politics/elections/2014/10/16/map-colorado-voters-party-affiliation-by-county/17379853/ (accessed November 22, 2017).

62. Florida, Richard. 2008. *Who's Your City: How the Creative Economy Is Making Where to Live the Most Important Decision of Your Life*. New York: Basic Books.

63. City-Data. 2014. Boulder, Colorado. http://www.city-data.com/city/Boulder-Colorado.html (accessed November 22, 2017).

64. University of Colorado-Boulder. 2017. https://www.colorado.edu/about (accessed November 22, 2017)

65. Florida, Richard. 2012. Insight—Rise Revisited: Creativity Index, June 27, 2012. http://martinprosperity.org/insight-rise-revisited-creativity-index/ (accessed November 22, 2017).

66. Other tongue-in-cheek terms for Boulder include "Disneyland for hippies" and "Boulder, Colorado: 16 square miles of utopia surrounded by reality."

67. U.S. Census 2010.

68. Colorado State University. 2017. Colorado State University System: About the System. http://www.csusystem.edu/about (accessed November 24, 2017).

69. Larimer County and City of Fort Collins. 2017. Intergovernmental Agreements. https://www.fcgov.com/planning/pdf/iga-doc.pdf (accessed November 24, 2017).

70. U.S. Census 2010.

71. U.S. Census 2010.

72. Weld County Colorado. 2017. Voter Statistics. https://www.weldgov.com /departments/clerk_and_recorder/elections_department/voter_statistics/ (accessed November 24, 2017).

73. Romano, Analisa. 2013. "Weld County Commissioners Propose Formation of New State, North Colorado." http://www.greeleytribune.com/news/6822670-113 /commissioners-county-state-colorado (accessed December 17, 2014).

74. The state of Colorado initiated more stringent background checks on gun sales in 2013 after the mass shooting at an Aurora theater in July 2012 that resulted in twelve fatalities, and the Sandy Hook school shooting in Newtown, Connecticut, in December 2012. Colorado's active response was also affected by the memory of the infamous 1999 mass shooting at Columbine High School in unincorporated Jefferson County, which was the first major school shooting in the United States, and resulted in the deaths of twelve students and one teacher.

75. This was the first time Coloradans voted both times in favor of the same Democratic candidate for president since they supported Franklin Delano Roosevelt in 1932 and 1936.

76. Counties voting against the secession included Elbert, Lincoln, Logan, Moffat, Sedgwick, and Weld, while Cheyenne, Kit Carson, Phillips, Washington, and Yuma Counties voted in favor.

77. Colorado Springs. 2017. History and Heritage. http://www.visitcos.com/colorado-springs/travel/history-heritage (accessed November 24, 2017).

78. Wyckoff, William. 1999. *Creating Colorado: The Making of a Western American Landscape, 1860–1940.* New Haven, Conn.: Yale University Press, 133–43.

79. El Paso County, Colorado. 2017. Elections. http://car.elpasoco.com/Election /Pages/default.aspx (accessed November 24, 2017).

80. Wyckoff 1999, 144.

81. Wyckoff 1999, 145.

82. Wyckoff 1999, 147–53.

83. Evraz North America. 2017. Evraz Rocky Mountain Steel: Pueblo, Colorado. http://www.evrazna.com/LocationsFacilities/RockyMountainSteelMills/tabid/71/ (accessed November 24, 2017).

84. Zillow. 2017. Colorado Home Prices and Values. http://www.zillow.com/co /home-values/ (accessed November 24, 2017).

85. The initial 1990 referendum limited the amount of a single bet to a $5 maximum; allowed only slot machines, black jack, and poker games; and limited the hours

of casino operation. In 2008, Colorado Amendment 50 was approved, which allowed the three gambling towns to raise the amount of a single bet to a $100 maximum, expand gaming to include roulette and craps, and extend casino hours.

86. Vuong, Andy. 2009. "Eased Gambling, Building Rules Give Central City a Second Chance." *Denver Post*, July 1, 1.

87. Stokowski, Patricia. 1996. *Riches and Regrets: Betting on Gambling in Two Colorado Mountain Towns*. Niwot: University of Colorado Press.

88. Denver Post. 2008. "Amendment 50 is Too Risky a Bet," September 24, 2008. http://www.denverpost.com/headlines/ci_10550155 (accessed January 2, 2015).

89. Denver Business Journal. 2006. "Revised 'Super Slab' Proposal Outlined," August 28, 2006. http://www.bizjournals.com/denver/stories/2006/08/28/daily8.html?page=all (accessed December 22, 2014).

90. Colorado Department of Transportation. 2012. Executive Summary, Colorado State Freight and Passenger Rail Plan, March 2012. https://www.codot.gov/projects/PassengerFreightRailPlan/StatePassengerRailPlan-Tasks/SPRP-ExecSummary (accessed November 24, 2017).

91. Colorado General Assembly. 2017. "Southwest Chief and Front Range Passenger Rail Commission." https://leg.colorado.gov/bills/sb17-153 (accessed August 14, 2017).

Chapter 6. Sustainable Futures

1. Much of this chapter is a restatement of research originally reported in Goetz, Andrew R. "Suburban Sprawl or Urban Centers: Tensions and Contradictions of Smart Growth Approaches in Denver, Colorado." *Urban Studies* 50 (11): 2178–95. Copyright © 2013 SAGE Publications. Reprinted by permission of SAGE Publications.

2. A previous wave of suburbanization in the United States started in the 1920s, although the size and scale of the post-1945 suburban era dwarfed that earlier period. Also, early forms of U.S. suburbanization can be traced to the mid-1800s with the beginning of the intraurban transportation revolution and the erosion of the walking city. See Jackson, Kenneth T. 1985. *Crabgrass Frontier: The Suburbanization of the United States*. New York: Oxford University Press.

3. Harris, Chauncy D., and Edward L. Ullman. 1945. "The Nature of Cities." *Annals of the American Academy of Political and Social Science* 242: 7–17; Knox, Paul L., and Linda McCarthy. 2005. *Urbanization: An Introduction to Urban Geography*. 2nd ed. Upper Saddle River, N.J.: Pearson Prentice Hall; Vance, James E., Jr. 1977. *The Scene of Man: The Role and Structure of the City in the Geography of Western Civilization*. New York: Harpers Collins; Muller, Peter O. 1981. *Contemporary Suburban America*. Englewood Cliffs, N.J.: Prentice Hall; Lewis, Pierce. 1983. "The Galactic Metropolis." In R. Platt and G. Macinko, eds., *Beyond the Urban Fringe: Land Use Issues of Nonmetropolitan America*. Minneapolis: University of Minnesota Press; Hartshorn, Truman A., and Peter O. Muller. 1989. "Suburban Downtowns and the Transformation of Metropolitan Atlanta's Business Landscape." *Urban Geography* 10: 375–95; Garreau, Joel.

1991. *Edge City: Life on the New Frontier.* New York: Doubleday; Harris, Chauncy D. 1997. "The Nature of Cities and Urban Geography in the Last Half Century." *Urban Geography* 18 (1): 15–35; Graham, Stephen, and Simon Marvin. 2001. *Splintering Urbanism.* New York: Routledge; Lang, Robert E. 2003. *Edgeless Cities: Exploring the Elusive Metropolis.* Washington, D.C.: Brookings Institution Press.

4. Gallagher, Leigh. 2013. *The End of the Suburbs: Where the American Dream Is Moving.* New York: Portfolio/Penguin.

5. Ewing, R., R. Pendall, and D. Chen. 2002. *Measuring Sprawl and Its Impact.* Washington, D.C.: Smart Growth America.

6. Real Estate Research Corporation. 1974. *The Costs of Sprawl: Detailed Cost Analysis.* Washington, D.C.: U.S. Government Printing Office; Barnett, Jonathan, ed. 2007. *Smart Growth in a Changing World.* Chicago: American Planning Association; Burchell, Robert W., George Lowenstein, William R. Dolphin, Catherine C. Galley, Anthony Downs, Samuel Seskin, Katherine Gray Still, and Terry Moore. 2002. *Costs of Sprawl—2000.* Transit Cooperative Research Program Report 74. Transportation Research Board—National Research Council. Washington, D.C.: National Academy Press; Newman, Peter W. G., and Jeffrey R. Kenworthy. 1999. *Sustainability and Cities: Overcoming Automobile Dependence.* Washington, D.C.: Island; Farr, Douglas. 2008. *Sustainable Urbanism: Urban Design with Nature.* Hoboken, N.J.: Wiley.

7. McCann, Barbara A., and Reid Ewing. 2003. *Measuring the Health Effects of Sprawl: A National Analysis of Physical Activity, Obesity, and Chronic Disease.* Washington, D.C.: Smart Growth America and Surface Transportation Policy Project; Plantinga, Andrew J., and Bernell, Stephanie. 2007. "The Association Between Urban Sprawl and Obesity: Is it a Two Way Street?" *Journal of Regional Science* 47 (5): 857–79; Raine, J., C. Spence, J. Church, N. Boulé, L. Slater, J. Marko, K. Gibbons, and E. Hemphill. 2008. *State of the Evidence Review on Urban Health and Healthy Weights.* Ottawa: CIHI.

8. Burchell, Robert W., David Listokin, and Catherine C. Galley. 2000. "Smart Growth: More Than a Ghost of Urban Policy Past, Less Than a Bold New Horizon." *Housing Policy Debate* 11 (4): 821–78.

9. Burchell, Lowenstein, et al. 2002.

10. Burchell, Listokin, and Galley 2000.

11. Krueger, Rob, and David Gibbs. 2008. "'Third Wave' Sustainability? Smart Growth and Regional Development in the USA." *Regional Studies* 42 (9): 1263–74.

12. Basolo, Victoria. 2003. "U.S. Regionalism and Rationality." *Urban Studies* 40: 447–62; Jonas, A. E. G., and McCarthy, L. 2009. "Urban Management and Regeneration in the United States: State Intervention or Redevelopment at All Costs?" *Local Government Studies* 35 (3): 299–314; Jonas, A. E. G., and Ward, K. 2002. "A World of Regionalisms? Towards a U.S.-U.K. Urban and Regional Policy Framework Comparison." *Journal of Urban Affairs* 24 (4): 377–401; Pastor, Manuel, Peter Dreier, J. Eugene Grigsby III, and Maria Lopez-Garza. 2000. *Regions That Work: How Cities and Suburbs Can Growth Together.* Minneapolis: University of Minnesota Press.

13. Jonas, A. E., Goetz, A. R., and Bhattacharjee, S. 2014. "City-Regionalism as a Politics of Collective Provision: Regional Transport Infrastructure in Denver, USA." *Urban Studies* 51 (11): 2444–56; Scott, J. W. 2007. "Smart Growth as Urban Reform: A Pragmatic 'Recoding' of the New Regionalism." *Urban Studies* 44 (1): 15–35.

14. Newman and Kenworthy 1999.

15. Reconnecting America. 2011. "Jumpstarting the Transit Space Race: 2011, a Catalog and Analysis of Planned and Proposed Transit Projects in the U.S." Reconnecting America, Washington, D.C. www.reconnectingamerica.org/assets/2011TransitSpace RaceIIFinal.pdf (accessed July 20, 2011).

16. Center for Transit-Oriented Development. 2011. http://www.ctod.org/portal/ (accessed July 19, 2011).

17. Rusk, David. 2004. *Denver Divided: Sprawl, Race, and Poverty in Denver.* Denver: University of Denver Morgridge College of Education.

18. Krueger and Gibbs 2008.

19. De Raismes, Joseph N., III, H. Lawrence Hoyt, Peter L. Pollock, Jerry P. Gordon, and David J. Gehr. 2000. "Growth Management in Boulder, Colorado: A Case Study." City of Boulder, Attorney's Office. http://www.bouldercolorado.gov/files/ City%20Attorney/Documents/Miscellaneous%20Docs%20of%20Interest/x-bgmcs1. jbn.pdf.

20. Steers, Stuart. 1997. "The Blacktop Jungle." *Westword*, June 19, 1997. http:// www.westword.com/1997-06-19/news/the-blacktop-jungle.

21. DRCOG (Denver Regional Council of Governments). 1997. *Metro Vision 2020 Plan.*

22. In the Metro Vision 2035 plan, the urban growth boundary/area was expanded to 980 square miles. Denver Regional Councl of Governments [DRCOG]. 2007. *Metro Vision 2035 Plan.* Denver, Colo. https://drcog.org/sites/drcog/files/resources /Regional%20Snapshot%20-%20Metro%20Vision%202035%20Goals.pdf (accessed January 4, 2015).

23. Jonas et al. 2014.

24. LoDo was the setting for many of Jack Kerouac's stories in *On the Road* based on the exploits of Denver native Neal Cassady. A Denver developer recently opened the Jack Kerouac Lofts in LoDo, but the LoDo of today is quite different from the LoDo of Cassady and Kerouac's era.

25. *Downtown Area Plan: A Plan for the Future of Downtown Denver.* 1986. Denver Partnership and Denver Planning Office, p. 46; Weiler, Stephan. 2000. "Pioneers and Settlers in Lo-Do Denver: Private Risk and Public Benefits in Urban Redevelopment." *Urban Studies* 37 (1): 167–79.

26. Forest City Stapleton. 2010. http://about.stapletondenver.com/about/history.

27. Leccese, Michael. 2005. "Denver's Stapleton: Green Urban Infill for the Masses?" *Terrain.org: A Journal of the Built and Natural Environments* 17 (Fall/Winter 2005), 125–33. https://www.terrain.org/archives/archives-issue-17/ (accessed November 24, 2017).

28. Continuum Partners. 2010. http://www.belmarcolorado.com/about.php.

29. Murray, Michael. 2002. "City Profile: Denver." *Cities* 19 (4): 283–94.

30. Robertson, Don, Morris Cafky, and E. J. Haley. 2004. *Denver's Street Railways*. Denver: Sundance; RTD (Regional Transportation District). 1995. *RTD Rapid Transit Planning History*. Denver: Regional Transportation District.

31. University of Denver graduate student Ryan Keeney has created a "storymap" that illustrates the spatial extent of streetcars and neighborhood development in Denver from 1872 to 1950. See https://dugis.maps.arcgis.com/apps/MapSeries/index.html?appid=00a2d498a2ac4c58ad140ac306110213 (accessed August 14, 2017).

32. Denver Metropolitan Study Panel. 1976. "Metropolitan Change in Denver: Past Approaches." Denver Metropolitan Study and National Academy of Public Administration, 11.

33. Ratner, Keith. 2001. "The Relationship of United States Rail Transit Development and Success with Urban Population, Employment and Congestion Characteristics." PhD diss., Department of Geography, University of Denver, 123; RTD (Regional Transportation District). 1995. *RTD Rapid Transit Planning History*. Denver: Regional Transportation District.

34. RTD 1995.

35. Goetz, Andrew R., Andrew E. G. Jonas, and Sutapa Bhattacharjee. 2011. "Regional Collaboration in Transport Infrastructure Provision: The Case of Denver's FasTracks Rail Transit Program." Final report, National Center for Intermodal Transportation.

36. Ratner 2001.

37. DRCOG. 1989. *Southeast/Southwest Transit Threshold Analysis*. Denver: Denver Regional Council of Governments.

38. Metropolitan Transportation Development Commission. 1990. *A Regional Solution to Metropolitan Transportation, Final Recommendations to the Colorado General Assembly*, 1.

39. Metropolitan Development Transportation Commission 1990, 7.

40. Hodges, Arthur. 1994. "Sick Transit." *Westword*, October 26, 1.

41. RTD (Regional Transportation District). 2011. *The 2010 Annual Report to DRCOG on FasTracks*. https://drcog.org/sites/drcog/files/resources/RTD%202010%20Annual%20Report%20to%20DRCOG%20on%20FasTracks_0.pdf (accessed August 17, 2017).

42. Leonard, S., and T. Noel. 1990. *Denver: Mining Camp to Metropolis*. Boulder: University of Colorado Press, 442.

43. RTD (Regional Transportation District). 1995. *RTD Rapid Transit Planning History*, 22.

44. Ratner 2001.

45. RTD 1995.

46. RTD 1995, 26.

47. Prendergast, Alan. 1997. "Divide the Ride: Pushing a $6 Billion Transit Plan, RTD Has Met the Enemy—the RTD Board. *Westword*, October 23, 1997.

48. Regional Transportation District. 2017. http://www.rtd-denver.com/FF-SouthwestCorridorLRT.shtml (accessed November 24, 2017).

49. Ratner 2001.

50. CDOT (Colorado Department of Transportation) and RTD (Regional Transportation District). 2006. *T-REX Transportation Expansion Project Fact Book*. Denver.

51. Regional Transportation District. 2017. http://www.rtd-denver.com/FF-SoutheastCorridor.shtml (accessed November 24, 2017).

52. Flynn, Kevin. 2001. "RTD to Begin Push for Transit Build-Out." *Rocky Mountain News* (Colo.), September 10. http://infoweb.newsbank.com/iw-search/we/InfoWeb?p_product=AWNB&p_theme=aggregated5&p_action=doc&p_docid=0EE7CC6 FF54590A5&p_docnum=3&p_queryname=2 (accessed January 4, 2015).

53. Goetz, Jonas, and Bhattacharjee 2011. Interview with regional civic group, April 2007.

54. The cost estimate in 2004 was $4.7 billion. The cost of FasTracks was estimated at $6.8 billion in 2011 owing to rapidly expanding costs of building materials since 2004; RTD (Regional Transportation District). 2011. *The 2010 Annual Report to DRCOG on FasTracks*. https://drcog.org/sites/drcog/files/resources/RTD%202010%20Annual%20 Report%20to%20DRCOG%20on%20FasTracks_0.pdf (accessed August 17, 2017).

55. RTD (Regional Transportation District). 2010. *The 2009 Annual Report to DRCOG on FasTracks*. http://www.drcog.org/documents/2009%20RTD%20Annual%20 Report%20to%20DRCOG%20on%20FasTracks.pdf (accessed August 17, 2017).

56. Migoya, David. 2012. "RTD Stunned by BNSF's Charge for Use of Northwest Rail Lines." *Denver Post*, June 4, 2012. http://www.denverpost.com/ci_20782125/rtd-stunned-by-bnsfs-charge-use-northwest-rail (accessed February 11, 2015). See also Goetz, Andrew R., Keith Ratner, Julie Cidell, Michael Minn, and Sylvia Brady. 2016. *Passenger Rail and Freight Rail Partnerships: Case Studies in Boston, Chicago, and Denver*. Research Report, National Center for Intermodal Transportation for Economic Competitiveness.

57. Migoya 2012.

58. RTD. 2015. Best Practices. http://www.rtd-denver.com/documents/best-practices-2015.pdf (accessed November 24, 2017). See also Goetz, Andrew R., Andrew E. G. Jonas, and Sylvia Brady. 2016. *Innovative Approaches to Improved Intermodal Transportation Infrastructure Funding and Financing Through Public-Private Partnerships: A Denver Case Study*. Research Report, National Center for Intermodal Transportation for Economic Competitiveness. http://www.ncitec.msstate.edu/wp-content/uploads/2012–19FR.pdf (accessed December 15, 2016).

59. RTD. 2017. EagleP-3 Project. http://www.rtd-denver.com/FF-EagleP3.shtml (accessed November 24, 2017).

60. The University of Colorado acquired naming rights for the commuter rail line to Denver International Airport as part of a five-year, $5 million deal with the Regional

Transportation District signed in August 2015. http://www.denverpost.com/2016/04/19/
why-the-train-to-denver-international-airport-is-named-the-university-of-colorado-a-
line/ (accessed December 15, 2016).

61. RTD. 2016. Inside RTD FasTracks, November 2016. http://www.rtd-fastracks.
com/media/uploads/main/Inside_RTD_FasTracks_NOVEMBER_2016_FINAL.pdf
(accessed December 15, 2016).

62. Aguilar, John. 2016. "A-Line Design Questions That Have Caused Travel Delays
Were Brought Up as Early as 2013." *Denver Post*, October 21, 2016. http://www.denver-
post.com/2016/10/21/rtd-a-line-design-delays-lightning-issues/ (accessed December 15,
2016).

63. RTD. 2014. RTD FasTracks, I-225 Rail Line: 2014 Fact Sheet. https://admin
.rtd-fastracks.com/media/uploads/i225/I-225_Fact_Sheet_2014.pdf (accessed January 4, 2015).

64. RTD. 2016. Inside RTD FasTracks, November 2016. http://www.rtd-fastracks.
com/media/uploads/main/Inside_RTD_FasTracks_NOVEMBER_2016_FINAL.pdf
(accessed December 15, 2016).

65. RTD. 2015. N Line. http://www.rtd-denver.com/NorthMetroRailLine.shtml
(accessed January 4, 2015).

66. Whaley, Monte. 2017. RTD's North Line Will Take Longer Than Expected,
Officials Say.. *Denver Post,* May 2, 2017. http://www.denverpost.com/2017/05/02/rtd-
north-line-construction-delays/ (accessed August 17, 2017).

67. City and County of Denver. 2015. TOD Strategic Plan. https://www.denvergov
.org/Portals/193/documents/DLP/TOD_Plan/TOD_Strategic_Plan_FINAL.pdf
(accessed January 4, 2015).

68. Regional Transportation District. 2015. RTD 2014 TOD Status Report. http://
www.rtd-fastracks.com/media/uploads/main/RTD_2014_TOD_Status_Report_FI-
NAL_Reduced.pdf (accessed December 15, 2016).

69. Regional Transportation District 2015.

70. Ratner, Keith A., and Andrew R. Goetz. 2013. "The Reshaping of Land Use and
Urban Form in Denver Through Transit-Oriented Development." *Cities* 30: 31–46.

71. Denver Regional Council of Governments. 2014. "Regional Snapshot: Metro
Vision 2035 Goals." https://drcog.org/sites/drcog/files/resources/Regional%20Snap-
shot%20-%20Metro%20Vision%202035%20Goals.pdf (accessed January 4, 2015).

72. Rusk 2004.

73. Denver Regional Council of Governments 2014.

74. Ratner and Goetz 2013.

75. Denver Regional Council of Governments 2014.

76. Regional Transportation District. 2015. "Facts and Figures." http://www.rtd-
denver.com/factsAndFigures.shtml (accessed December 15, 2016).

77. Denver Regional Council of Governments 2014 (accessed January 5, 2015).

78. Hendee, Caitlin. 2014. "Denver a Top 10 City for Increased Commuting by Bike." *Denver Business Journal*, May 13, 2014. http://www.bizjournals.com/denver/news/2014/05/13/denver-a-top-10city-for-increased-commuting-by.html?page=all (accessed January 5, 2015).

Conclusion

1. Leonard, Stephen J., and Thomas J. Noel. 1990. *Denver: Mining Camp to Metropolis*. Niwot: University Press of Colorado.

2. Leonard and Noel 1990; Quillen, Ed. 1994. "DIA Follows Colorado Tradition." *Denver Post*, April 5; Dempsey, Paul Stephen, Andrew R. Goetz, and Joseph S. Szyliowicz. 1997. *Denver International Airport: Lessons Learned*. New York: McGraw-Hill.

3. Brookings Institution. Metropolitan Policy Program. 2010. *State of Metropolitan America: On the Front Lines of Demographic Transformation, Overview*. Washington, D.C.: Brookings, 30.

4. The complete list of "Industrial Core" cities includes Augusta–Richmond County, Georgia–South Carolina; Birmingham, Alabama; Buffalo, New York; Cleveland, Ohio; Dayton, Ohio; Detroit-Warren, Michigan; Grand Rapids, Michigan; Harrisburg, Pennsylvania; Louisville, Kentucky-Indiana; Memphis, Tennessee-Mississippi-Arkansas; New Orleans, Louisiana; Providence, Rhode Island; Scranton, Pennsylvania; Toledo, Ohio; Tulsa, Oklahoma; Virginia Beach–Norfolk–Newport News, Virginia–North Carolina; Wichita, Kansas; and Youngstown, Ohio-Pennsylvania.

5. Hafley, Taylor. 2014. "Changing Geographic Patterns of High- and Low-Income Groups in Eight United States Metropolitan Areas." MA thesis, University of Denver.

6. U.S. Census 2010.

Index

Acknowledgments

We wish to thank original series editor Judith Martin, who first approved our proposal to write this book. We especially enjoyed her visit to Denver in 2010 and the opportunity to show her the city. It is unfortunate that she is not here to see the finished product, but we are extremely grateful for her heart-felt support of our efforts. We would also like to thank Bob Lockhart of the University of Pennsylvania Press for his continued support after Judith's untimely passing. Bob has been very patient with our revision process, and we very much appreciate his willingness to stay engaged with this book.

We want to acknowledge many of our colleagues and students at the University of Denver. The faculty, students, and staff in the Department of Geography and the Environment have been supportive and helpful as we have completed this project. In particular, we wish to acknowledge some of our current and former graduate students, Sutapa Bhattacharjee, Sylvia Brady, and Greg Kwoka, who conducted research that contributed to some of the material in this book. We also want to thank our students in a first-year seminar course, "Geography of Metropolitan Denver," who read our initial manuscripts and provided useful comments. We have benefited from discussions with other University of Denver colleagues who share our interests in urban studies and Denver, including Fred Cheever (who will be missed greatly), Doug Clark, Nick Cutforth, Susan Daggett, and the Rocky Mountain Land Use Institute, Jim Griesemer, Richard Lamm, Bill Philpott, Tom Romero, Dean Saitta, Susan Schulten, and Chuck Wilson (who helped us plan Judith Martin's visit to Denver). We also acknowledge the funding support of the National Center for Intermodal Transportation at the University of Denver and Mississippi State University for several research projects that contributed to this book.

We would like to thank colleagues at other universities, agencies, and companies. Andrew Jonas of the University of Hull (UK) has been a collaborator on several research reports and journal articles that are reflected in some of the chapters in this book. We thank Andy for his contributions as well as his feedback and commentary during his visits to Denver. Thanks as well to Keith Ratner of Salem State University, who collaborated with us on several research projects that contributed to this book. We wish to thank the Denver Regional Transportation District, the Denver Regional Council of Governments, the City and County of Denver, Denver International Airport, the Denver Public Library, the Beck Archives of Rocky Mountain Jewish Historical Society at the University of Denver, Colorado Public Radio, and the Colorado Department of Transportation for the use of illustrations and their willingness to help us in our ongoing research. We acknowledge Sage Publications, the publisher of the journal *Urban Studies*, in which some of the original research that appears in this book was published.

Finally, we want to acknowledge the love and support from our families. For Andrew, this includes my wife, Andrea, and my two children, Alex and Annalise, who have shared the Denver experience with me. For Eric, this includes my wife, Jennifer Miller, who provided insightful comments on this work and has been a great partner in exploring urban life together.